FURNITURE YOU CAN MAKE

a Rockwell Publication

Rockwell International

Tool Group
400 North Lexington Avenue
Pittsburgh, Pennsylvania 15208

BIRCHARD PUBLIC LIBRARY OF SANDUSKY CO...
FREMONT, OHIO

Foreword

The projects in this book are aimed at helping you build handsome, sturdy furniture pieces for considerably less money than you would have to pay at a store. Most of them are well within the woodworking capabilities of the average do-it-yourselfer. However, a few of the furniture projects will challenge and delight the expert. There are tables, desks, chairs, screens, storage units, children's furniture, and other furniture items ranging in style from traditional to modern.

Most of the plans for the furniture pieces first appeared in *Flying Chips* (a former Rockwell publication). We would like to thank the Formica Corporation (subsidiary of Cyanamid) and the American Plywood Association for certain laminated plastic and plywood furniture projects.

Before attempting to build any of the furniture projects that appear in this book, be certain to review and understand each step of construction and to verify all dimensions. While every effort has been made to ensure accuracy in the designs and drawings appearing in this book, the possibility of error always exists and the publisher cannot accept responsibility for materials improperly used or designs not first verified.

Rockwell International
Tool Group

Copyright © 1978 Rockwell International Corporation
Published by Rockwell International

Brief quotations may be used in critical articles and reviews. For any other reproduction of this book, including electronic, mechanical, photocopying, recording or other means, written permission must be obtained from the publisher.

Text prepared and book designed by
Robert Scharff & Associates

Library of Congress Catalog Card Number: 78-66287
Manufactured in the United States of America

Contents

RUSTIC TABLE	1
MODERN WALL UNIT	4
OCCASIONAL TABLE	14
EARLY AMERICAN LOWBOY	20
WINDSOR CHAIR	27
QUEEN ANNE OCCASIONAL TABLE	31
MOKÉ ROOM SCREENS	35
CHILD'S ROCKER	40
COFFEE TABLE	44
ENTERTAINMENT CENTER	46
END TABLE	52
MODERN CHAIR	57
CHINA CABINET	60
COMPACT DESK	64
COCKTAIL TABLE	66
STUDENT'S DESK	69
SHAKER PEDESTAL TABLE	73
BOOK CABINET	78
SCHOOL DESK AND CHAIR	84
NESTED TABLES	88
SOFA	91
FOLDING DINING TABLE	94
EARLY AMERICAN NIGHT STAND	99

PLANTER TABLE	102
PLASTIC LAMINATED FURNITURE	105
MODERN COCKTAIL TABLE	108
FURNITURE CUBE	109
TELEVISION CABINET	110
UTILITY CABINET	112
ART PEDESTAL	114
DINING ROOM PEDESTAL TABLE	116
BEDSIDE TABLE	118
CONSOLE TABLE	120
INCH/MILLIMETER CONVERSIONS	122

Photo 1: A rustic styled table.

RUSTIC TABLE

This unusual rustic table (Photo 1) is not only a challenge to build, there is the additional challenge of finding appropriate materials to work with. The table shown here is made from a large oak burl, discovered at a saw mill in the Laurel Mountains of Pennsylvania. However, just as suitable would be a 2" slice from the butt portion of a large log or a diagonally cut 2" slice from any available log.

If a chain saw is not available for cutting the table top, the wood can be cut at a local saw mill. Use a disk sander with a medium grit disk as shown in Photo 2, to sand the table top. Using a large 7" sander of this type makes quick work out of a tough job. Do this sanding outdoors, if possible, because of the large amount of sawdust involved. Do the finish sanding with a belt sander and then a finish sander.

Because it adds to the rustic effect, the bark has been left on the table, even though it may eventually peel off. The bark should not fall off, however, if the tree from which the table top has been taken is cut at the right time of the year. Unfortunately, this period varies from region to region. It is probably best to ask a local lumberman for the proper cutting time in each particular area. When working with green wood, it will probably be necessary to resand and refinish the top again after it dries. Therefore, it might be a good idea to rough sand the wood, coat it with boiled linseed oil, and let it air dry thoroughly before completing the table.

The legs (Fig.1) can be squared on a band saw or table saw to 1-3/4" by 2", then cut to an oversize length of 19". Next, lay out and cut the tapers freehand on the band saw (Photo 3). Tilt the band saw table to 45° and chamfer freehand the four edges of each leg 3/8" by 45° (Photo 4). Hand plane all of these rough surfaces and slightly round the remaining sharp edges (Photo 5). It is not necessary to be exact.

Leave the surfaces unsanded to maintain a rustic hand hewn effect. On a lathe, turn the small end of each leg to a 1" diameter making this dowel section 1-1/2" long (Photo 6). Note that a 1" hole bored in a scrap block is used to achieve an exact 1" diameter. Accuracy is important here, because if kiln dried wood is used for the legs, and air dried or green wood for the top, a tight fitting joint will make it unnecessary to use glue or fasteners to hold the legs in place. The top will shrink as it dries and becomes increasingly tighter on the already dry legs.

Photo 2: Leveling the top surface of the table with a disk sander.

Photo 5: Setup for hand planing the leg surfaces.

Photo 3: Cutting leg tapers on a band saw.

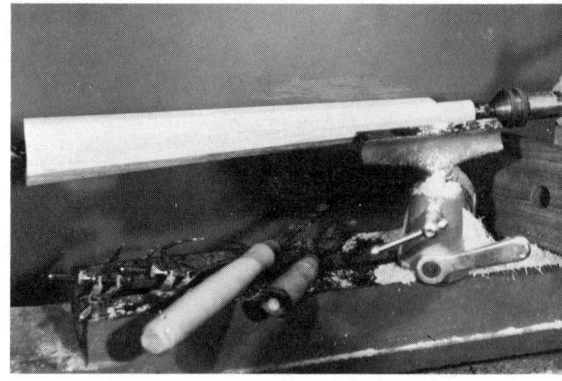

Photo 6: Turning the dowel portion of the legs on a lathe.

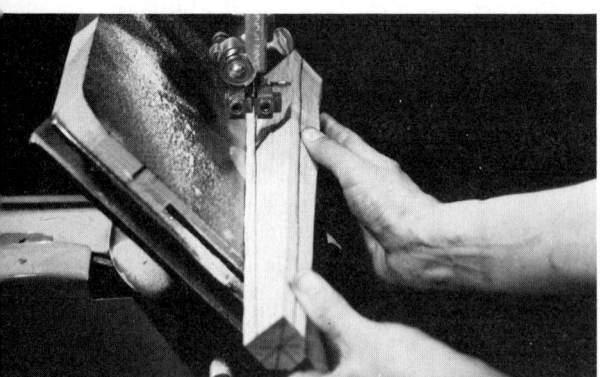

Photo 4: Chamfering the edges of the legs on a band saw.

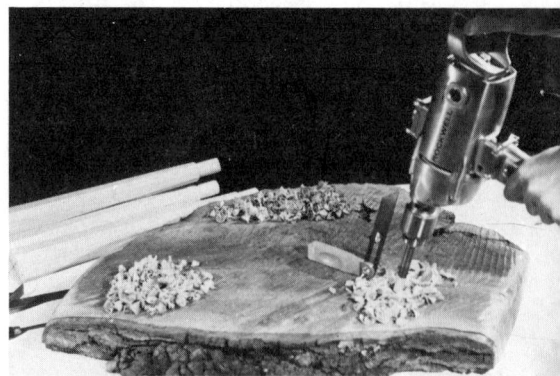

Photo 7: Drilling holes for the legs in the table top.

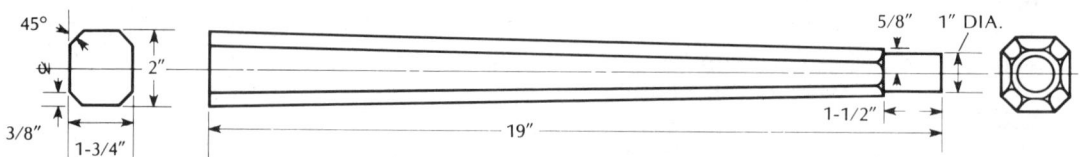

Fig. 1: Dimensions for the table legs.

In the bottom of the table top, bore three 1" diameter holes, 1-1/2" deep at a 15° angle, approximately 5-1/2" from the edge. Space the holes to form an equilateral triangle on the bottom as shown in Photo 7. Mount the legs with a wooden mallet. Cut the legs to a proper length and angle with a hand or back saw. A 17" table height was used for the table shown in Photo 8. Sand the bottom of each leg with a disk sander so they accurately conform to the floor. Chamfer the bottom corners of the legs with a spokeshave or block plane and install furniture glides.

Finish the table top with linseed oil. The legs can be stained with an oil-base black enamel, which should be applied sparingly with a cloth in spots and streaks, to give an aged appearance. Then, before the enamel sets, apply an additional coat of dark oak stain with a cloth.

Photo 8: Using a guide to level the table legs.

MATERIALS

Quantity	Description
1	2" Top (thickness)
3	1-3/4" x 2" x 19" Legs
2	Medium grit sanding disks
—	Assorted sanding belts
—	Black paint
—	Stain
—	Boiled linseed oil

MODERN WALL UNIT

Photo 1: This versatile, self-contained wall unit includes: seven shelves, a desk, a table, a magazine shelf, and three drawer units.

This modern-style, self-contained wall unit (Photo 1) is a good way to put empty wall space to use. Not only is the wall unit practical, it is stylish as well. The projecting desk unit and table can be folded back into the wall unit if more floor space is needed in the room; and, the table-supporting grillwork presents an appealing patterned design when folded against the wall (Photo 2). The various component parts of the wall unit: shelves, drawers, cabinets, the desk, the folding table, and the magazine shelf, for example, are shown in Fig. 1. The project is made of birch plywood, but oak, walnut, or mahogany can be substituted.

Begin the project by building the uprights which are made in sections from 3/4" plywood (Fig. 2). Each upright is assembled from four parts: (A), (B), (C), and (D), as shown in Fig. 2. The assembly is held together by glue, applied between the parts, and by two No. 6 by 1-1/4" flathead wood screws, fastened at each heel, where the upright pieces (A) and (D) overlap (Fig. 3). A hole 1/2" in diameter and 4" deep is bored at the top end of each upright for the adjusting tension nut (Fig. 3). Hammer the thread on one end, jamming the nut tight, to keep the rubber tip from turning (Fig. 4).

The shelves, drawer cabinets, and desk are all supported, at least partially with dowels. The shelves are supported by 3/8" dowels, each 6" long, which run through the uprights from front to back where the shelves overlap (Fig. 3).

The sides of the desk, the desk drawer, the drawer cabinets, and the magazine shelf receive added support from 1/2" dowels, which run through the uprights from side to side (Fig. 5). They should measure 3" long, and can be used on one side of an upright (as for the magazine rack), or jut through on both sides (as for the adjacent drawer units). The positioning of the dowels for the tilting magazine shelf is shown in Fig. 6. The dowel holes are bored in the assembled uprights on a drill press, using a fence and an extra guide strip, both clamped to the table (Photo 3).

Do not cut the shelf lengths until the uprights have been assembled and positioned. Cut 6" long blind grooves, 3/8" wide and 1/4" deep, in each shelf, centered and 3/16" from the end. These are used to hold the shelves in place on the 3/8" dowels (Fig. 7). Note the two half shelves in the center section which allow for clearance when the table is in a raised position (Fig. 2). These half shelves are doweled from the back of the uprights, as shown in Fig. 8. The ends of the shelves are notched out to fit around the uprights (Photo 4).

The tilting magazine shelf is grooved for the 1/2" dowel and notched as shown in Fig. 9. The angled notches on the edges of the magazine shelf are made on a table saw. Use a dado head with the stock held against a miter gauge set at 25°.

Complete details for the table are given in Figs. 10 and 11. Screw fasten the odds and ends trough to the two inner uprights, (Fig. 11), making the table measure exactly 29" from the floor to the top. A magnetic catch is used to hold the table top in a vertical position (Photo 2).

All three cabinet units have the same overall dimensions, as shown in Figs. 12-17. The drawers are assembled with butt joints; details are given in Fig. 18. The simple desk construction details are shown in Figs. 19 and 20.

Exposed plywood edges can be covered with flexible wood trim and contact cement per manufacturer's instructions. This type of veneer, often called edging tape, should be applied with hand pressure, and then tapped down with a rubber headed mallet to insure a good bond.

Finish the project with a penetrating resin stain, following the manufacturer's instructions.

MATERIALS

Desk Unit

Quantity	Description	Quantity	Description
2	3/4" x 13" x 19" Sides	1	3/8" x 1-1/8" x 27" Shelf facing strip
2	3/4" x 13" x 28-1/2" Top and bottom	1	Magnetic catch
1	1/8" x 20-1/4" x 28-1/4" Hardboard back	1	1" dia. Lid knob
1	3/4" x 19-1/2" x 28" Desk lid	1	1-1/4" x 27" Continuous hinge
1	3/4" x 7-5/8" x 27" Shelf	4	No. 8 x 2" Flathead wood screws
1	1/8" x 8" x 27" Hardboard shelf cover		

Five Drawer Cabinet

Quantity	Description	Quantity	Description
2	3/4" x 16" x 14-1/2" Sides	1	1/2" x 5-1/4" x 9-1/4" Drawer back
2	3/4" x 16" x 28-1/2" Top and bottom	2	1/2" x 5-3/4" x 16" Drawer sides
1	1/8" x 15-3/4" x 28-1/4" Hardboard back	1	1/8" x 9-3/4" x 15-3/4" Hardboard drawer bottom
1	3/4" x 16" x 14-1/2" Cabinet upright	1	3/4" x 6-3/4" x 16-3/4" Drawer front facing
1	3/4" x 3/4" x 16" Front drawer slide frame	1	1/2" x 5-3/4" x 15" Drawer front
2	3/4" x 3/4" x 10-1/4" Front drawer slide frames	1	1/2" x 5-1/4" x 15" Drawer back
6	3/4" x 3/4" x 15-1/4" Side drawer slide frames	2	1/2" x 5-3/4" x 16" Drawer sides
4	1/4" x 3/4" x .16" Bottom drawer slides	1	1/8" x 15-1/2" x 15-3/4" Hardboard drawer bottom
2	3/4" x 11" x 4-1/8" Drawer front facings	1	3/4" x 8-1/2" x 16-3/4" Drawer front facing
2	3/3/8" x 9-1/4" Drawer fronts		
2	1/2" x 2-3/4" x 9-1/4" Drawer backs	1	1/2" x 7-3/4" x 15" Drawer front
4	1/2" x 3-3/8" x 16" Drawer sides	1	1/2" x 7-1/8" x 15" Drawer back
2	1/8" x 9-3/4" x 15-3/4" Hardboard drawer bottoms	2	1/2" x 7-3/4" x 16" Drawer sides
1	3/4" x 6-3/4" x 11" Drawer front facing	1	1/8" x 15-1/2" x 15-3/4" Hardboard drawer bottom
1	1/2" x 5-3/4" x 10-3/4" Drawer front	5	1" dia. Drawer knobs

MATERIALS

Table Support

Quantity	Description	Quantity	Description
2	3/4" x 1-1/2" x 28-1/4" Sides	5	3/4" x 3/4" x 19" Horizontal grillwork pieces
2	3/4" x 1-1/2" x 19" Top and bottom		
1	1/8" x 28-1/4" x 20-1/2" Hardboard back	4	3/4" x 3/4" x 26-3/4" Vertical grillwork pieces

Odds and Ends Trough

Quantity	Description	Quantity	Description
2	3/4" x 4" x 27" Sides	1	1/8" x 5-1/2" x 28-1/2" Hardboard bottom
2	3/4" x 4" x 5-1/2" Ends		

Table Top

Quantity	Description	Quantity	Description
4	No. 5 x 1-1/2" Flathead wood screws	2	3/8" x 1-1/4" x 28-1/2" End edging strips
1	3/4" x 27-3/4" x 55-1/2" Top		
2	3/8" x 1-1/4" x 56-1/4" Side edging strips	2	1" x 2-1/2" Butt hinges
		1	1-1/4" x 27" Continuous hinge

Sliding Door Cabinet

Quantity	Description	Quantity	Description
2	3/4" x 16" x 14-1/2" Sides	2	1/4" x 14" x 14" Sliding doors
2	3/4" x 16" x 28-1/2" Top and bottom	1	9/16" x 27" Top plastic track
1	1/8" x 15-3/4" x 28-1/4" Hardboard back	1	5/16" x 27" Bottom plastic track
		2	1/4" x 1" dia. Cup pulls

Two Drawer Cabinet

Quantity	Description	Quantity	Description
2	3/4" x 16" x 14-1/2" Sides	1	1/2" x 6-7/8" x 26" Top drawer front
2	3/4" x 16" x 28-1/2" Top and bottom	1	1/2" x 6-5/8" x 26" Bottom drawer front
1	1/8" x 15-3/4" x 28-1/4" Hardboard back	1	1/2" x 6-1/4" x 26" Top drawer back
1	3/4" x 3/4" x 27" Front drawer slide frame	1	1/2" x 6" x 26" Bottom drawer back
2	3/4" x 3/4" x 15-1/4" Side drawer slide frames	2	1/2" x 6-7/8" x 16" Top drawer sides
2	1/4" x 3/4" x 15-1/4" Side drawer slide frames	2	1/2" x 6-5/8" x 16" Bottom drawer sides
		2	1/8" x 15-3/4" x 26-1/2" Hardboard drawer bottom
2	3/4" x 7-5/8" x 28" Drawer front facings	4	1" dia. Drawer knobs

Uprights

Quantity	Description	Quantity	Description
4 (A)	3/4" x 1-1/2" x 93" Upright cabinet supports	4	1/2" x 9" Threaded rods (with washer and two hex nuts)
4 (B)	3/4" x 1-1/2" x 91-3/4" Upright cabinet supports	4	Rubber chair tips
4 (C)	3/4" x 7-1/2" x 7" Upright supports	14	1/2" x 3" Dowels
4 (D)	3/4" x 9" x 7" Upright supports	8	No. 6 x 1-1/4" Flathead wood screws

MATERIALS

Shelves

Quantity	Description	Quantity	Description
5	3/4" x 9-1/2" x 29-3/4" Full shelves	14	3/8" x 6" Dowels
2	3/4" x 5-1/2" x 29-3/4" Half shelves		

Magazine Shelf

Quantity	Description	Quantity	Description
1	3/4" x 13-7/8" x 29-3/4" Shelf	2	1/2" x 3" Dowels
1	3/8" x 1-1/4" x 29-3/4" Edging strip	2	3/8" x 6" Dowels

Photo 2: When more room space is needed, the desk and table can be folded into the wall unit.

Photo 3: A fence and an extra guide strip are used to bore the dowel holes in uprights on a drill press with a machine spur bit.

Photo 4: Making the notches on the edges of the full shelves on a table saw, using a dado head and a miter gauge.

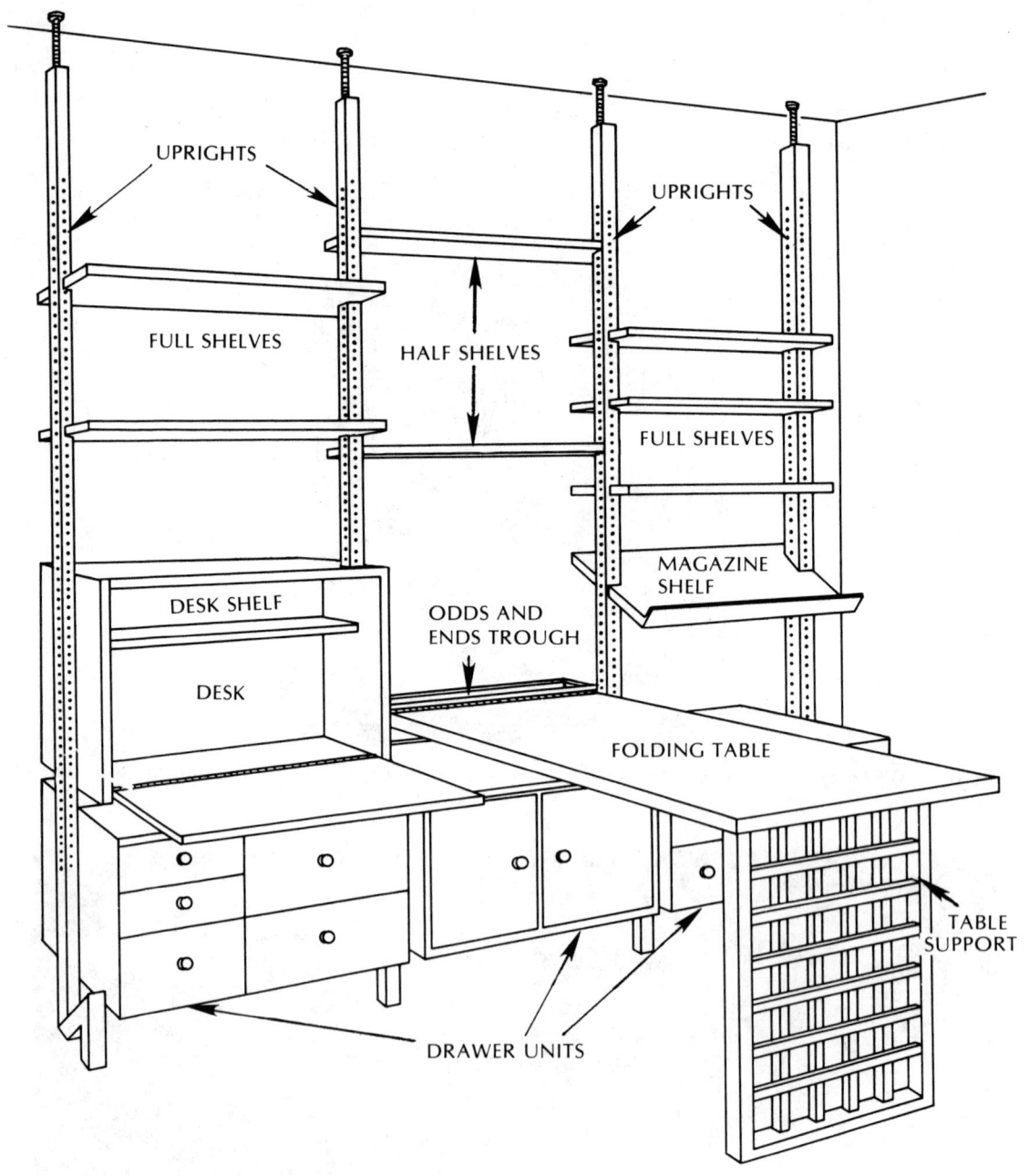

Fig. 1: Component parts of the modern wall unit.

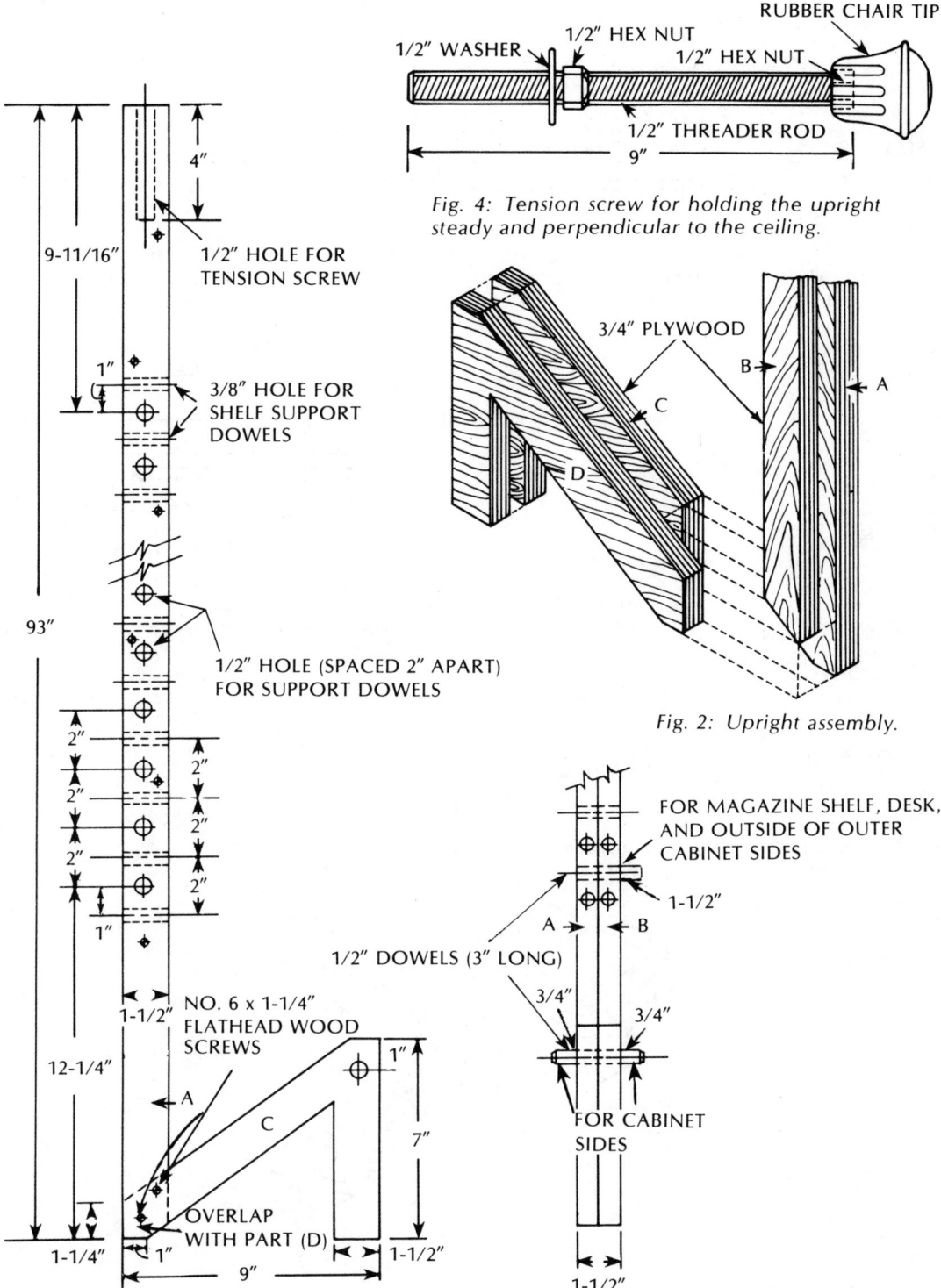

Fig. 4: Tension screw for holding the upright steady and perpendicular to the ceiling.

Fig. 2: Upright assembly.

Fig. 3: Details for the uprights.

Fig. 5: The 1/2" dowels help to support the magazine shelf, the desk, and the drawer units.

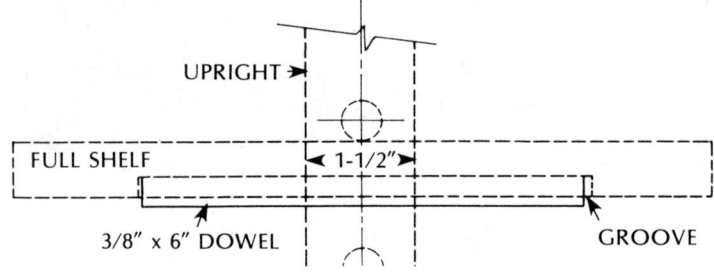

Fig. 7: The dowel in a blind groove for supporting a full shelf.

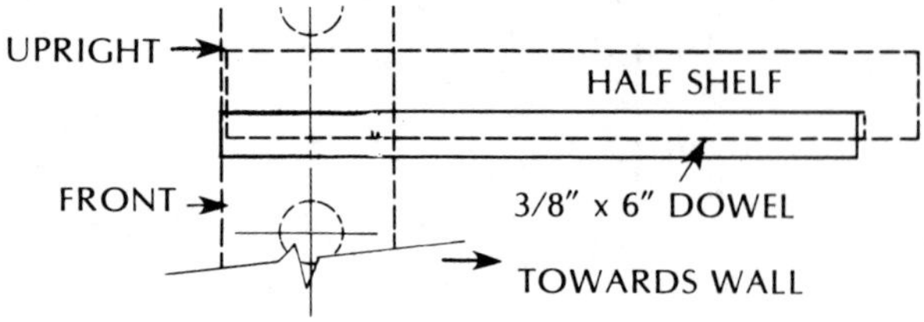

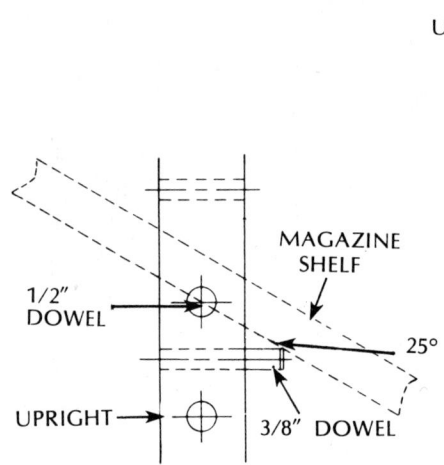

Fig. 8: The dowel and groove arrangement for a half shelf.

Fig. 6: Dowel positioning for the magazine shelf.

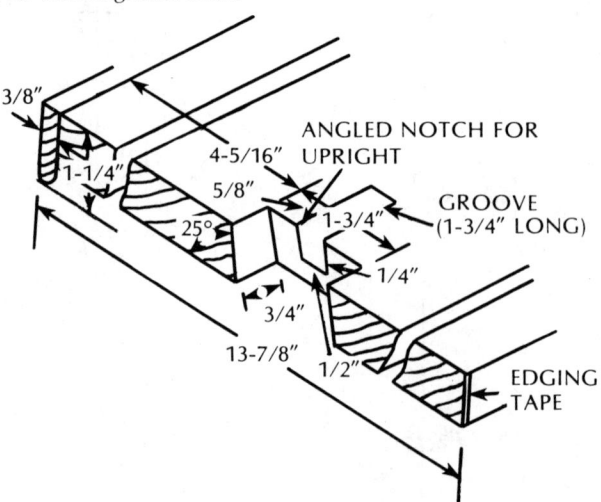

Fig. 9: Details for the end of the magazine shelf (bottom view).

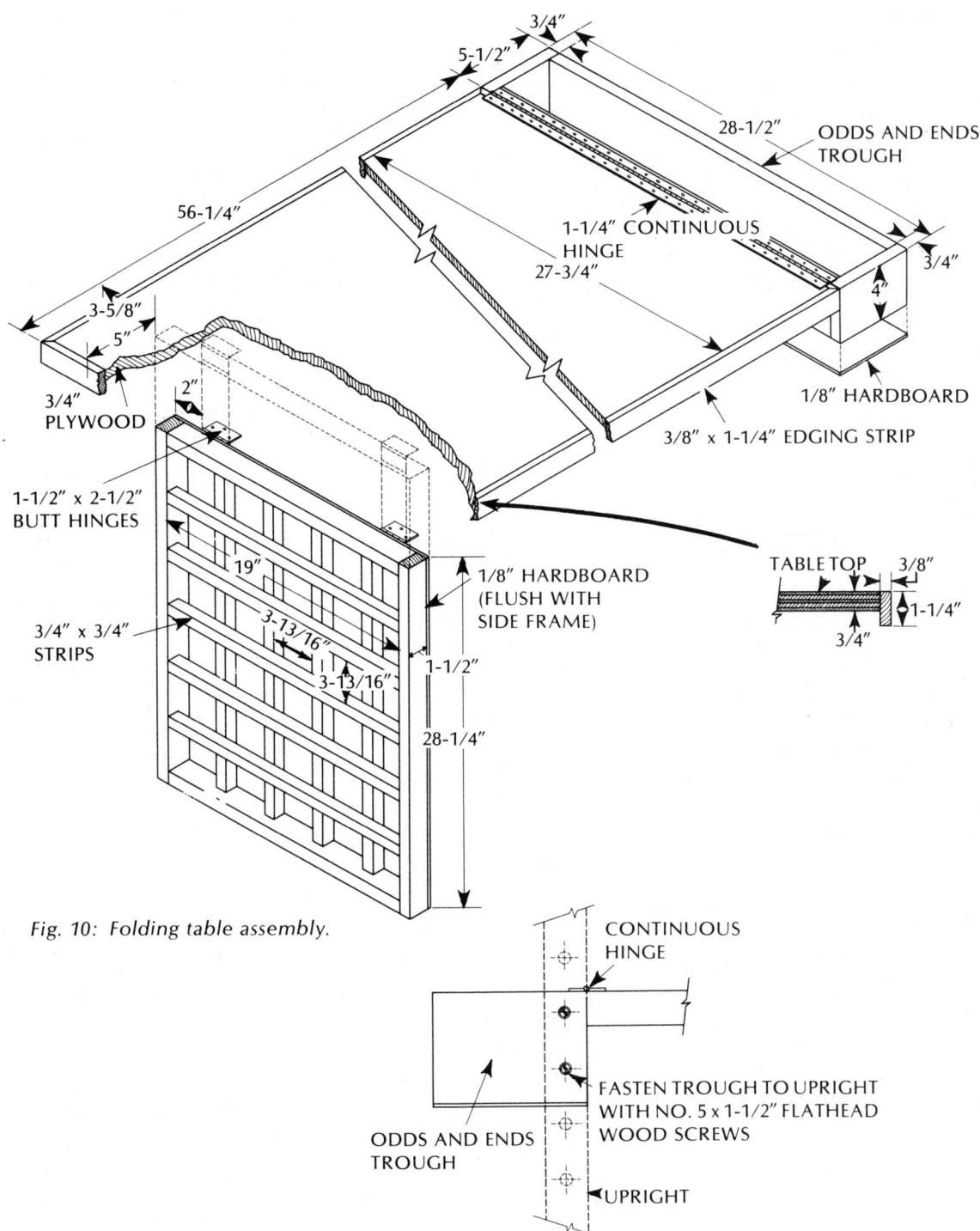

Fig. 10: Folding table assembly.

Fig. 11: Details for fastening the table and trough to the two center uprights.

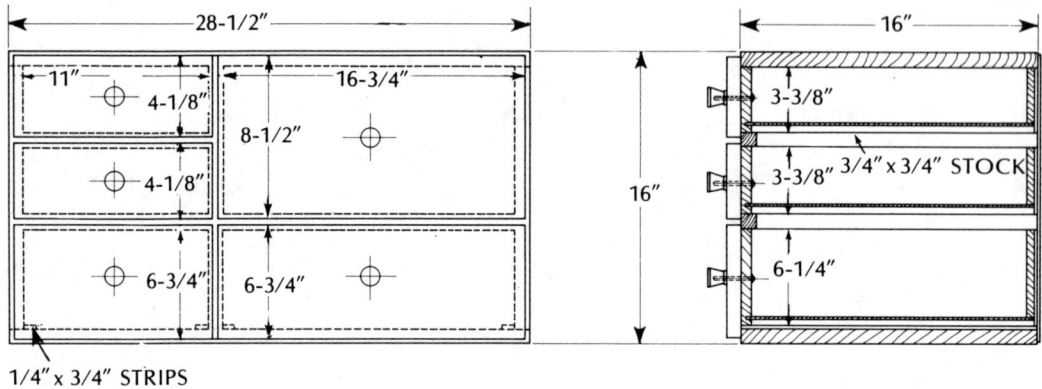

Fig. 12: Five drawer cabinet details.

Fig. 13: Cross section of the five drawer unit.

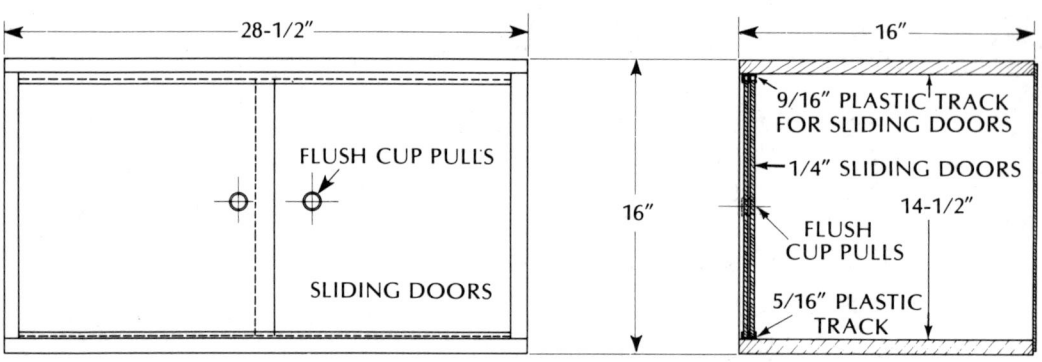

Fig. 14: Sliding door cabinet details.

Fig. 15: Cross section of the sliding door cabinet.

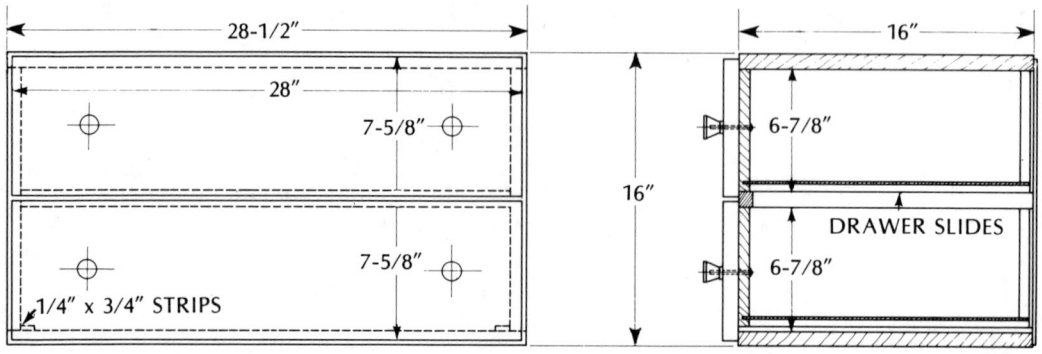

Fig. 16: Two drawer cabinet details.

Fig. 17: Cross section of the two drawer unit.

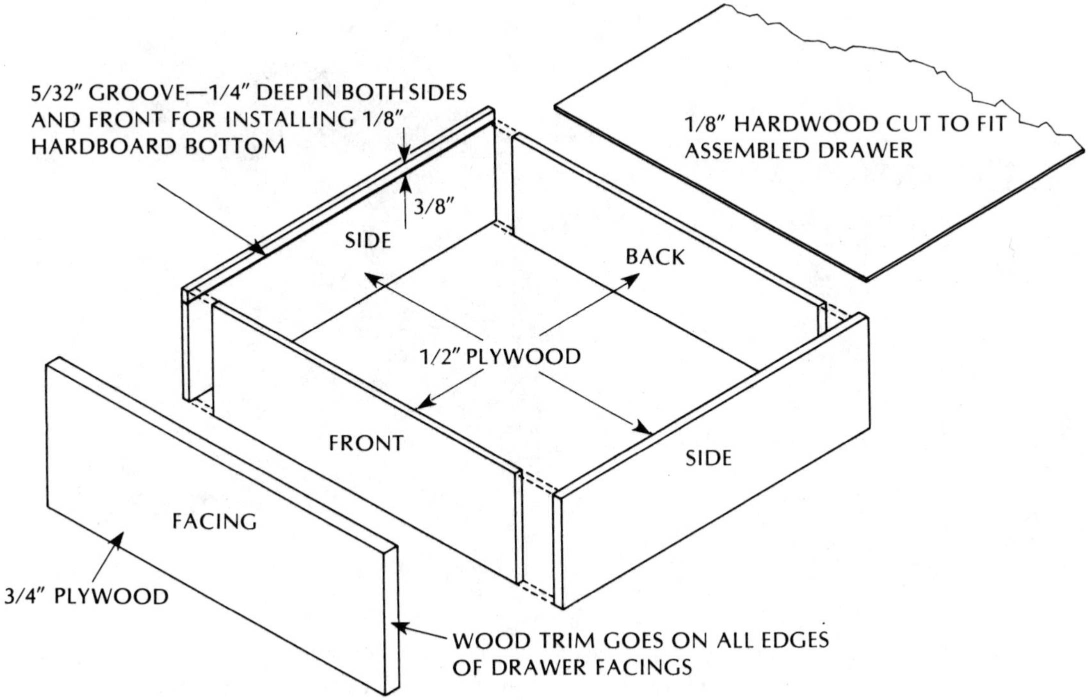

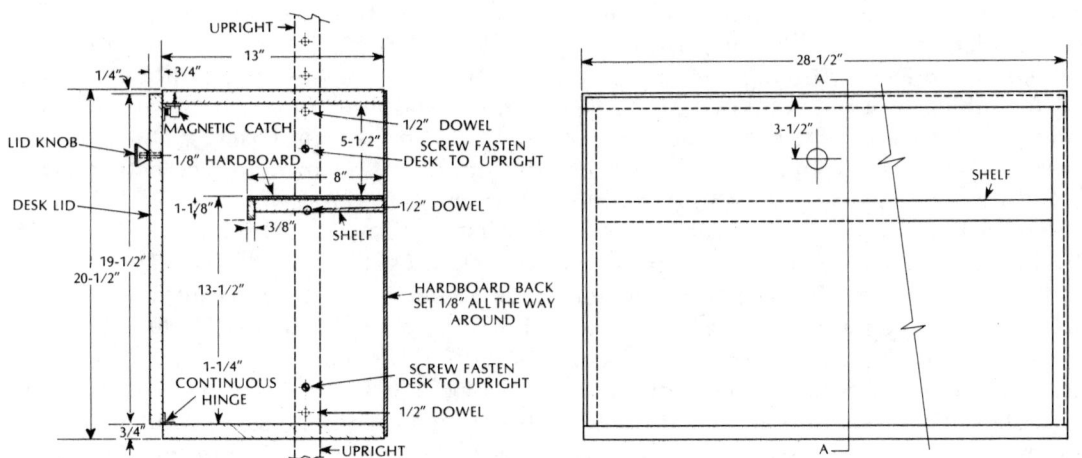

Fig. 18: The drawers are assembled with simple butt joints and glued.

Fig. 19: Cross section of the desk.

Fig. 20: Front view of the desk.

OCCASIONAL TABLE

Photo 1: A simple, clean-looking table with a slate top.

The heart of this straightforward table design (Photo 1) is the interlocking corner joint (Photo 2), which is made entirely on a table saw. The frame is so basic, it will look good in almost any wood or size; the top can be anything from severe in appearance—glass, for instance—to fancy (an inlaid design, laminations, or a large ceramic plaque). The included illustrations and list of materials are for a 21" square oak table with a slate top. Three other possibilities are shown in Fig. 1. The big slate-covered coffee table is not recommended for anyone who does not like to move furniture; it will weigh about 250 pounds when finished.

Before deciding to use slate for the table top, check to see if it is available first. Ask for blackboard slate, which comes in pieces 1/4" to 3/8" thick, and tell the supplier which side of the slate will be face up—the smooth or rough side. The rough side has a warmer appearance and does not show scratches. It is a good idea to build the table before ordering the slate or other material for the table top. Remember, the top material should be cut 1/16" undersize.

The materials list calls for oak construction; however, walnut, cherry, mahogany, or maple can be substituted. Maple or cherry with a slate top will look best if it is stained a fairly dark golden brown, instead of a reddish brown.

Saw blade spacers are needed for several steps of cutting the table frame. It would be a good idea to make an assortment of spacers, as shown in Photo 3: two 1/4" thick, two 1/8" thick, and several from various thicknesses of cardboard and paper. Masonite or good plywood is all right for the thicker spacers. They should be about 2-1/2" in diameter with a 5/8" hole through the center.

First cut four 1-1/4" by 1-1/4" by 21-1/16" oak squares, four 1-1/4" by 1-1/4" by 16" oak squares, and three or four 1-1/4" by 1-1/4" by 8" oak squares. These cuts must be perfectly square.

Cut the 1/2" thick tenons on all of the horizontal members, using two fine-tooth blades to minimize splintering. Use two 1/4" spacers between the blades; make trial cuts and add cardboard spacers as necessary to leave 1/2" of wood between the cuts (Fig. 2A).

If a tenoning jig is available, cut the tenons as shown in Photo 4. If a tenoning jig is not available, make the jig shown in Photos 5 and 6. Screw a good straight 3/4" by 4" by 12" (or longer) board to a table saw miter gauge; then screw a 1-3/4" by 1-3/4" by 6" hardwood block to it, making sure the block is square with the table. Use masking tape shims for the final positioning of the cuts (Photo 6). Make three or four good tenons in the 1-1/4" by 1-1/4" by 8" scrap blocks, which will be used for practicing cross-mortise cuts.

Next, use a stop block clamped to the miter gauge to complete the tenon (the 1-9/32" length will leave 1/32" of the tenon sticking out of the joint; this will have to be sanded flush later), as shown in Photo 7. The details for the completed tenon appear in Fig. 2A.

Use a 1/4" spacer between the blades and add paper spacers as necessary to cut a mortise in scrap wood that fits the tenon correctly. The tenon should slide into the mortise without being forced. Set up the table saw the same way as was done for cutting the tenons; make the first cuts both ways in all the legs (Photo 8). Make trial cuts first in the 1-1/4" by 1-1/4" by 8" scrap blocks to get the mortise positioned exactly in the center of the leg. Clean out the mortises by spacing the blades closer together and making repeated cuts (Fig. 3). Do not change the blade elevation. Chisel out any remaining splinters.

Then, cut the 11/16"-deep cross mortises in the tenons (Fig. 2B) with the same blades and spacers that were used to cut the mortises before (Photo 9). Use a stop block to position the cross mortises to line them up with the mortises in the legs when the joint is assembled. Be sure to make trial cuts first in the completed scrap tenons made earlier. Make an extra cut or two between the first cuts, and clean out the mortises with a chisel.

Assemble the table without glue to make

Photo 2: Interlocking corner joint on the table.

sure everything fits (Fig. 4). Do not force the joints together; use a rasp to relieve tight fits. Number all of the joints so the pieces can be put back together in the same order in the final assembly.

Take the table apart and coat all of the joint surfaces with clear epoxy. Assemble the table and put it upright on a flat surface for 24 hours to dry. No clamps or jigs are necessary, but the legs should be checked by eye to be sure they are not crooked.

Fill any cracks in the joints with clear epoxy. Allow it to dry; then finish-sand the frame. The two pairs of corner protectors shown in Photo 10 will keep the corners from being rounded off when sanding them flush. A portable disk sander or belt sander used with a fine abrasive (and great care) will make short work of this heavier sanding work, however, a rasp can also be used for this job. The finish sanding is best done with a pad sander.

Stain and finish the frame. Use a dark oak wiping stain, followed a week later with linseed oil as was used on the table shown in Photo 1.

For the top, have the slate cut about 1/16" smaller than the inside of the frame.

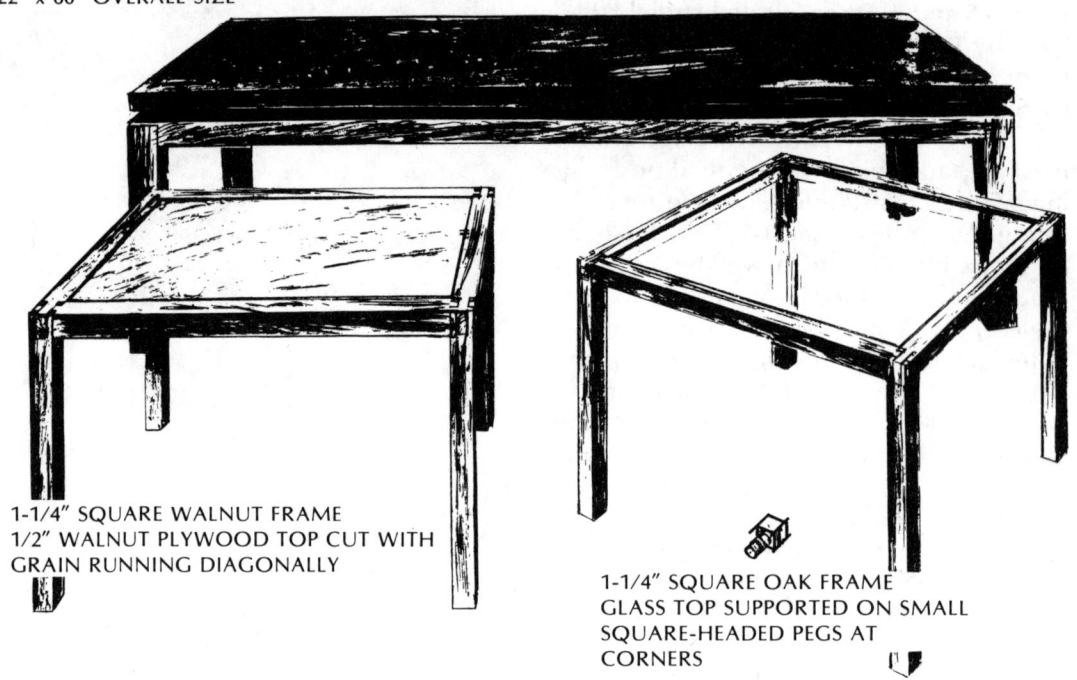

1-3/4" SQUARE OAK FRAME
1" SLATE TOP RAISED 5/8" ABOVE THE FRAME
22" x 60" OVERALL SIZE

1-1/4" SQUARE WALNUT FRAME
1/2" WALNUT PLYWOOD TOP CUT WITH GRAIN RUNNING DIAGONALLY

1-1/4" SQUARE OAK FRAME
GLASS TOP SUPPORTED ON SMALL SQUARE-HEADED PEGS AT CORNERS

Fig. 1: Three variations of the basic design.

MATERIALS

Quantity	Description
4	1-1/4" x 1-1/4" x 21-1/16" (finished size) Oak squares
4	1-1/4" x 1-1/4" x 16" (finished size) Oak squares
3 or 4	1-1/4" x 1-1/4" x 8" Scrap oak squares for trial cuts
1 piece	Blackboard slate approximately 18-1/2" square (cut to fit finished table)
4	5/8" x 1/2" x 19" Maple, pine or poplar strips
8	No. 8 x 1" Flathead wood screws
-	Clear epoxy cement
-	Suitable finishing materials for the frame and top
-	Scrap wood for fixtures, blade spacers

The slate should be finished with crude oil, or with neatsfoot oil as a second choice. Wipe a coat on with a cloth, allow it to soak in for a few minutes, then, wipe off all the excess oil. After completing the first oiling, it will be necessary to re-oil the slate three or four times in the following few weeks, until dry streaks stop showing up on the surface.

The supports for the slate top can be made from maple, pine, or poplar. Miter the ends to fit the frame (Fig. 5). Staining them or painting them flat black will add a professional touch, even though they do not show when the top is on.

Clamp the supports to the frame, using cardboard pads to prevent the clamps from denting the wood. Set the slate in place and adjust the height of the supports until the slate is flush with the top of the frame. Remove the slate, drill (Photo 11), and screw the supports into the frame (Fig. 6).

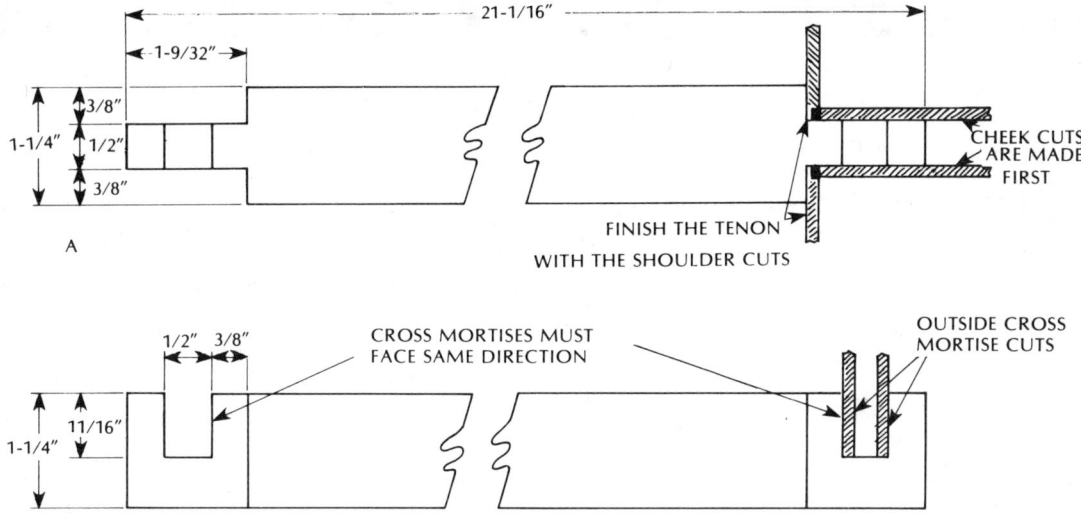

Fig. 2: (A) Details for the tenons; (B) details for cross mortises in the tenons.

Photo 3: Saw blade spacers for use on the table saw.

Photo 4: Cutting tenons with a tenoning jig.

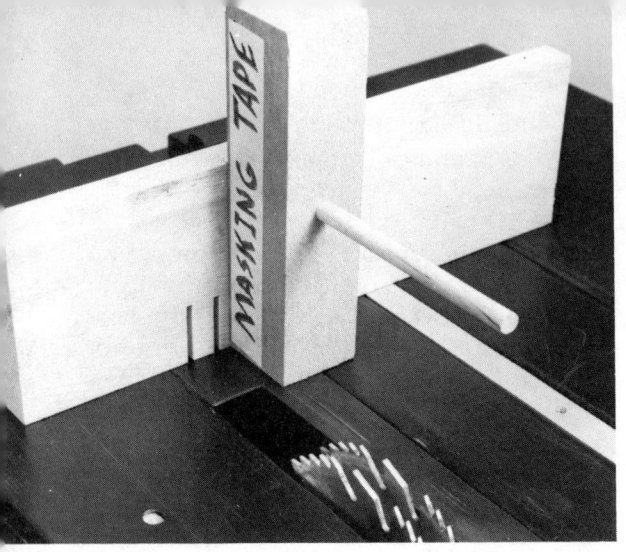

Photo 5: Homemade jig for cutting tenons. Note the 3/8" dowel, used to keep the clamp from falling into the saw blades if it should vibrate loose.

Photo 6: Cutting tenons with the homemade jig.

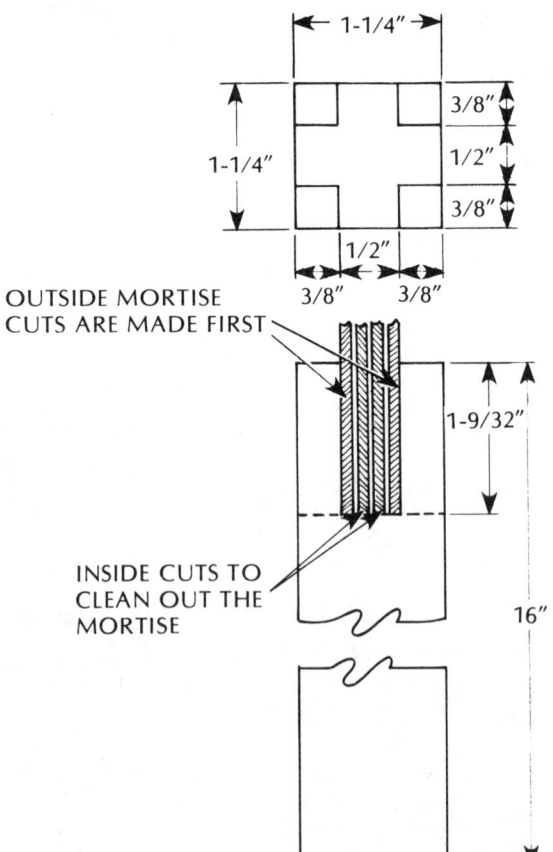
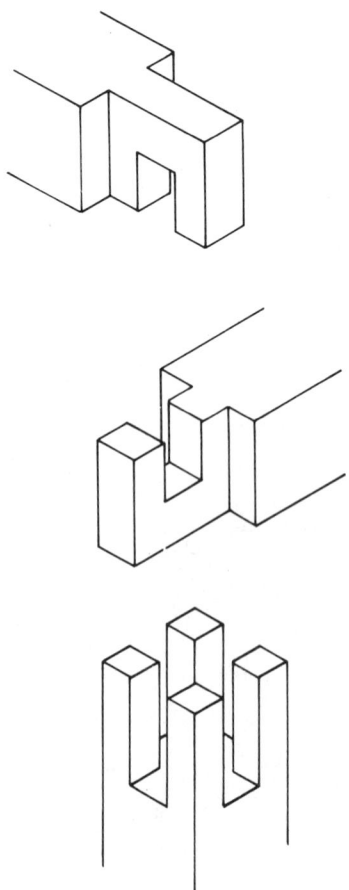

Fig. 3: Details for the mortises; make the outside cuts first.

Fig. 4: Positioning for the joint assembly.

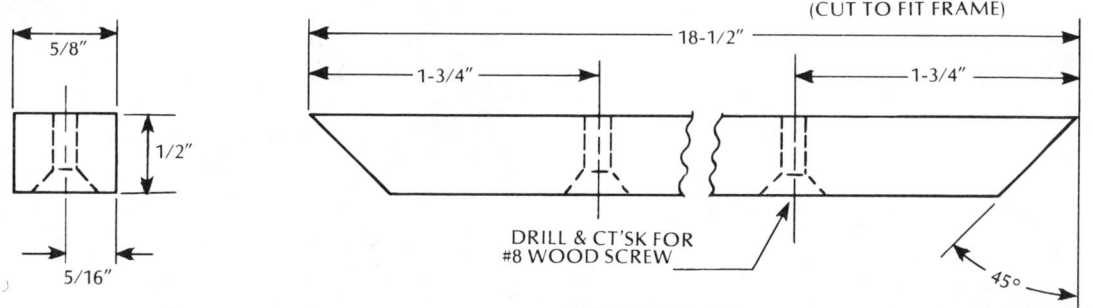

Fig. 5: Details for support rails to hold slate top.

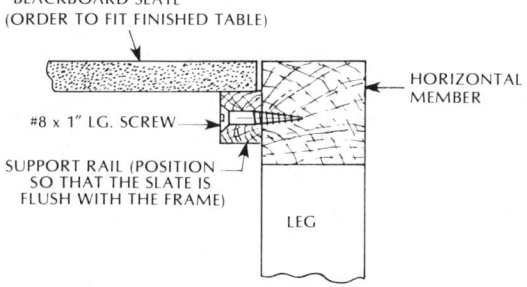

Fig. 6: Corner details for the top of the table.

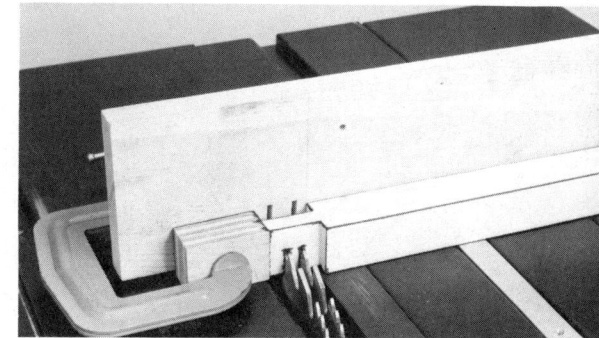

Photo 9: Cutting cross mortises on the tenons. Note: The blade guard is removed for clarity.

Photo 7: Completing the tenon with the two shoulder cuts. Note: The blade guard is removed for clarity.

Photo 10: Corner protectors prevent the corners from being rounded off when sanding.

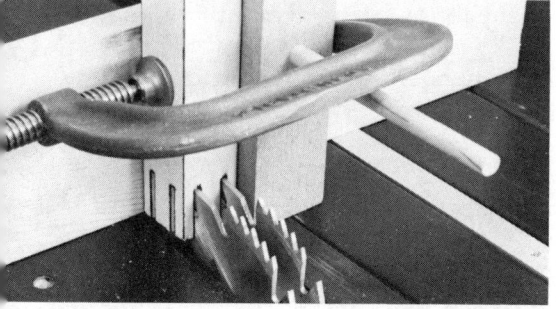

Photo 8: Making the first mortise cut (either the homemade jig pictured above or the tenoning jig can be used again).

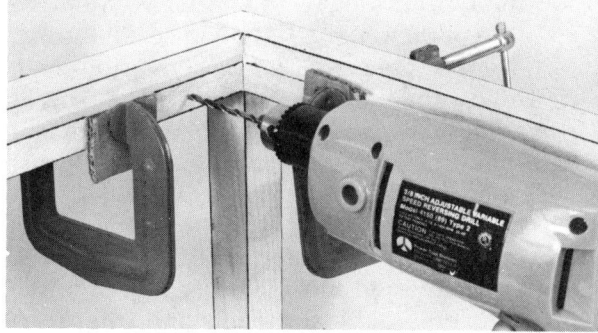

Photo 11: Drilling into the frame for screws to hold the slate top supports.

EARLY AMERICAN LOWBOY

Photo 1

This is a reproduction of an Early American lowboy (Photo 1). The design lends itself to almost any decor.

Suitable woods for the exterior of the lowboy are mahogany, cherry, walnut, or curly maple. More common woods — birch or other hardwoods — are used for constructing the exterior framework. Plywood or hardboard can be used for the dust panels, drawer bottoms, and back panel.

Make a cardboard template of the cabriole leg (Fig. 1) and trace the pattern on two adjacent sides of the leg stock. Glue up stock as required for the width (Fig. 2); then, cut the legs on a band saw. After one side of the outline has been cut (Photo 2), the waste pieces are replaced, using small brads, and the other marked side is cut. No additional length is needed for turning the foot on a lathe (Photo 3). Next, 3/8" mortises are made on a drill press with a 3/8" hollow chisel (Photo 4), to house the tenons of the side panels, the front and back stretchers and the apron (Fig. 3).

Assemble the stretchers and stiles with the mating legs and make a dry fitting (before gluing), to make sure all of the pieces join properly (Photo 5). The intermediate and bottom stretchers are separated by four vertical mullions, which are mortised into them. Details for this mortise and tenon joint appear in Figs. 1 and 3. The dust panels are inserted into grooves in the stretchers. They are also inserted between the outside stiles and one side of the four horizontal muntins and between the muntins at the center. The tenons of the stiles fit into the same stretcher grooves. This is possible because the stiles are rabbeted around the top of the legs. The stretchers are themselves tenoned into the legs (Fig. 3).

The four horizontal muntins and the two back vertical mullions are all joined to the stretchers with mortise and tenon joints. The two front vertical mullions are tenoned

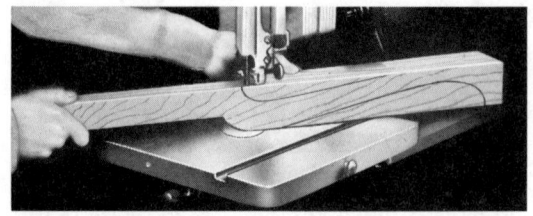

Photo 2: Cutting the cabriole leg on a band saw.

MATERIALS

Quantity	Description
4	2-3/4" x 2-3/4" x 29-1/4" Legs
1	1" x 1-1/2" x 26-1/2" Top stretcher (front)
1	1" x 1-5/16" x 26-1/2" Top stretcher (back)
1	1" x 1-1/2" x 26-1/2" Intermediate stretcher (front)
1	1" x 1-5/16" x 26-1/2" Intermediate stretcher (back)
1	3/4" x 3/4" x 25" Bottom stretcher (front)
1	3/4" x 2-1/2" x 26-1/2" Apron
1	3/4" x 1-1/2" x 26-1/2" Bottom stretcher (back)
2	1" x 1-1/2" x 5-7/8" Center mullions (front)
2	1" x 1-5/16" x 5-7/8" Center mullions (back)
2	1" x 1-1/2" x 14-1/2" Stiles (top)
2	3/4" x 1-1/2" x 13-3/8" Stiles (bottom)
2	1" x 1-1/2" x 13-3/8" Stiles (intermediate)
2	1" x 2-1/2" x 13-3/8" Muntins (intermediate center)
2	3/4" x 2-1/2" x 13-3/8" Muntins (bottom center)
1	3/4" x 17" x 30" Top
1	3/16" x 10-1/2" x 26" Back panel
2	3/4" x 12-5/8" x 14-1/2" Side panels
4	3/16" x 5-3/4" x 13-3/8" Dust panels (end)
2	3/16" x 8-1/2" x 13-3/8" Dust panels (center)
2	1-3/16" x 1-3/16" x 3-7/16" Finials
2	1/4" x 1-1/4" x 1-3/4" Caps
8	1" x 1" x 1-3/8" Leg corner blocks
1	3/4" x 3-1/4" x 25-1/2" Top drawer front
2	1/2" x 3" x 15-1/2" Top drawer sides
1	1/2" x 2-1/2" x 24-1/2" Top drawer back
1	3/16" x 15-1/4" x 24-1/2" Top drawer bottom
2	3/4" x 5-1/4" x 7-1/4" End drawer fronts
4	1/2" x 5" x 15-1/2" End drawer sides
2	1/2" x 4-1/2" x 6-1/4" End drawer backs
2	3/16" x 6-1/4" x 15-1/4" End drawer bottoms
1	3/4" x 5-1/4" x 10" Center drawer front
2	1/2" x 5" x 15-1/2" Center drawer sides
1	1/2" x 4-1/2" x 9" Center drawer back
1	3/16" x 9" x 15-1/4" Center drawer bottom
4	1/4" x 2" x 15" Drawer runs
4	1/2" x 3/4" x 15" Drawer guides
1	1-3/4" x 1-3/4" x 1" Drawer knob
4	Handles (Chippendale design brass)
1	Escutcheon (Chippendale design brass)
6	No. 10 x 1-1/2" Flathead wood screws (for fastening top)
1	No. 8 x 5/8" Flathead wood screw (for drawer knob)
8	No. 6 x 1/2" Flathead wood screws (for drawer guides)
24	No. 18 x 1/2" Escutcheon pins (for drawer runs)

into the bottom front stretcher and the apron, which are flush together, as shown in Fig. 4.

After all of the pieces, including the side and back panels, are glued in place, the two top stretchers, which have dovetailed ends, as shown in Fig. 1, are inserted into the proper dovetail mortises on the top ends of the legs. Be sure to check the structure for squareness to make sure it is true when completed.

Cut all of the drawer fronts 1/2" longer and 1/4" wider than the openings in the frame, to allow for rabbets at the top and

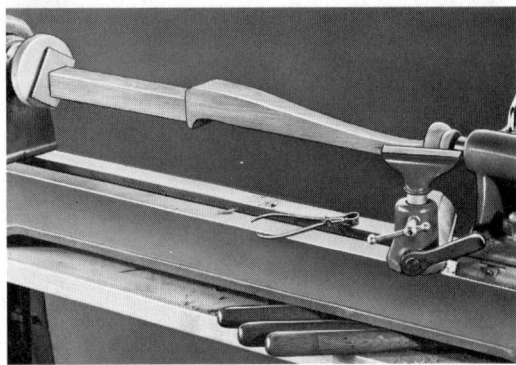

Photo 3: Turning the foot on a lathe, using an offset centering device fastened to the faceplate.

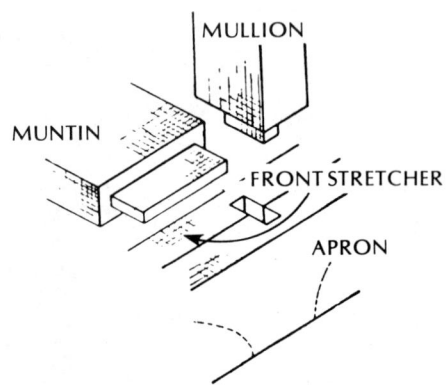

Fig. 4: Construction of the lower front section of the frame.

Photo 4: Cutting mortises in the legs on a drill press, using a 3/8" hollow chisel. All mortises are 13/16" deep.

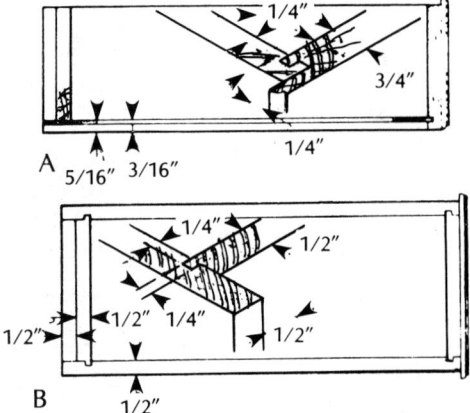

Fig. 5: (A) Rabbet and groove jointing the drawer front to the sides; (B) dado and rabbet jointing the drawer sides to the back.

ends of all drawer fronts. The front and sides of the drawers are joined with standard rabbet and groove joints (Fig. 5A); the sides and back of the drawers are joined with dado and rabbet joints (Fig. 5B).

As was stated before, the apron is tenoned into the front legs (Fig. 3), and is glued to the bottom front stretcher. The two hanging finials are turned to shape on a lathe, and are glue-jointed to the apron with a 3/8" dowel. Finial dimensions are shown in Fig. 6.

The shell design on the center bottom drawer is made with the jig shown in Photo 6. To make the jig, lay out the shell design on a piece of scrap material the same size as the drawer front; then, tack the jig to the back of the drawer front. When drawing the design on the jig, lay out the center line first, locating the knob center 7/16" from the base, and scribe a 3-5/16" arc around this center point. Mark off a 3/4" distance on the arc, beginning at 3/8" on each side of the center line. Then, draw guide lines through these marks to the center point, to align the jig for cutting the shell.

The rough cutting is done on a table saw with a molding cutterhead and 90° V-groove cutter knives. A 7" wide auxiliary rip fence, which is clamped to the standard rip fence is needed. Adjust the molding cutterhead for a 5/16" deep cut (Fig. 7). Scribe index lines on the auxiliary fence,

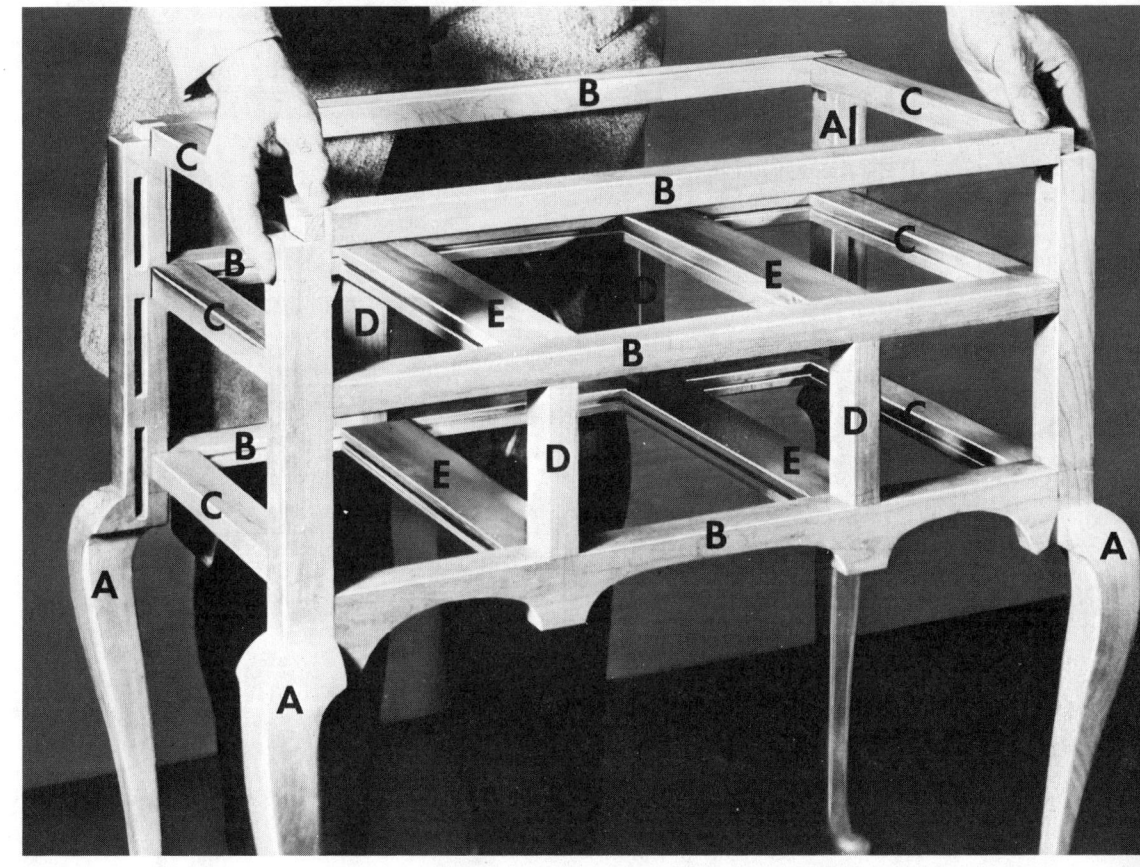

Photo 5: Dry fitting (before gluing) the legs (A), stretchers (B), stiles (C), mullions (D), and muntins (E) to be sure all of the pieces fit properly.

where the cutter knife arc crosses the table top, both front and back, to control the length of the cut. Provide a positive stop for the cutter knife height, so all of the cuts will be the same (Photo 7). Adjust the jig guides and raise the cutter knives for the first cut, always holding the work steady. Advance the jig and the drawer front to the index stop lines on the auxiliary fence; then, lower the cutterhead. Adjust the jig to a new position on the drawer back and repeat the operation for each cut (Photo 8). Finish the shell with hand tools. Then, cut the rabbets on the top and sides of all the drawer fronts, and mold the drawer edges with 1/2" quarter round cutter knives (Fig. 3). Details for the center drawer knob are given in Fig. 8.

The top of the lowboy is glued up from 3/4" solid stock and cut to a 17" by 30" size. The front and side edges are molded on a saw in two steps. The bottom of the top edge is molded with 1/8" quarter round cutter knives, the upper part with ogee cutter knives (Fig. 3).

Sand the project with first a medium-grit, and then a fine-grit abrasive. Apply a stain on the exterior of the lowboy. If mahogany or walnut is used, apply a wood filler after staining. Follow this with two thin coats of white shellac and a coat of synthetic varnish. The finishing work completes an authentic reproduction of an Early American lowboy.

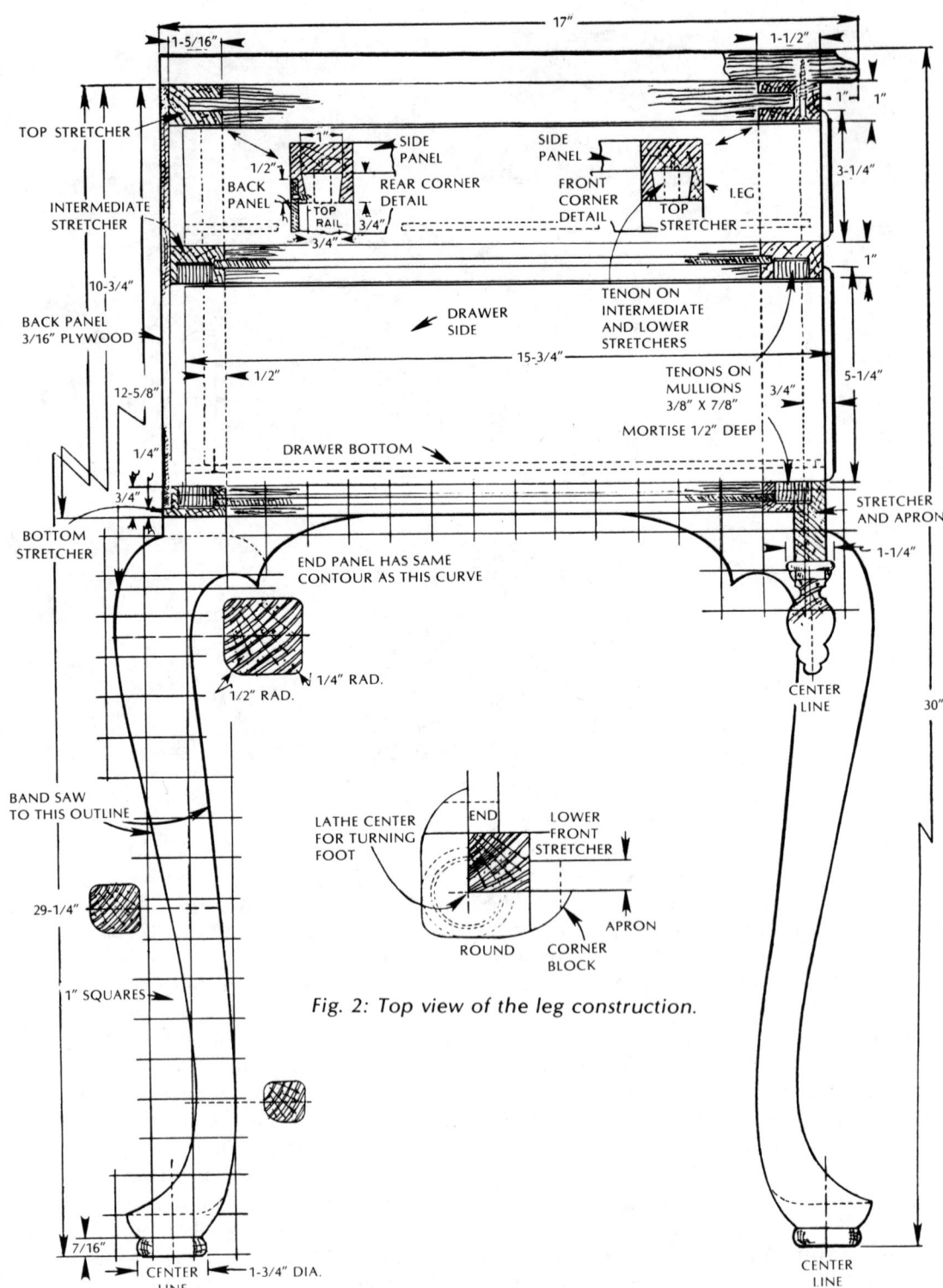

Fig. 2: Top view of the leg construction.

Fig. 1: Cross section of the lowboy.

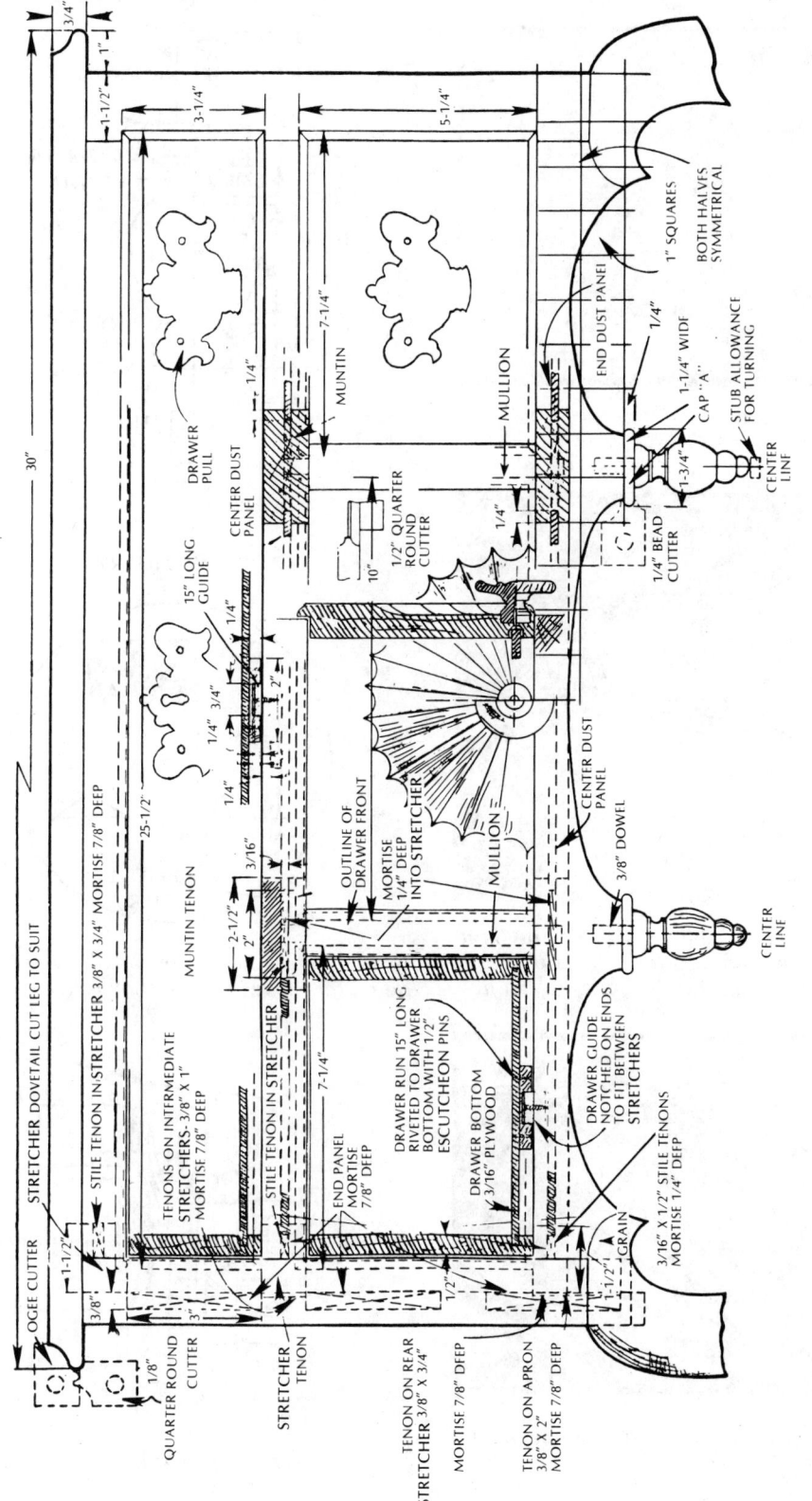

Fig. 3: Front view of the lowboy.

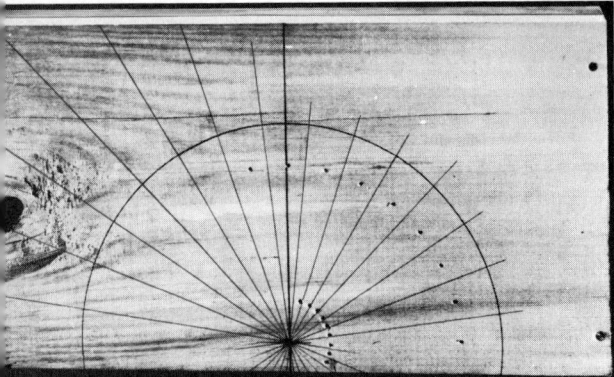

Photo 6: A jig used for cutting the shell relief on the center bottom drawer front.

Photo 7: Cutting the shell design on the table saw, using a molding cutterhead and 90° V-groove cutter knives and the shell-design jig.

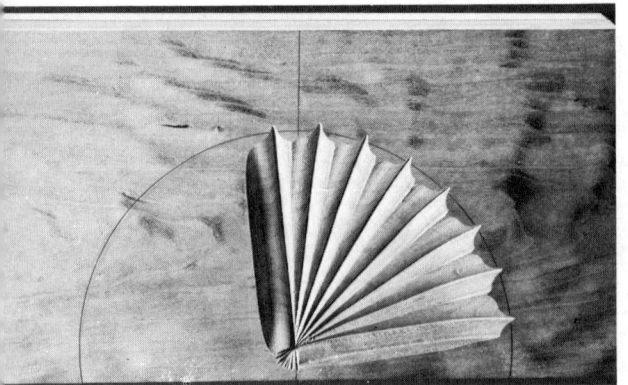

Photo 8: Partially finished shell relief on the drawer front.

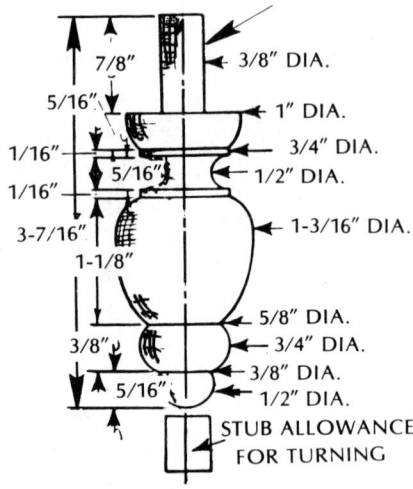

Fig. 6: Finial details.

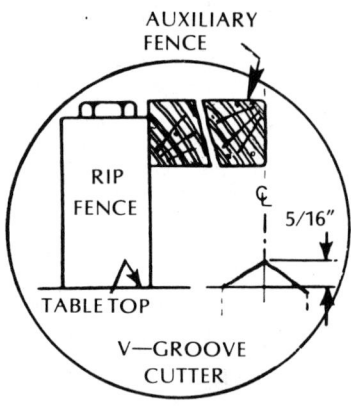

Fig. 7: Alignment of the auxiliary fence and the cutter knives for the shell relief operation.

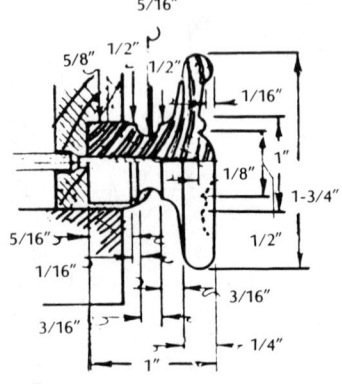

Fig. 8: Drawer knob details.

WINDSOR CHAIR

Photo 1: An eighteenth century style Windsor chair.

One of the most popular chair styles in America at the beginning of the eighteenth century was the Windsor chair featured here (Photo 1). Many graceful varieties and shapes evolved from the original design. Windsor chairs of both the fan or comb-backed and hoop-back type were once in vogue. Most of these variations were of purely American development.

Begin the project by gluing together some 1" stock for the chair seat. The dished portion of the seat is optional, but it can be turned on the outboard end of a lathe. Be sure to use a steady rest on the lathe when turning the four long spindles used on the back of the chair. The arm support spindles, as well as the legs and leg stretchers, can be turned on the lathe with a wood turning duplicator attachment such as shown in Photo 2. All of the essential dimensions for the spindles and legs are given in Figs. 1 and 2.

Both the curved back rest and arm rest are made of 3/4" plywood; 3/4" by 1-1/2" by 2" blocks are glued to the front ends of the arm rests for the hand grip blocks—which have a 3/4" radius after being turned (Fig. 1 and 3). The base stock of these pieces

27

can be covered with a veneer or painted to match the finish of the chair.

The scrolled back (Fig. 3) consists of two panels and is held in place with short tenons set into the mortises of the curved back rest, arm rest, and chair seat, as shown in Fig. 3.

Before drilling any of the spindle holes, temporarily assemble the lower scrolled back panel and the front spindles; then mark off the approximate drilling angles on both the arm rest and the chair seat with a straight edge, by using the points indicated in Figs. 4 and 5.

If the chair is made of walnut or mahogany, apply a walnut filler, followed by two or three thin coats of white shellac. For a satin smoothness, apply a coat of rubbed-effect synthetic varnish.

MATERIALS

Quantity	Description
1	1" x 22" x 20" Chair seat (solid stock)
1	3/4" x 24-1/2" x 16-1/2" Arm rest (plywood)
1	1/4" x 4" x 8" Lower back panel
1	1/4" x 3" x 22-5/8" Upper back panel
1	3/4" x 15" x 23-1/2" Back rest (plywood)
2	1-3/4" x 1-3/4" x 17-3/4" Front legs
2	1-3/4" x 1-3/4" x 16-3/4" Back legs
2	1-1/2" x 1-1/2" x 20" Lower leg stretchers
1	1-1/2" x 1-1/2" x 17" Upper leg stretcher
2	1-1/2" x 1-1/2" x 14-3/4" Side leg stretchers
2	1-3/4" x 1-3/4" x 10-5/8" Front arm supports
2	7/8" x 7/8" x 10-3/8" Rungs
2	7/8" x 7/8" x 9-1/2" Rungs
2	7/8" x 7/8" x 9" Rungs
2	7/8" x 7/8" x 8-3/4" Rungs
4	7/8" x 7/8" x 30-1/2" Long back rungs
2	3/4" x 1-1/2" x 2" Hand grip block (for arm rest)

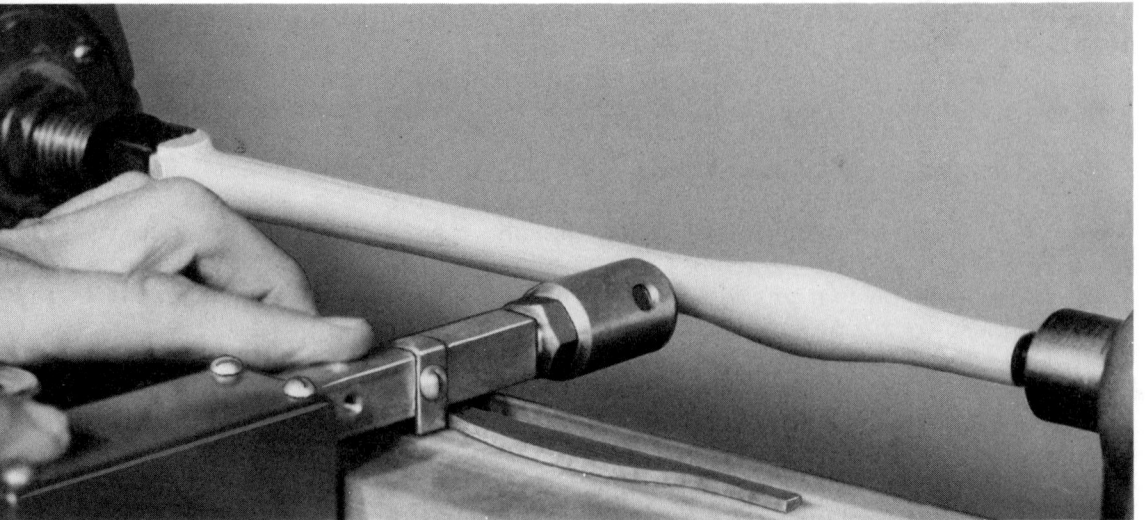

Photo 2: All of the spindles, including the front arm rests and legs, can be turned on the lathe, using a wood turning duplicator and the proper templates.

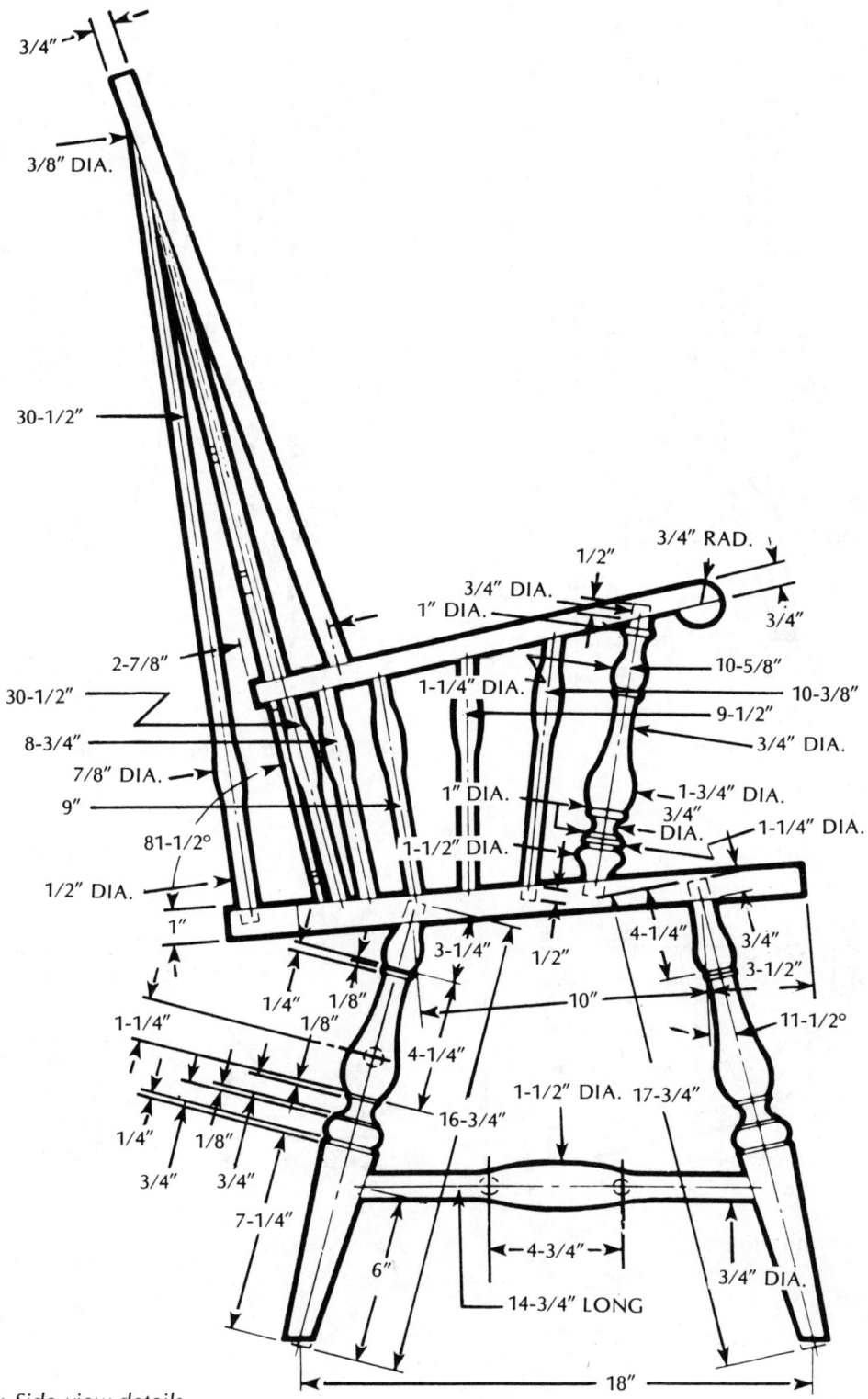

Fig. 1: Side view details.

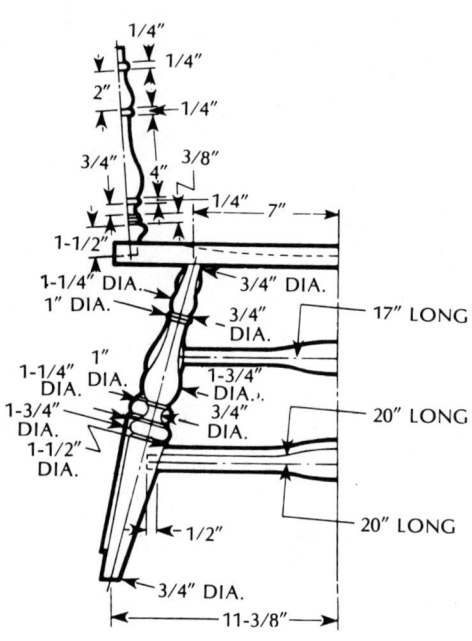

Fig. 2: Front view details.

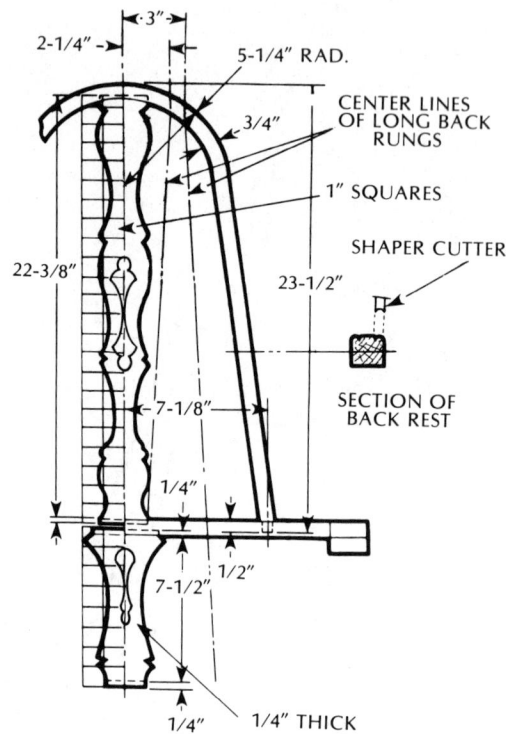

Fig. 3: Details for the back panels and the back rest.

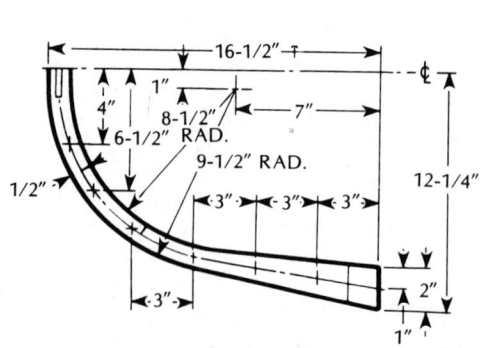

Fig. 4: Arm rest details.

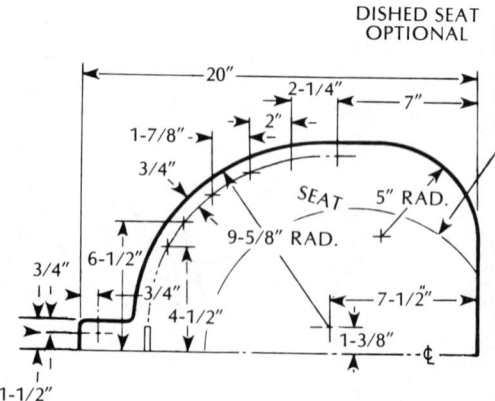

Fig. 5: Chair seat details.

QUEEN ANNE OCCASIONAL TABLE

Photo 1: An eighteenth century style occasional table.

The eighteenth century design of this table (Photo 1) was taken from a distinguished original antique masterpiece. The table shown here is an authentic copy of the original, reproduced for the Woodford mansion collection by Edward Austin Walton, a nationally known authority on period furniture.

The cabriole legs are made from glued-up stock that must be 2-1/4" square. The foot pad of the leg is turned on a lathe, as shown in Photo 2. Details for the foot pad are given in Fig. 1. Cut out a full size outline of the leg (Fig. 2) on a piece of cardboard, as a template for marking off the two adjoining sides of the leg stock. First, cut one side on a band saw; then, tack the pieces that have been cut away back onto the stock with small brads, and proceed to cut the other side (Photo 3). After this operation is completed, the remainder of the work on the legs is done by hand, except for the upper portion of the foot pad which can be sanded with a sanding drum on the drill press (Photo 4), or some other adaptable power tool. The rough cutting to shape can be done with a hand spokeshave, holding the leg in a vise or on a lathe. Finish the leg with first a medium-grit, and then fine-grit abrasive paper.

For the dowel joints holding the legs to the stretchers, bore dowel holes in the top of the legs on a drill press, using a 3/8" machine spur bit (Photo 5). Eighteen 3/8" dowel holes must be drilled altogether, three for each joint. The 1-1/4" front stretcher takes two 5/16" dowels (Fig. 3); the front legs must be drilled accordingly. After boring all of the dowel holes in the side, back, and front stretchers, shape the bottom edge of the stretchers using a molding cutterhead and combination 1/8" quarter round and 1/4" bead cutter knives on a table saw (Fig. 4). Counterbore three pocket holes in the side and back stretchers (Photo 6) for fastening the table top to the stretchers. The screw holes for the No. 7 by 1-1/4" flathead wood screws (Fig. 2) are made with a 9/64" drill bit.

The table top dimensions are 3/4" by 18-7/8" by 30". After the stock for the table top has been cut to size on a table saw, the top is molded with 1/8" quarter round and 1/2" quarter round molding cutterhead knives, as shown in Fig. 4. The 1/4" by 19" by 15-5/8" drawer bottom panel is set and glued into 1/4" dadoes in the drawer front and sides.

The drawer runners are made as shown in Fig. 5. They are then counterbored and screw fastened to the side stretchers with No. 7 by 1-1/2" flathead wood screws (Fig. 2). The drawers are made with the conventional rabbet and groove joint at the front, as shown in Fig. 6. A completed assembly of the drawer front and side is shown in Photo 7. The back and sides of the drawer unit are joined with dado and rabbet joints. In keeping with the style of the furniture, a turned drawer handle should be made; this is held in place with a tapered pin (Fig. 7).

For a mellow finish, apply a brown mahogany stain and let it dry overnight. Then, use a brown mahogany wood filler. Finally, apply two coats of satin polyurethane varnish. A penetrating resin finish may also be used.

MATERIALS

Quantity	Description
4	2-1/4" x 2-1/4" x 25-3/8" Legs
2	3/4" x 5-1/4" x 14-7/8" Side stretchers
1	3/4" x 5-1/4" x 19-3/8" Back stretcher
1	3/4" x 1-1/4" x 19-3/8" Front stretcher
2	3/4" x 1-3/8" x 14-3/4" Drawer runners
1	3/4" x 18-7/8" x 30" Top
1	3/4" x 4" x 19-3/8" Drawer front
2	1/2" x 4" x 16" Drawer sides
1	1/2" x 3-1/2" x 19" Drawer back
1	1/4" x 19" x 15-5/8" Drawer bottom panel
1	1-1/8" x 1-1/8" x 3-1/8" Drawer handle
1	3/16" x 1/4" x 1" Drawer handle pin
18	3/8" x 1-3/4" Hardwood dowels
4	5/16" x 1-3/4" Hardwood dowels
6	No. 7 x 1-1/2" Flathead wood screws
9	No. 7 x 1-1/4" Flathead wood screws

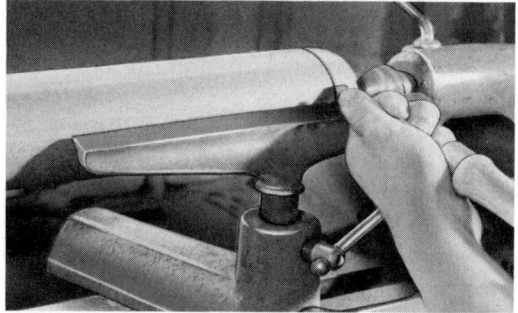

Photo 2: Turning the foot portion of the cabriole leg on a lathe.

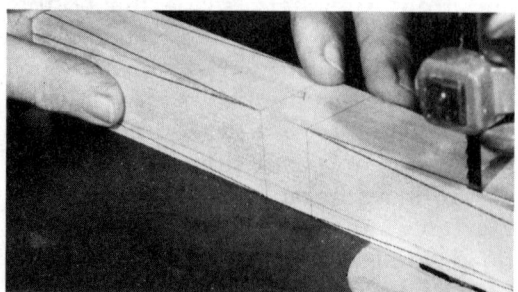

Photo 3: After transferring the outline of the adjoining sides of the leg from a template, cut to size on a band saw.

Photo 4: Sanding the foot portion above the pad to a perfect contour on a drill press, using a 3" sanding drum.

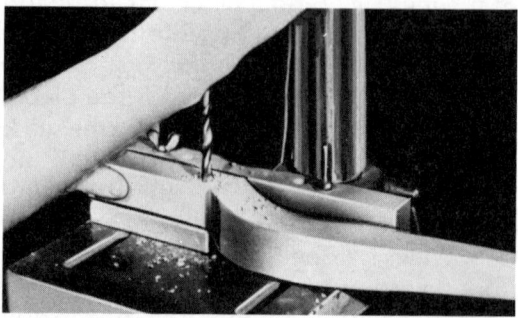

Photo 5: Boring dowel holes with a machine spur bit and a support block.

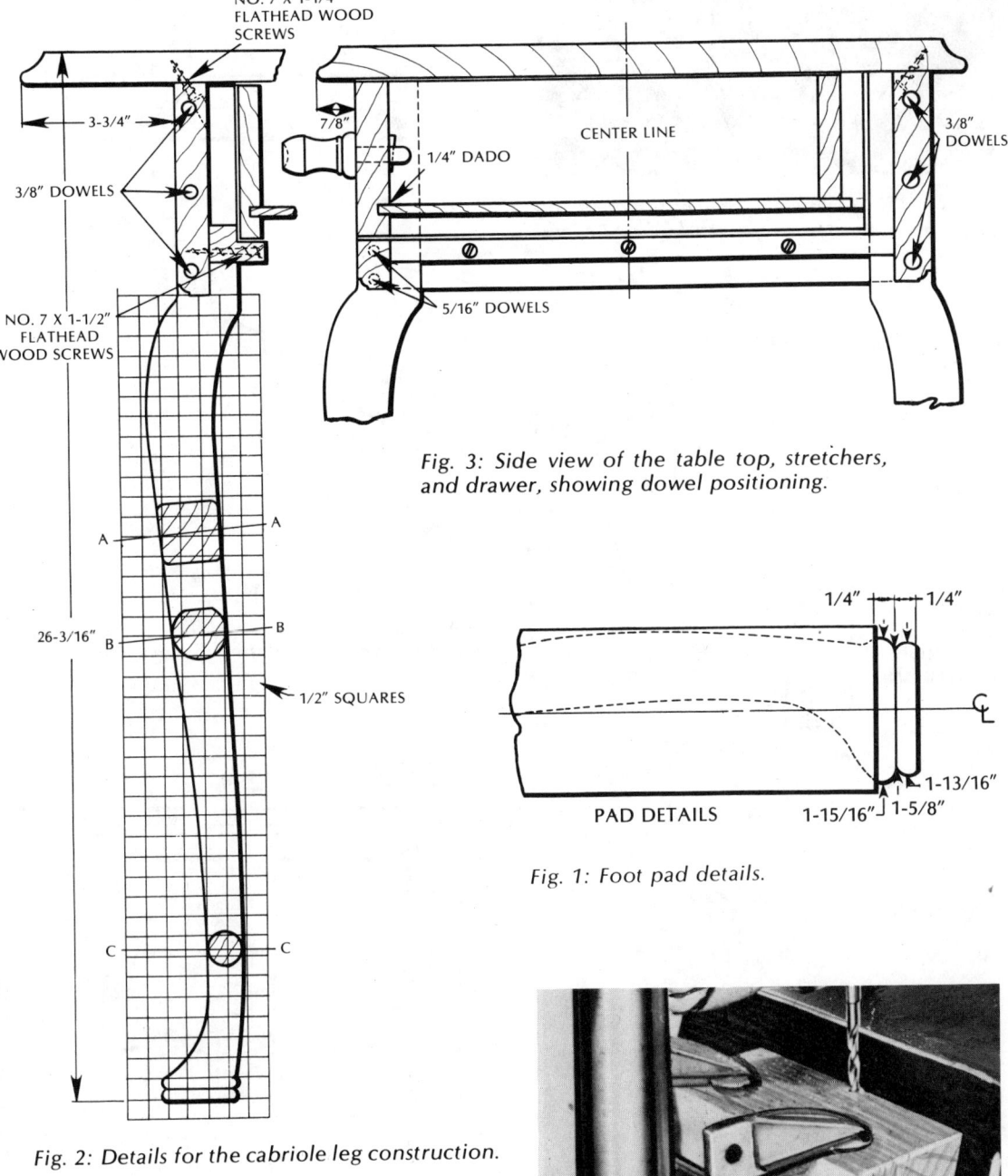

Fig. 3: Side view of the table top, stretchers, and drawer, showing dowel positioning.

Fig. 1: Foot pad details.

Fig. 2: Details for the cabriole leg construction.

Photo 6: Counterboring pocket holes into the side and back stretchers, using a 15° beveled block.

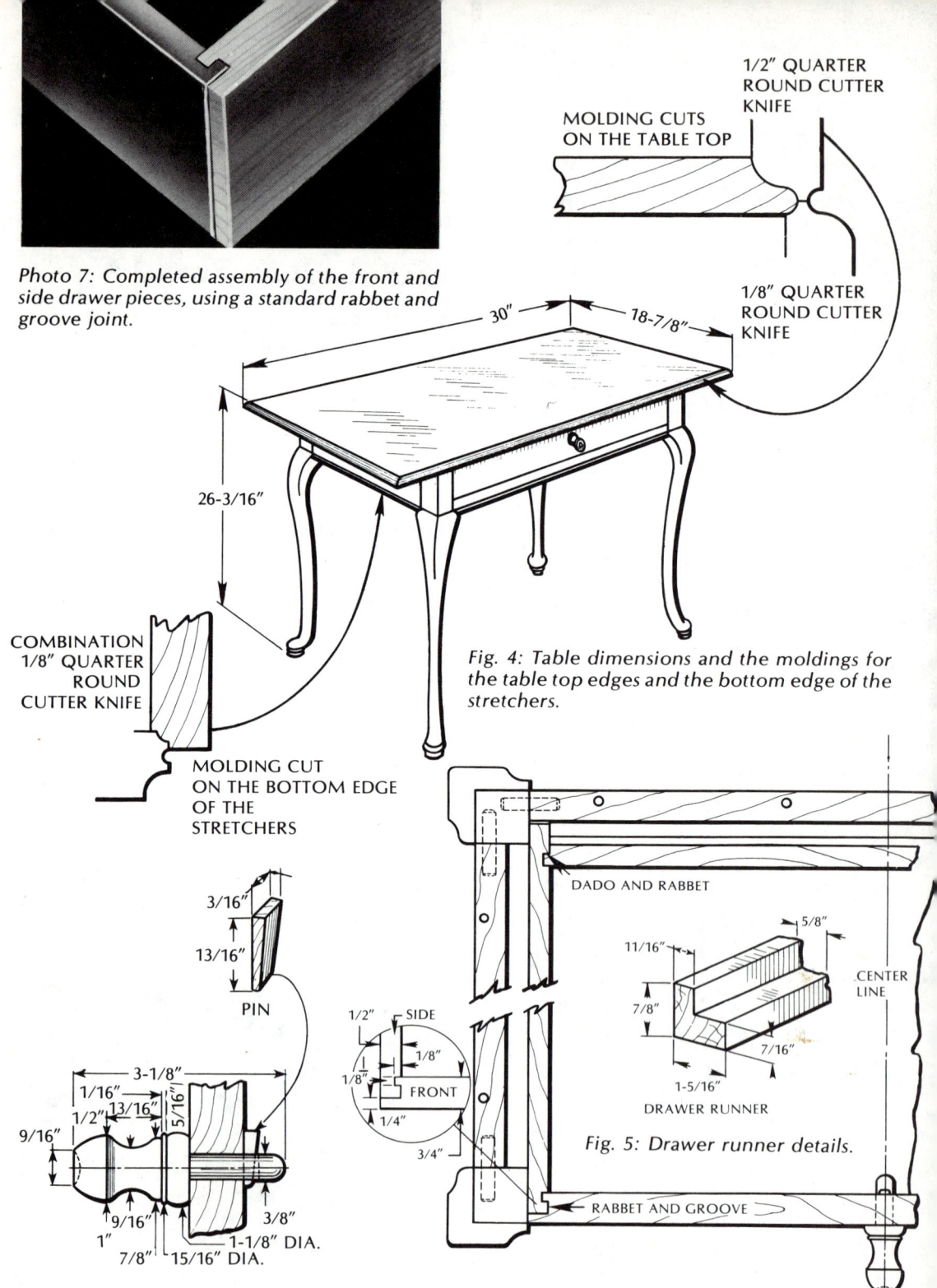

Photo 7: Completed assembly of the front and side drawer pieces, using a standard rabbet and groove joint.

Fig. 4: Table dimensions and the moldings for the table top edges and the bottom edge of the stretchers.

Fig. 5: Drawer runner details.

Fig. 7: Drawer handle and drawer handle pin details.

Fig. 6: Top view of the stretchers and drawer.

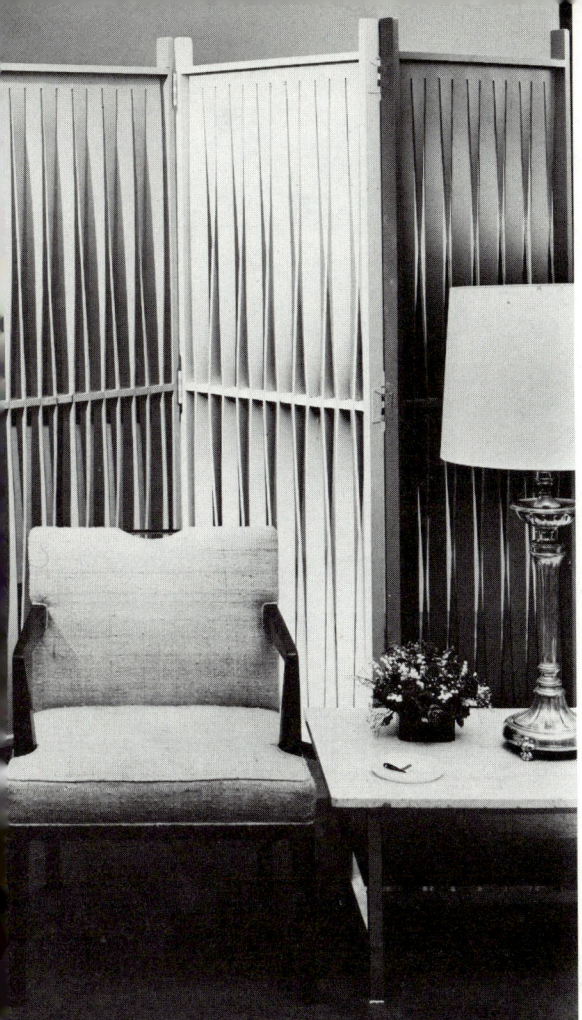

Photo 1: Moké room screen with a twisted slat design.

MOKÉ ROOM SCREENS

These light-weight portable screens can be used in a variety of ways around the house, especially where it is necessary to define or enclose an area without sacrificing valuable space.

All four of the designs shown here use the same type and size of outside frame, which is made of 3/4" by 2" birch or some other hardwood stock. For added strength, the top and bottom rails are set into 3/4" dadoes, 1/4" deep, in the outside frames. Also, along the center of each frame piece, a 1/4" by 1/4" groove is cut for the 1/4" plywood insert. The frame stock is assembled with 6d finishing nails. Glue is used around the panel insert after the designs have been cut.

The twisted slat design (Fig. 4) is made by cutting a series of saw slots in the plywood spaced 2" apart (Photo 2 and Fig. 5). A separator board (Fig. 6), made of 3/4" thick scrap stock, is used to twist the plywood strips in alternate directions. The twisted slats are temporarily inserted in spaced 1/4" slots cut in the separator board (Photo 3). After the slats are all in place on the separator board, insert eleven 1-3/4" blocks and two 1-5/8" blocks between the open spaces, applying glue to each block (Photo 4). The 1-5/8" blocks are used for the ends between the frame and the first slat. When all of the blocks have been inserted, remove the separator board.

For the screen designs shown in Figs. 7 and 9, lay out the patterns on brown wrapping paper, using the squares method (Figs. 8 and 10). Trace the design onto the plywood, using thumb tacks or tape to hold the wrapping paper down. Also, drill 1/8" holes at the corners of each section

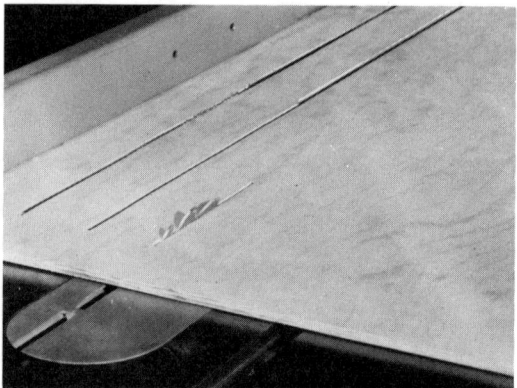

Photo 2: Cutting the slots in the plywood on a table saw for the twisted slat design screen. Note: The blade guard is removed for clarity.

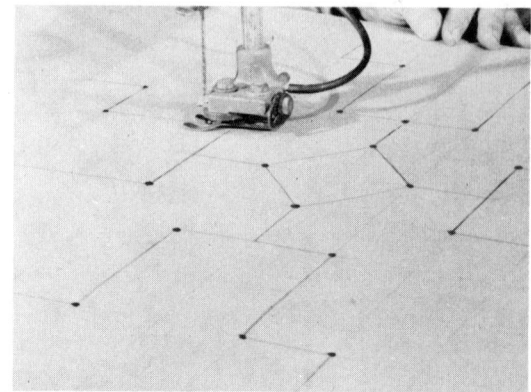

A

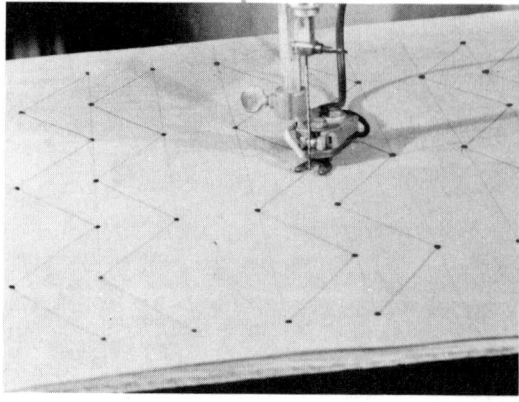

B

Photo 3: Twisting the plywood strips in alternate directions and inserting them into the 1/4" slots of the separator board.

Photo 5: (A) Cutting the design shown in Fig. 7 on a scroll saw; (B) the design shown in Fig. 9 is also cut on a scroll saw by inserting the blade in the corner holes of the pattern.

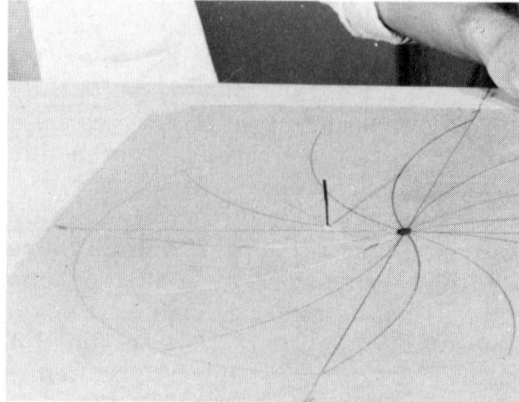

Photo 4: Gluing the spacer blocks in place, using the separator board to hold the plywood slats.

Photo 6: Using a scroll saw with a jigsaw blade to cut the screen design shown in Fig. 11.

Fig. 1: Moké screen with a patterned insert.

Fig 2: Moké screen with a weave design.

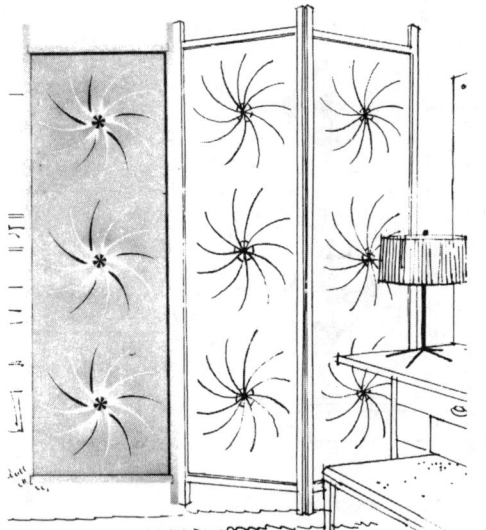

Fig. 3: Nebula pattern moké screen.

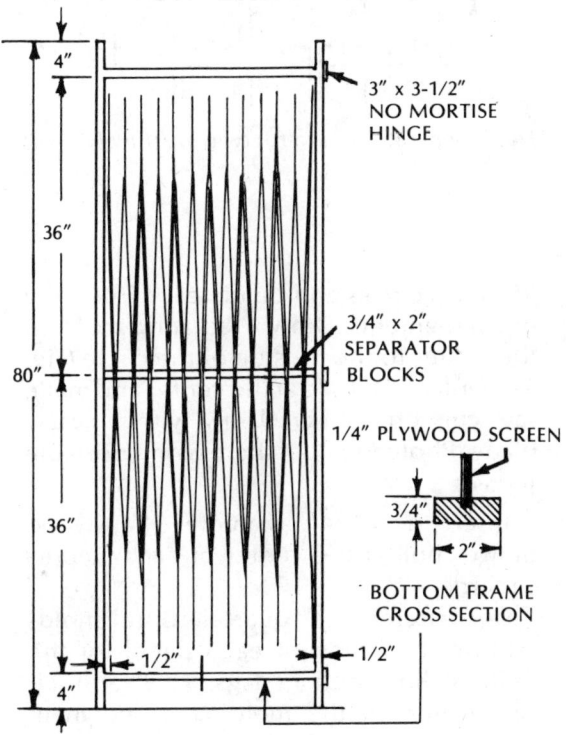

Fig. 4: Twisted slat design.

for inserting a scroll saw blade to cut the design (Photos 5A and 5B). These cuts can also be made with a portable jigsaw. Insert three 8-1/2" by 8-1/2" squares made from 1/4" plywood for the design shown in Fig.

7. To make the screen design shown in Fig. 9, six 1/4" dowels, each 36" long, must be woven between the saw cuts.

The design shown in Fig. 11 is made of three Nebula patterns on each panel. Draw

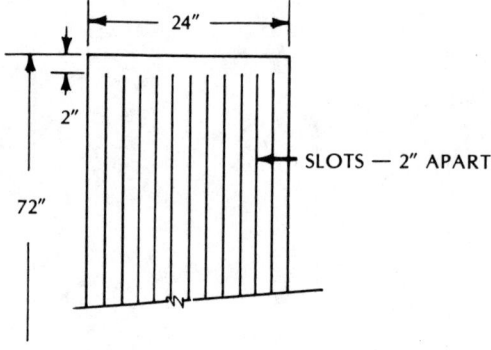

Fig. 5: Cutting details for the plywood panel.

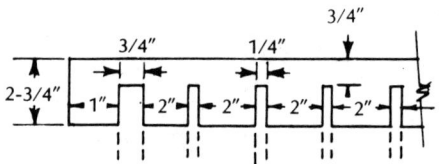

Fig. 6: Separator board for twisting the plywood slats.

9" radius circles and divide each into nine equal segments. Draw a radiating arc from the center to the outside of the circle (Fig. 12). Drill a 1/4" hole at the center and make saw cuts on the scroll saw with a jigsaw blade (Photo 6) or cut them with a portable jigsaw.

Insert a 1-1/4" diameter hardwood drawer pull at the center of each Nebula pattern.

Use mitered 1/4" quarter-round moldings on the inside of each panel for the designs illustrated in Figs. 7, 9, and 11. Application of the molding is shown in Fig. 11.

Smooth all sharp corners with a medium-grit abrasive. Apply an enamel undercoat and one or two coats of semi-gloss enamel.

For the designs shown in Figs. 7 and 9, remove the screen inserts and wood poles and paint the frame a contrasting color before replacing them.

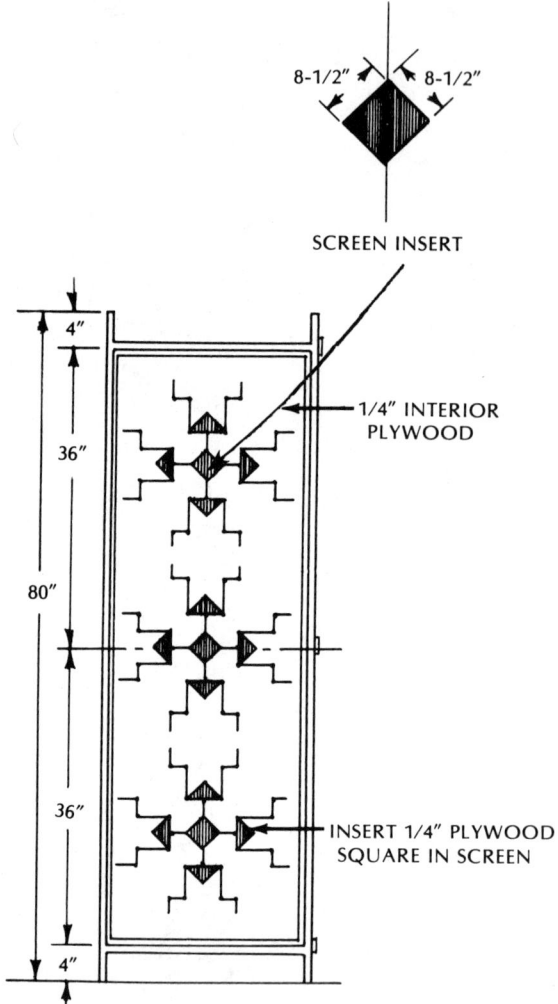

Fig. 7: Patterned insert design.

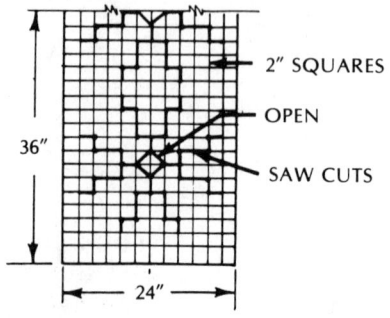

Fig. 8: Cutting details for the plywood panel.

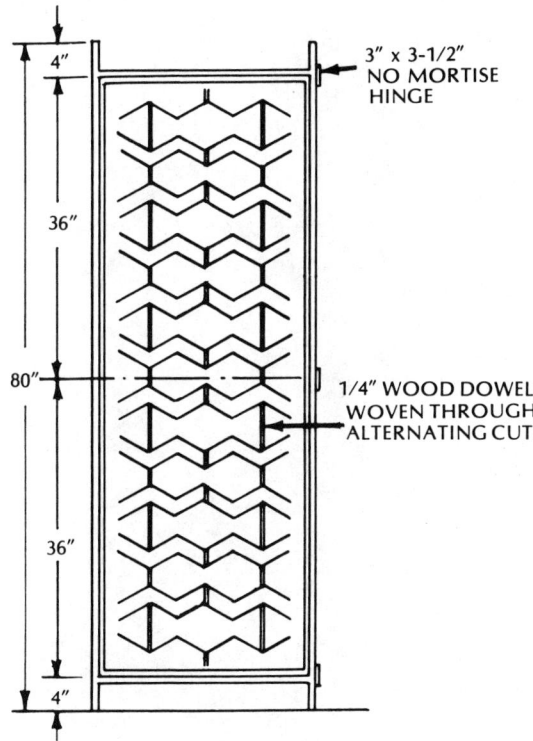

Fig. 9: Weave design, using 1/4" dowels to raise the pattern.

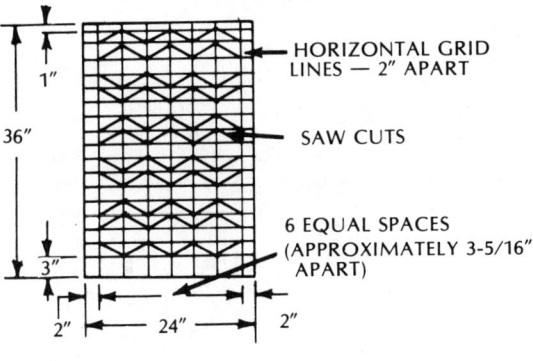

Fig. 10: Cutting details for the weave design.

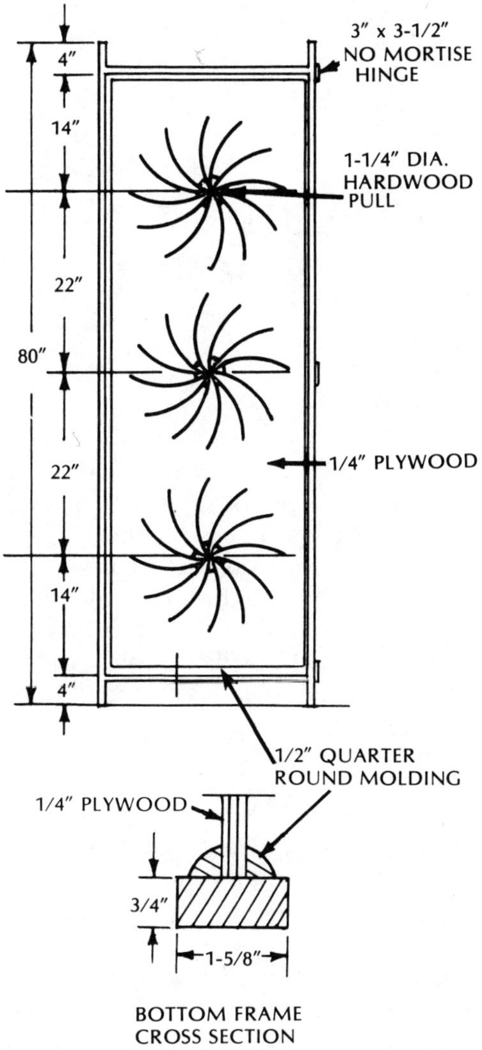

Fig. 11: Nebula pattern design.

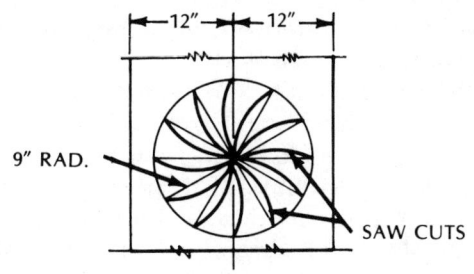

Fig. 12: Cutting details for the Nebula pattern.

CHILD'S ROCKER

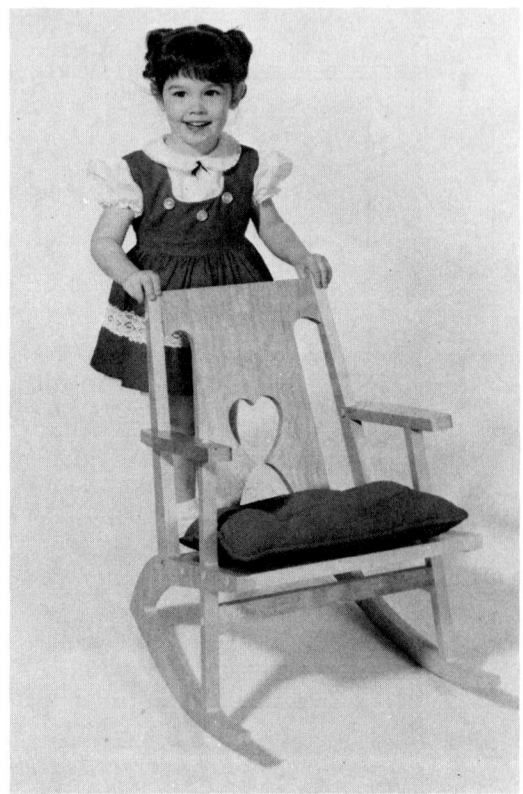

Photo 1: A rocking chair for youngsters.

The sturdy little rocker pictured here (Photo 1) is a perfect gift for children on their birthday, or any occasion for that matter. The miniature chair is something a young son or daughter can call their very own. Not only will the rocker be a joy to present as a gift, it will be easy for the father or grandfather who has a shop at home to build.

The entire rocker is constructed from 3/4" birch plywood or any other veneer plywood desired. One piece, measuring 48" square, is all that is needed.

Use the squares method to transfer the shape of the side of the rocker to the plywood (Fig. 1). The sides can be cut out on a band saw or scroll saw. Note that both sides are cut at one time by tacking the two pieces of plywood together (Photo 2).

A table saw or radial saw is used to cut the rocker back, the seat board (Fig. 2), and the arm rests (Fig. 3) to shape. A 4° angle is required on the sides of the seat board (Photo 3), as well as on the ends of the front (Fig. 4) and rear braces. These are also cut on a table or radial saw. A taper cutting jig is needed to cut the sides of the back panel (Photo 4). Note the 4° angle on the bottom edge of the back (Fig. 5). The design on the back is cut out with a scroll saw or band saw. Cut the arm rest notches on the table saw or radial saw. If a table saw is used, set the miter gauge at 11-1/2° to the right for the right arm rest

MATERIALS

Quantity	Description
2	3/4" x 20" x 25-1/2" Sides
1	3/4" x 12-1/2" x 16" Back
1	3/4" x 12-7/8" x 13" Seat board
2	3/4" x 2" x 12" Arm rests
1	3/4" x 3/4" x 13" Rear brace
1	3/4" x 1-1/2" x 13-1/2" Front brace
16	No. 6 x 1-1/2" Flathead wood screws
2	No. 6 x 1-1/4" Flathead wood screws
4	5d Nails
18	Screw hole plugs
10	Hardwood dowels

and 11-1/2° to the left for the left arm rest. Use a stop clamp to ensure uniformity in the cuts on both arm rests (Photo 5). If a radial saw is used, the arm is rotated 11-1/2° to the right and left to make the angle cuts.

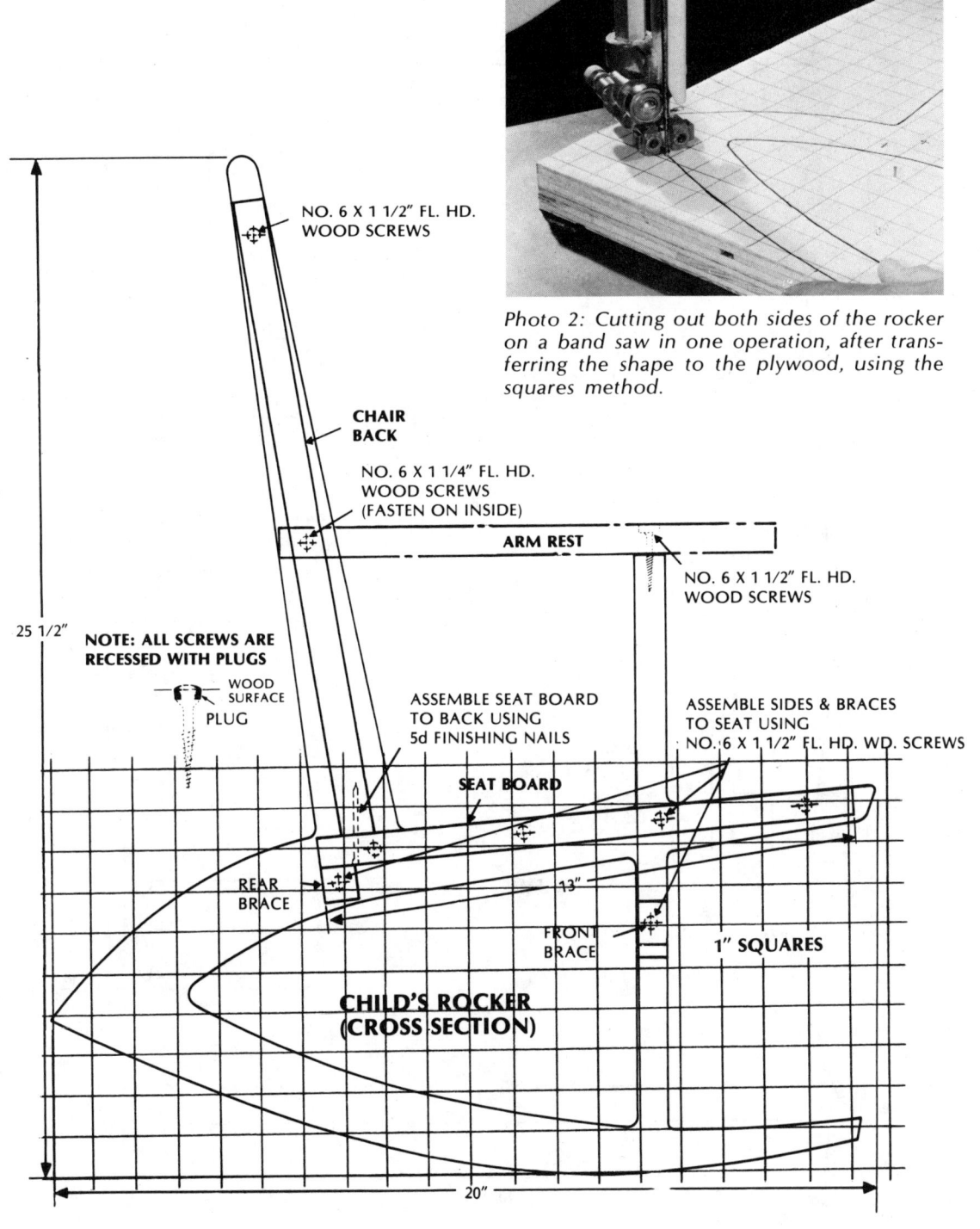

Photo 2: Cutting out both sides of the rocker on a band saw in one operation, after transferring the shape to the plywood, using the squares method.

Fig. 1: Side view details of the rocker.

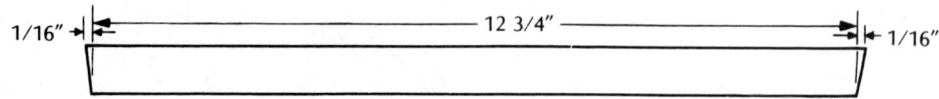

Fig. 2: Seat board details.

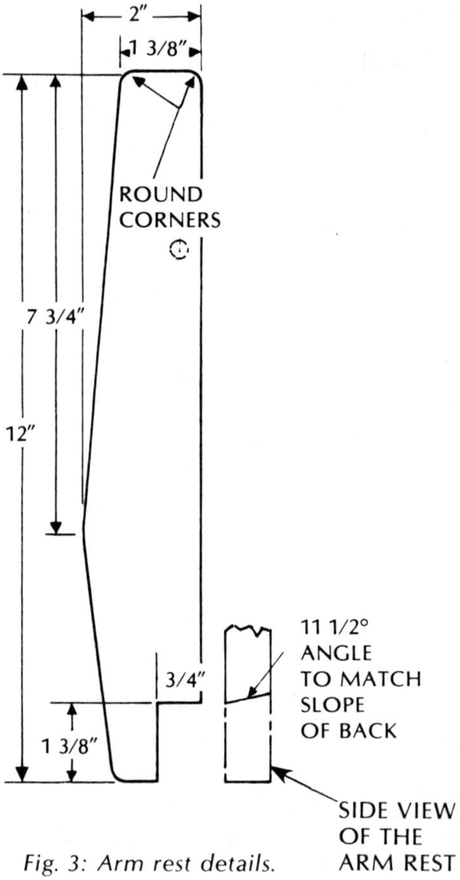

Fig. 3: Arm rest details.

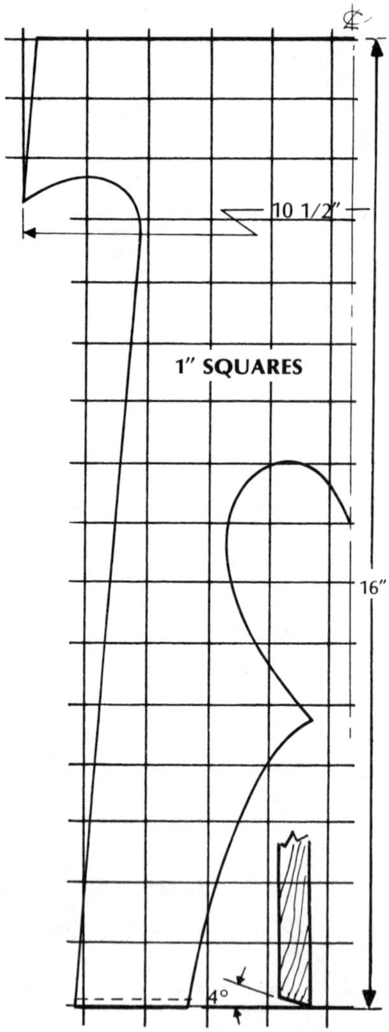

Fig. 5: Details for the back of the rocker.

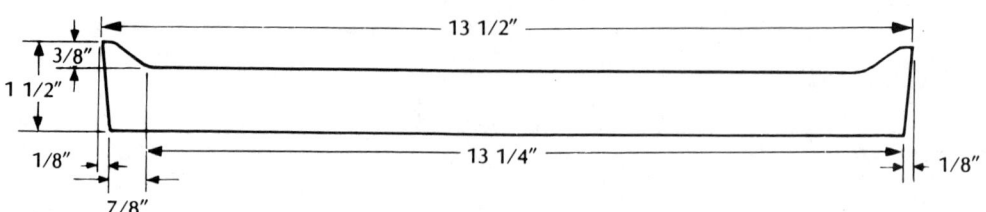

Fig. 4: Front brace details.

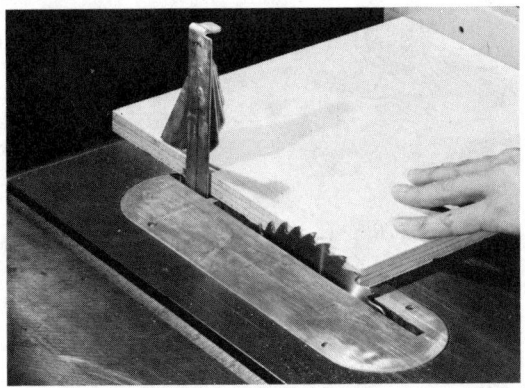

Photo 3: Cutting a 4° angle on the sides of the seat board. Note: Blade guard removed for clarity.

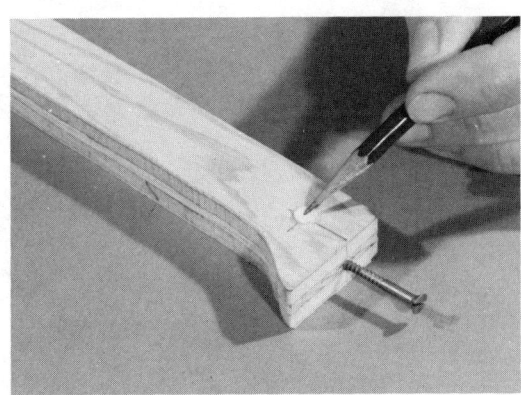

Photo 6: Screwing into a hardwood dowel gives added strength when screw fastening into end grain.

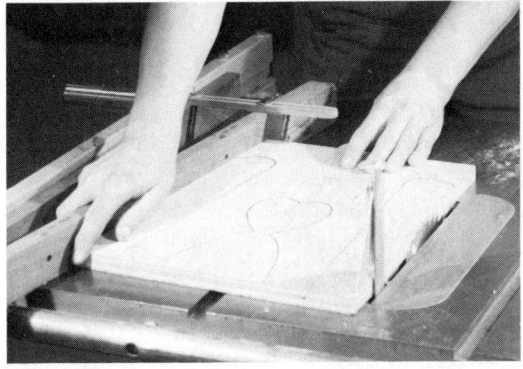

Photo 4: Using a taper cutting jig on a table saw to cut the sides of the back. Note: Blade guard removed for clarity.

Photo 5: Cutting the notches in the arm rests on a table saw; a stop clamp ensures the uniformity of the cuts. Note: Blade guard removed for clarity.

Predrill all holes in the sides and arm rests for the screws and screw hole plugs before assembly. Glue, sixteen No. 6 by 1-1/2" flathead wood screws, two No. 6 by 1-1/4" flathead wood screws, and 5d nails are needed to assemble the rocker. When screw fastening into the end grain, hardwood dowels may be added for additional strength, as shown in Photo 6.

An adjustable screw setter greatly simplifies the assembly of the rocker. In one operation, it predrills, countersinks, and counterbores for the flathead wood screws and wood plugs used in the assembly.

Flexible wood veneer makes it easy to cover the exposed plywood edges. The veneer, also called edging tape, is fastened with contact cement. Apply it with hand pressure, then tap it down with a rubber headed mallet to achieve a good bond. Make sure all of the corners are rounded and any sharp edges are sanded smooth. Complete the project with a clear semi-gloss wood finish, sanding lightly between coats.

A 12" by 12" knife edge or box style cushion will add comfort and enhance the beauty of the project.

COFFEE TABLE

Here is a coffee table that really earns its keep. In addition to its spacious coffee service area, the unit also has a built-in magazine rack and two storage wells under the table top.

After all the parts are cut as shown in the panel layout (Fig. 1), proceed as follows:

1. Cut the quarter rounds to fit the dimensions of part D, allowing enough extra length on each side to make a 45° mitered joint for each corner. Glue-nail the quarter rounds to part D. Fill the joints with wood dough; sand as needed. Cover Section D with the vinyl material; smooth and staple to the underside of D.

2. Assemble the remaining sections of the unit, but do not fasten them to the base or platform yet. First fasten Section D to the assembled unit by screwing it in place through the underside of the triangular H sections as shown in Fig. 2.

3. Assemble the raised platform. Fasten the entire unit to its base (Section C), and the base to the platform as detailed in the side view (Fig. 3).

When you have completed the assembly, the coffee table can be finished as desired. MDO plywood needs no preparation and is finished with conventional paints for an exceptionally smooth and durable surface. Sanded panels require very little preparation, most of which is "touch sanding" (in the direction of the grain only) to smooth any filler or spackle applied to minor openings in the panel face or to remove blemishes. Do not paint over dust, spots of oil, or glue. Any knots or pitch streaks should be touched up with sealer or shellac before painting.

Either water- or oil-base paints can be used to get flat, semigloss, or gloss finishes. Some oil-base paints are self-priming; otherwise, use recommended material. Stains may be used to obtain a natural looking finish on the plywood's grain patterns and on neatly made mechanical repairs. Two methods that give pleasing results are: color toning, which uses companion stains and nonpenetrating sealers; and, light stain, which uses a pigmented sealer, tinting material (stain, thin enamel, or undercoat), and a finish coat (varnish or lacquer). Whatever finishing method you use—paint or stain—always use top-quality materials and follow the manufacturer's instructions.

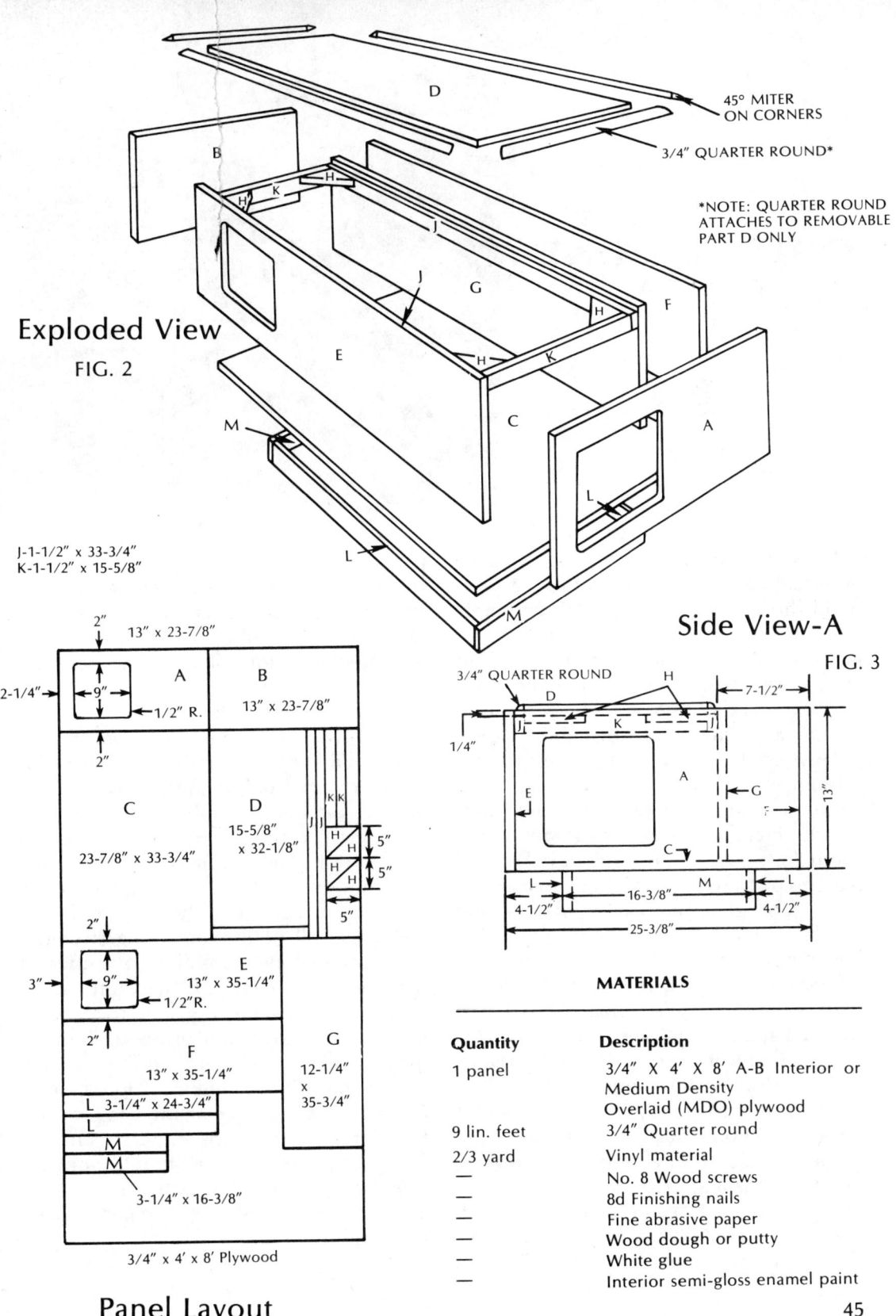

ENTERTAINMENT CENTER

Turn an ordinary room into a home entertainment center with this easy-to-build three-module unit. Used separately or as an all-in-one storage wall, the center gives you fixed spaces for records and stereo speakers. Four 16" adjustable shelves can accommodate a television set, stereo amplifier and turntable, tapes, games, books, or decorator items. One cabinet provides space for liquor, bar equipment, and glassware. There is a built-in wine rack, too. Another cabinet makes room for snack tables and trays. And, a plastic-covered drop leaf shelf, adjacent to the liquor and glassware storage areas makes an ideal service bar for food and beverages.

Each measuring 2-1/2" wide by 7-1/2" high, all three modules can be constructed from 6 panels of 3/4" and 3 panels of 1/4" A-A, A-B, or B-B Interior, or Medium Density Overlay (MDO), American Plywood Association (APA) grade-trademarked plywood. Smooth surfaced and flat, these grades are ideal for paints or stain finishes.

Before starting, study the plans on the next five pages most carefully to make sure you understand all the details. Then, following the layouts in Figs. 1 and 2, draw all parts on the plywood panels using a straightedge and a carpenter's square for accuracy. Use a compass to draw corner radii. Be sure to allow for saw kerfs when plotting dimensions; if in doubt, check the width of your saw cut.

Once the parts have been cut and sanded, assemble them by sections; that is, any part that can be handled as an individual completed unit. Construction by section makes final assembly easier. For the strongest possible joints, use a combination of glue and nails (or screws). To glue and nail, check for a good fit by holding the pieces together. Pieces should contact at all points for lasting strength. Mark the nail locations along the edge of the piece to be nailed. In careful work where nails must be very close to an edge, you may wish to predrill using a drill which must be slightly smaller than the nail size. Always predrill for screws. Apply glue to clean surfaces, according to manufacturer's instructions. Press surfaces firmly together until a "bend" appears, then nail or screw, check for square, and apply clamps, if possible, to maintain pressure until the glue sets.

MATERIALS

Quantity Description

6 panels	3/4" x 4' x 8' Plywood
3 panels	1/4" x 4' x 8' Plywood
8	3/8" x 3/8" x 14-1/2" Wood strips for shelf rests in R-S section
2	1/4" x 1-1/4" Dowel to hold shelf J in position (see details)
2	1/4" x 1-1/2" Dowel to hold shelf J in position (see details)
1	3/4" x 1-1/2" x 28-1/2" Wood strip for under shelf C
1	3/4" x 1-1/2" x 28-1/2" Wood strip for edge of shelf D1
4	3/4" x 3/4" x 28-1/2" Wood strips for stops to position N
4	3/4" x 3/4" x 13" Wood strips to position N
1	28-7/8" x 14-1/4" Plastic laminate sheet for shelf D
1	28-3/4" x 23-3/4" Plastic laminate sheet for shelf M
1	28-7/8" x 15-1/2" Plastic laminate sheet for shelf D1
1 yard	35" Wide speaker enclosure fabric (glue and tack in place)
3 sets	Furniture glides
7	Door handles of your choice
8 sets	Friction catches for doors L and K and shelf M
4	29-1/8" x 1-1/2" Continuous hinges for doors L
2	19" x 1-1/2" Continuous hinges for doors K
1	28-3/4" x 1-1/2" Continuous hinge for shelf M
32	Shelf supports to fit sides of cabinets
1 pair	Fall supports for shelf M
-	Finishing nails for nail gluing all parts together
-	Glue for nail gluing (urea resin type recommended) and for applying formica D, D1, and M
-	Fine abrasive paper for smoothing out edges and surfacing putty
-	Surfacing putty for filling exposed plywood edges and countersunk nail holes
-	Paint or stain for finishing
-	No. 9 Wood screws for reinforced construction if speakers are installed (Consult components distributor for recommendations)
Options	1" Fiberglass insulation batten for lining speaker enclosures

FIG. 1

Of course, if you have power tools, such as a table saw or radial saw, you can miter, rabbet, and dado easily. These joints are much stronger than the butt joints just described. Details on how to make these professional joints are given in the books *Getting the Most Out of Your Table Saw* and *Getting the Most Out of Your Radial Saw.*

O
30″ x 87″
Q
Q
Q
Q
Q
Q
Q
Q
8 PIECES - 12″ x 6-15/16″
1/4″ x 4′ x 8′
3/4″ x 1-1/2″
NOTCH FOR DOOR STOP
6″
1/4″
7-1/4″
5-5/8″
R
O
30″ x 87″
R
R - 15-3/16″ x 28-1/2″
S
4-5/8″
7-1/4″
S
15-3/16″ x 13-7/8″
1/4″ x 4′ x 8′
S
S
P
2″
O
30″ x 87″
12″ x 13-1/2″ HIGH
P
3″
P
1/4″ x 4′ x 8′

FIG. 2

B
N
FABRIC
B
A
F
F
A
O
B
F
B
Q
P
P
P
Q
B
B
N
FABRIC
B
F
F
C
K
K
A
I
O
A
C
M
T
R
S
E
L
L
C

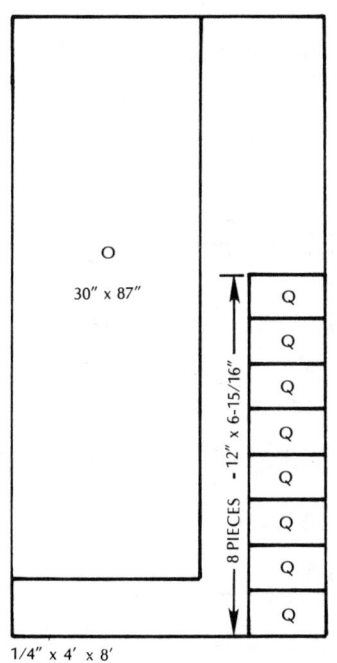

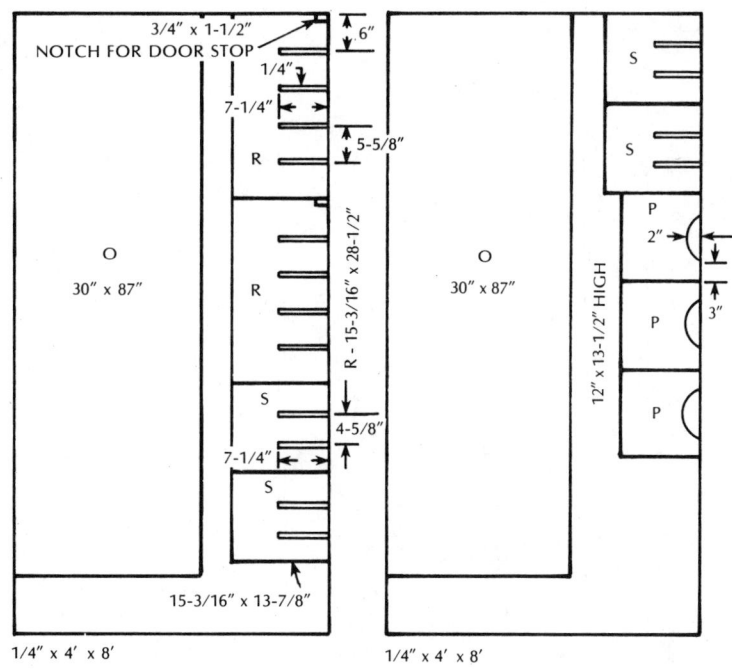

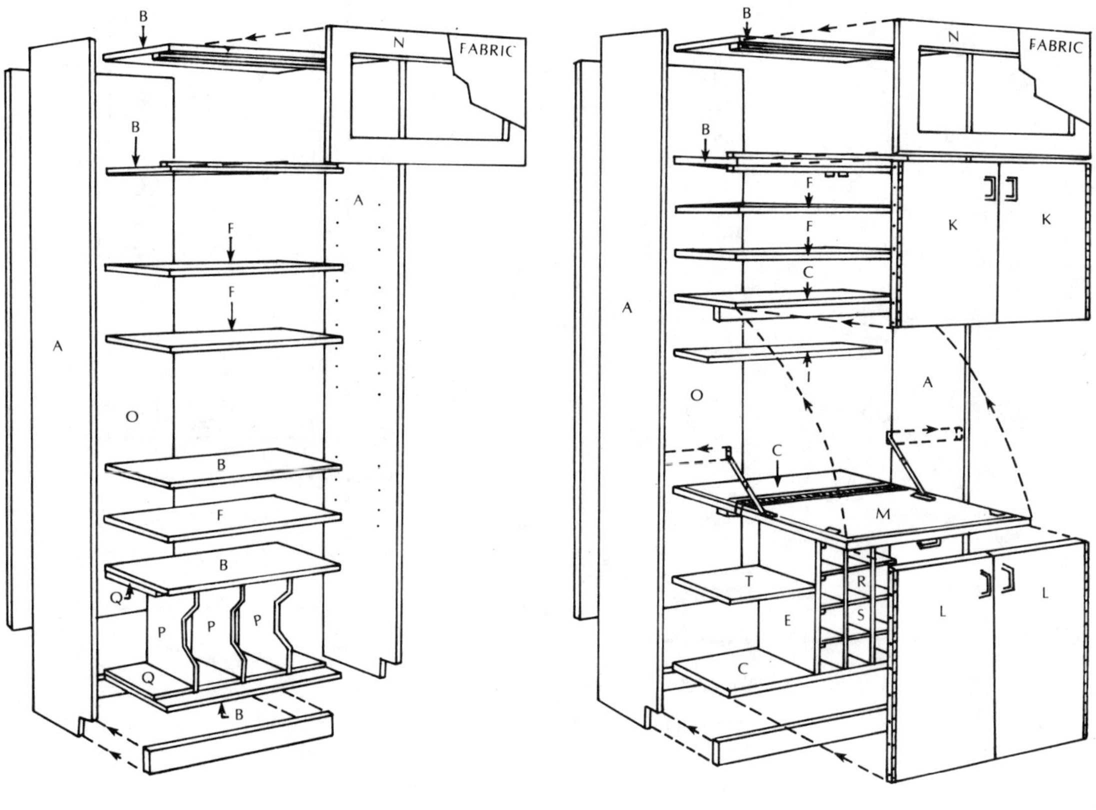

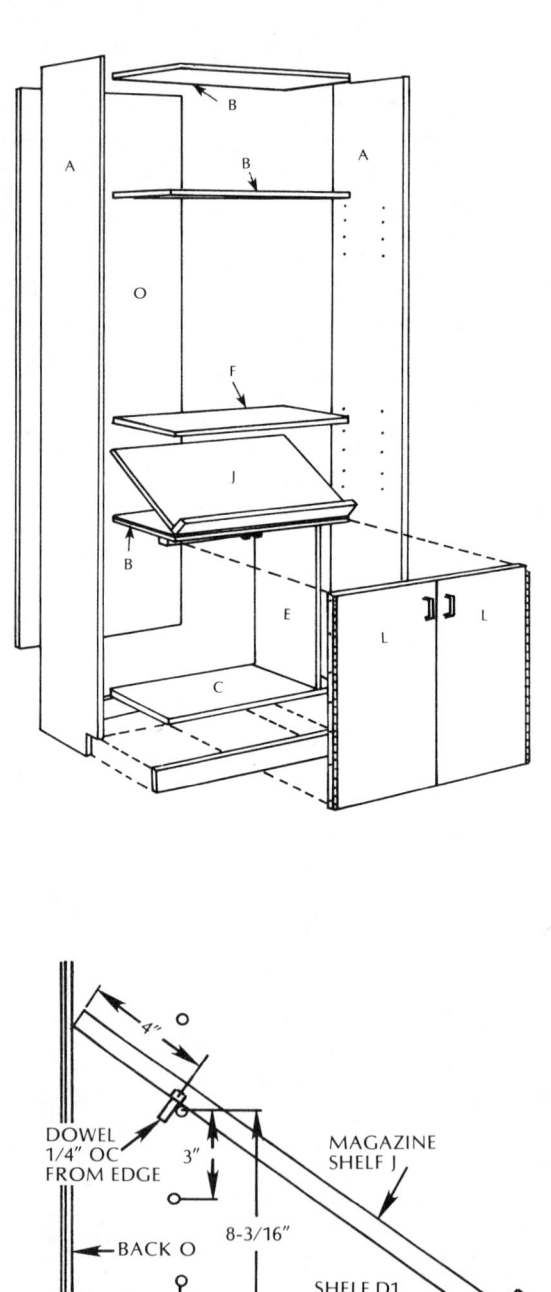
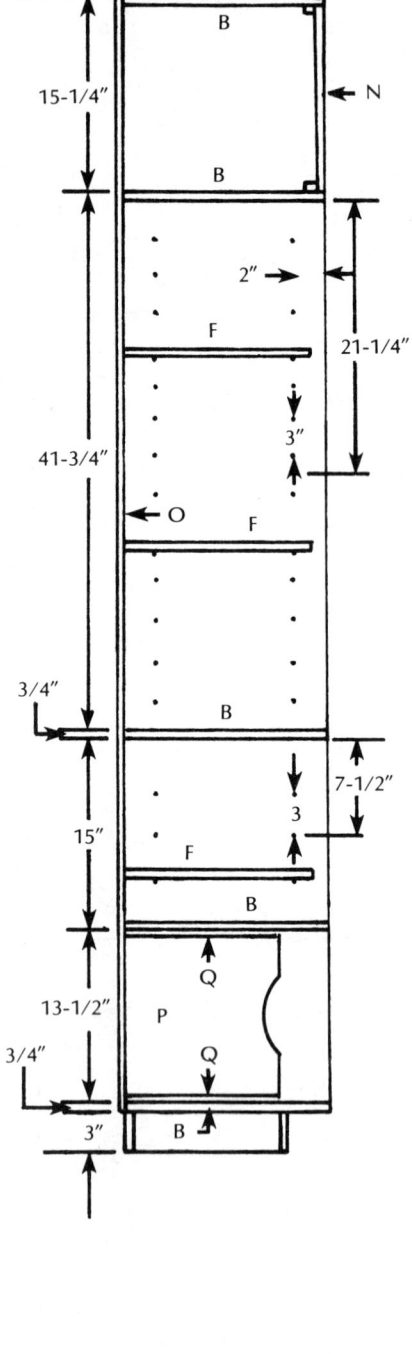

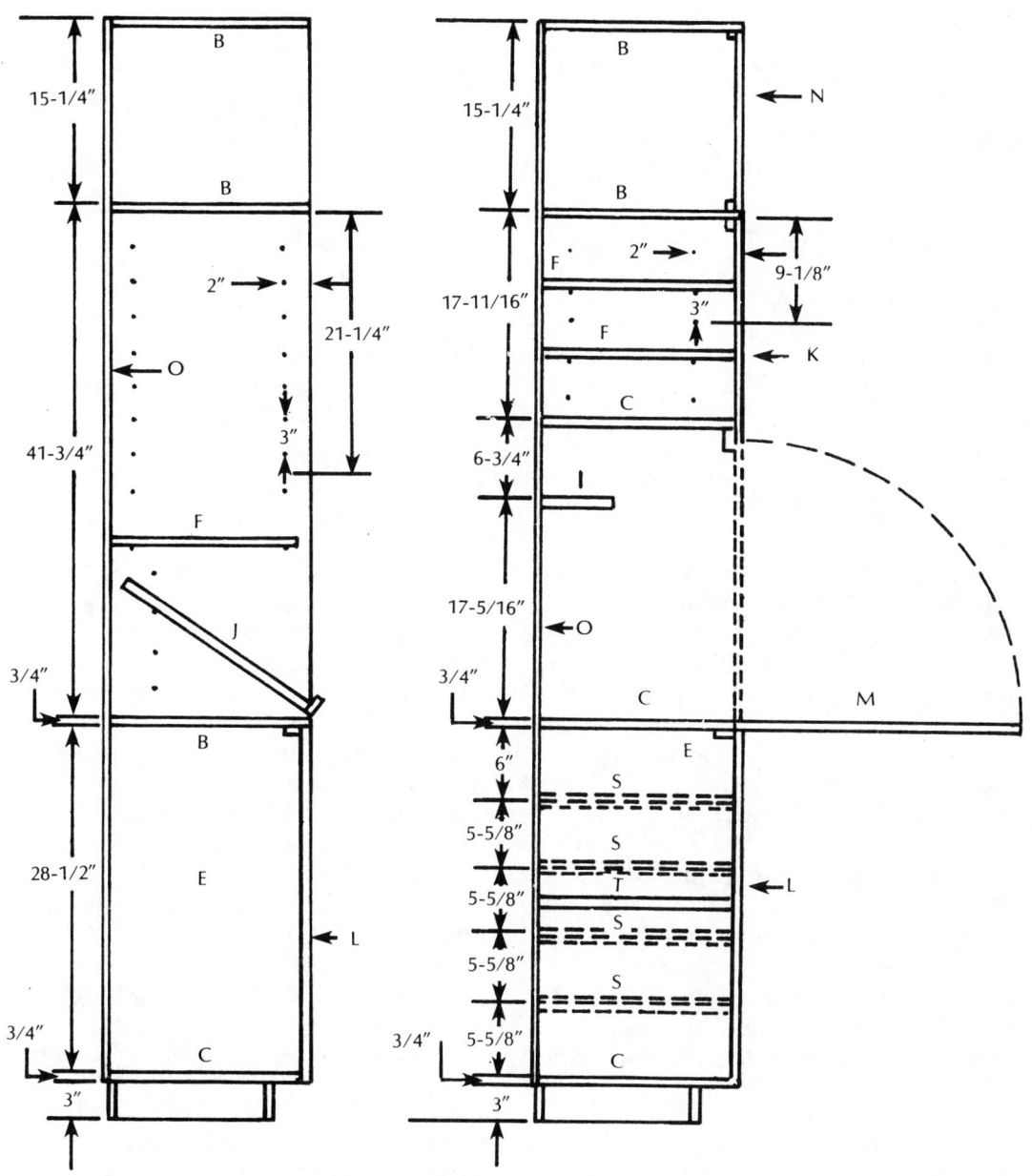

Side View

END TABLE

Photo 1: A drawer-type end table.

The traditional styling of this drawer-type end table (Photo 1) allows it to be easily matched with a wide variety of living room furniture. Making it also offers the homeshop owner the opportunity of cutting flutes with a high-speed router.

Select a hardwood to match the furniture presently in the living room. Cut the legs from 2" by 2" stock, with each leg 14-5/8" long. Draw the leg taper on two faces of the stock. The leg should be tapered 1" from the bottom—2" on all four sides at the top and 1" on each side at the bottom (Fig. 1). Cut the two side tapers on a band saw (Photo 2), replace the cut pieces in their original position with small brads, and finish cutting the other two tapers (Photo 3). Clean the tapered cuts by running them over the jointer.

Before making any further cuts on the legs, make the flutes on the four tapered sides, 2" from the top and 2" from the bottom (Fig. 1). For this operation, you will require a jig to hold the leg while routing the flutes (Fig. 2). Make the center flute first on all four sides of all four legs, using a hardwood template, as shown in Photo 4 and Fig. 3. Next, move spacer blocks C and D, as indicated in Fig. 4, and replace the hardboard template. Ride the template guide along the opening in the template and make the second groove. Cut the second flute on all four sides of each leg with this same setting. The third flute is made by moving the spacer blocks C and D, as shown in Fig. 5. The same procedure is used on all four sides of each leg. Photo 5 shows the template removed with three flutes cut in the legs.

After all the flutes are made, the upper end of each leg is notched out to fit against the sides, as shown in Fig. 1. The first cuts are made on a table saw with the leg lying flat. The last two cuts are made with the stock in an upright position.

The table sides, back, and front have mitered corner joints with 1/4" by 3/4" splines (Fig. 6B). The drawer slide frame is made from 3/4" by 2" hardwood stock and assembled with short mortise and tenon joints, as shown in Fig. 8. Drawer guide strips are glued in place after the legs are screw-fastened to the drawer slide frame (Fig. 1). The table top and upper drawer guide strips are glued in place last.

The drawer is made in the conventional way with rabbet and groove joints at the front and a 1/4" by 1/4" dado and rabbet

MATERIALS

Quantity	Description
4	1-7/8" x 1-7/8" x 14-5/8" Legs
2	3/4" x 7-1/4" x 24" Sides
1	3/4" x 7-1/4" x 15" Back
2	3/4" x 1-1/2" x 7-1/4" Stiles (front)
1	3/4" x 3/4" x 12" Top rail (front)
1	3/4" x 1-1/2" x 12" Bottom rail (front)
1	3/4" x 15" x 24" Top
1	3/4" x 2" x 13-1/2" Drawer slide frame (front)
2	3/4" x 2" x 20-7/8" Drawer slide frame (sides)
1	3/4" x 2" x 10-1/4" Drawer slide frame (back)
2	3/4" x 1" x 22-1/2" Bottom drawer side guides
2	3/4" x 2" x 22-1/2" Top drawer side guides
2	3/4" x 1-1/4" x 22-1/2" Top drawer guides
1	3/4" x 5" x 12" Drawer front
2	1/2" x 5" x 23" Drawer sides
1	1/2" x 4-3/8" x 11-1/2" Drawer back
1	1/8" x 11-1/2" x 12-3/4" Drawer bottom (hardboard)
1	3-1/2" C.C. Drawer pull
4	3/4" dia. Furniture glides

Leg Routing Jig

Quantity	Description
1 (A)	2" x 2-1/4" x 4-1/8" Support block
1 (B)	1-1/2" x 2" x 2-3/4" Support block
2 (C)	1/2" x 3/4" x 2" Spacer blocks
2 (D)	5/16" x 1/2" x 1-1/16" Spacer blocks
1 (E)	3/4" x 4-1/8" x 18-1/8" Jig base board
1 (F)	1/4" x 4-1/8" x 18-1/8" Hardboard template
4	No. 10 x 1" Flathead wood screws

Photo 4: With the leg stock mounted in a jig fitted with a hardboard template, the three flutes are cut with a high speed router. The four center flutes on all four legs are cut first.

Photo 2: Two sides of the legs are taper cut on a band saw fitted with a 1/4" skip tooth blade.

Photo 5: The table leg with the template removed, after the third flute has been cut.

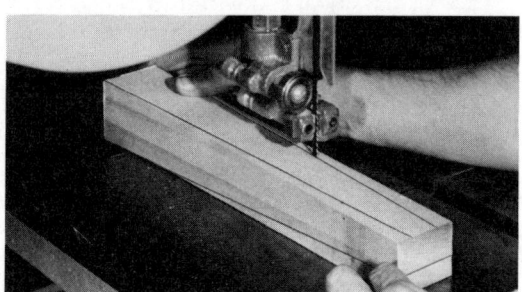

Photo 3: By tacking the cut wedges to the legs with brads, the other two sides are taper cut on the band saw.

Photo 6: A 1/4" round end router bit and a template guide are used to rout the drawer front design.

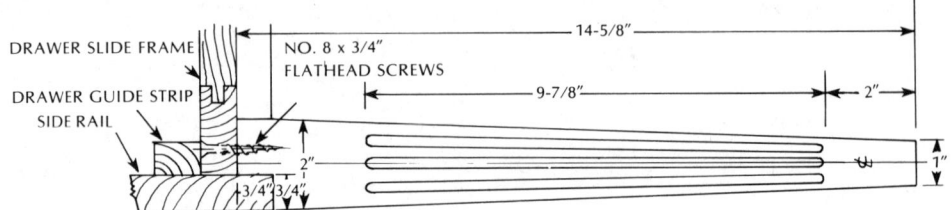

Fig. 1: Details of the table leg, showing the leg screw—fastened to the drawer slide frame.

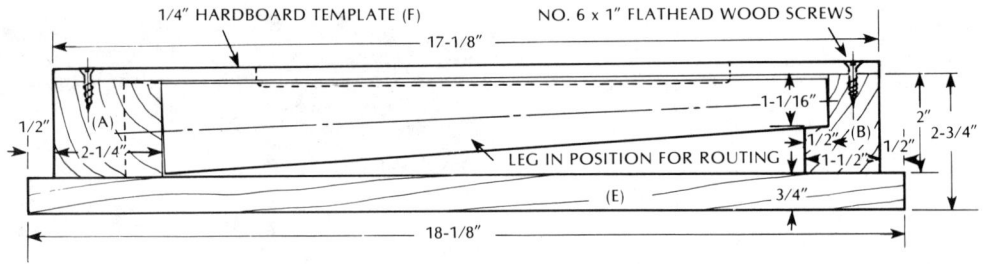

Fig. 2: Side view of the routing jig used for fluting the table legs.

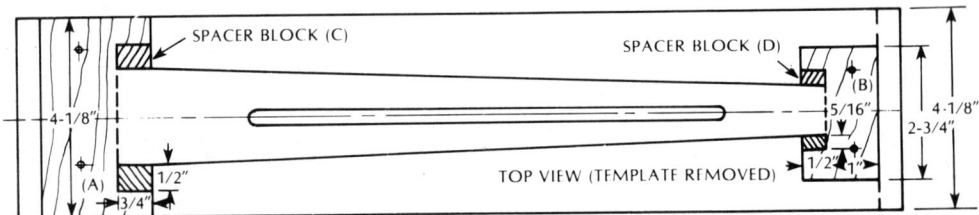

Fig. 3: Setup for fluting the table legs with a router—first operation.

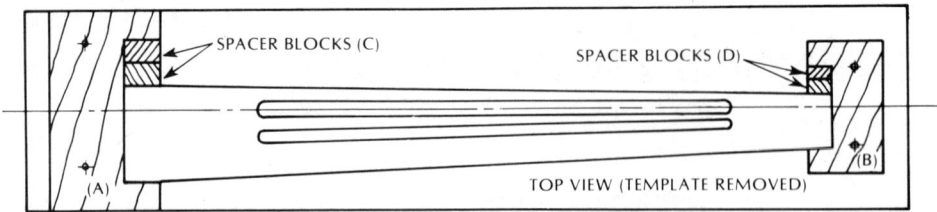

Fig. 4: Setup for fluting the table legs with a router—second operation.

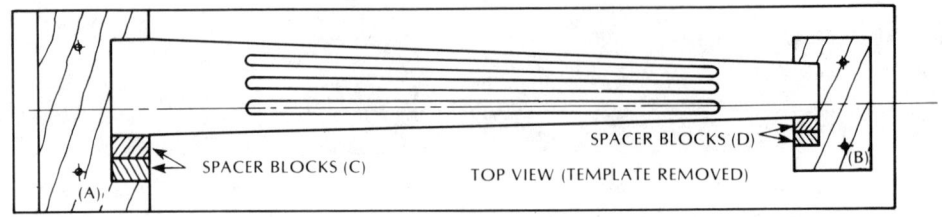

Fig. 5: Setup for fluting the table legs with a router—third operation.

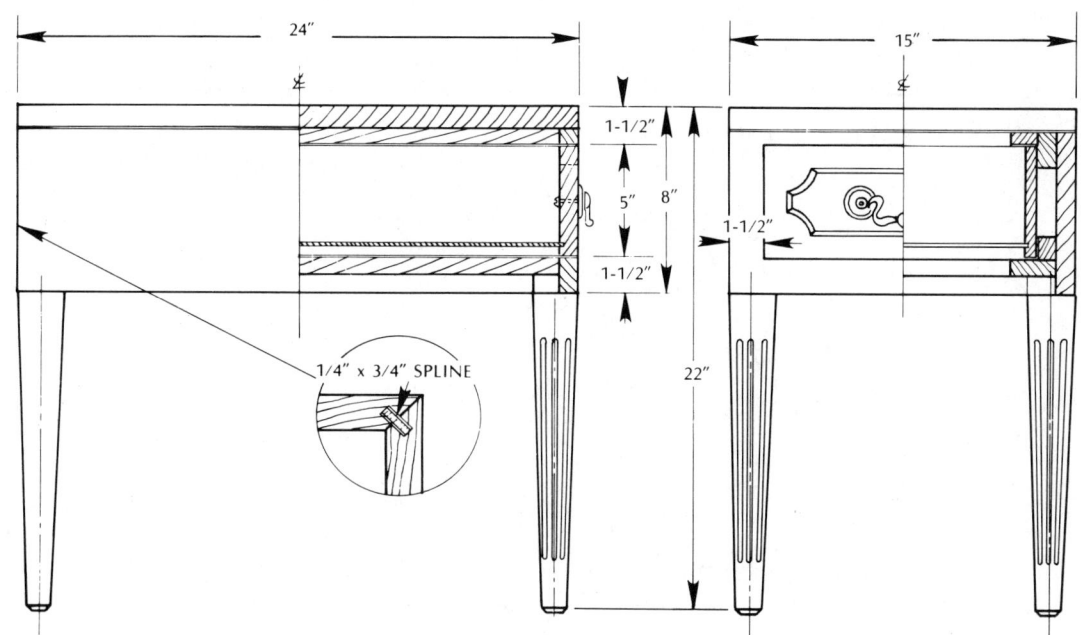

Fig. 6: (A) Side view of the end table; (B) corner construction of the side rail.

Fig. 7: Front view of the end table.

joint at the back (Fig. 9). A 1/4" flute on the drawer front is made with a hardboard template (Fig. 10), using a template guide and round end router bit (Fig. 11) mounted in a high speed router (Photo 6).

Sand all sharp edges with medium- and fine-grit abrasive paper. Finish with a filler if open grained wood is used and stain it to match the other pieces of furniture in the room where it will be placed. Finish with a penetrating resin material or satin synthetic varnish.

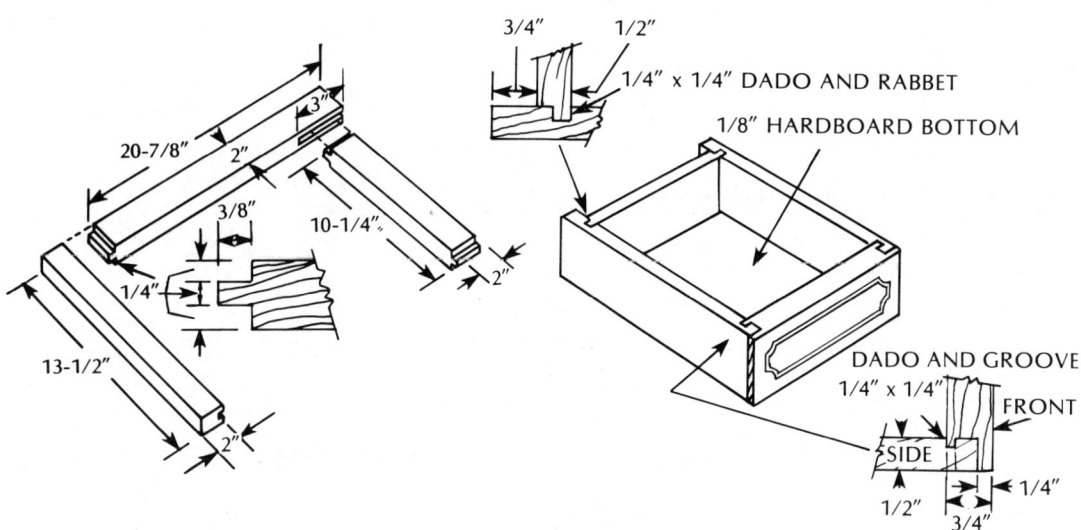

Fig. 8: Details of the drawer slide frame, showing mortise and tenon joints.

Fig. 9: Details for the drawer, showing the joints used.

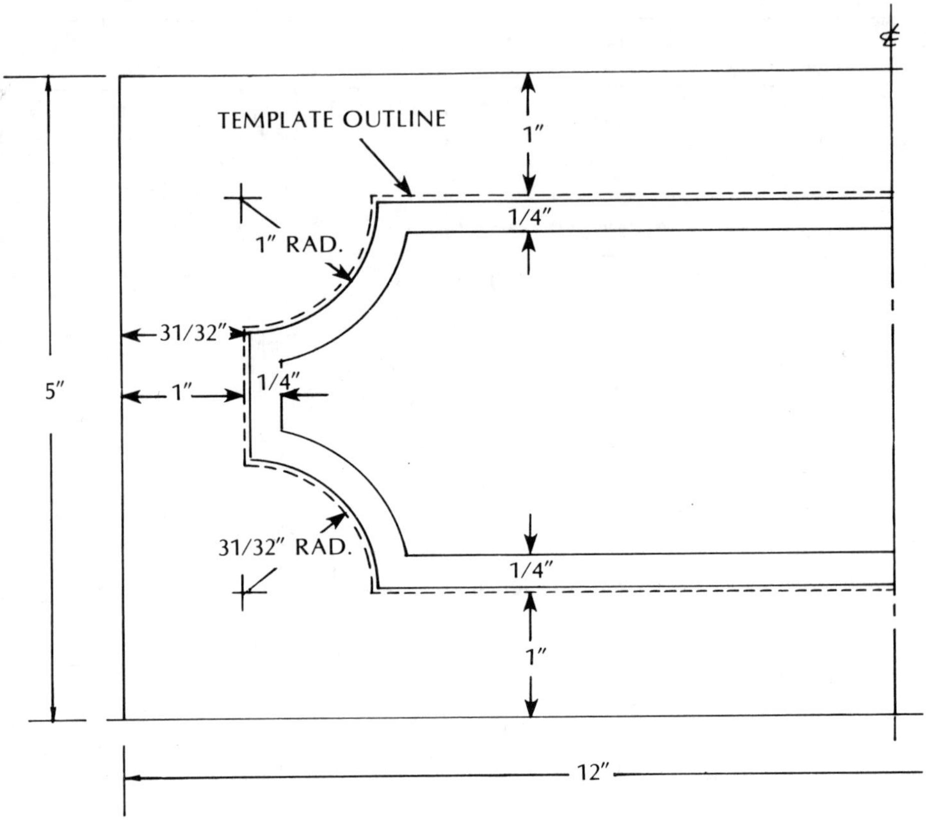

Fig. 10: Fluting details on the drawer front.

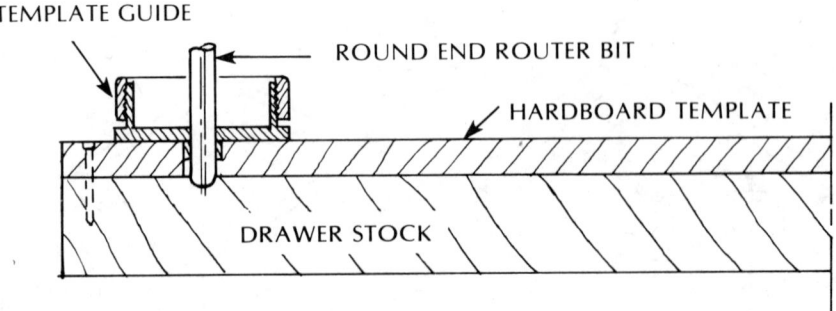

Fig. 11: Routing template, template guide, and router bit used on the drawer front.

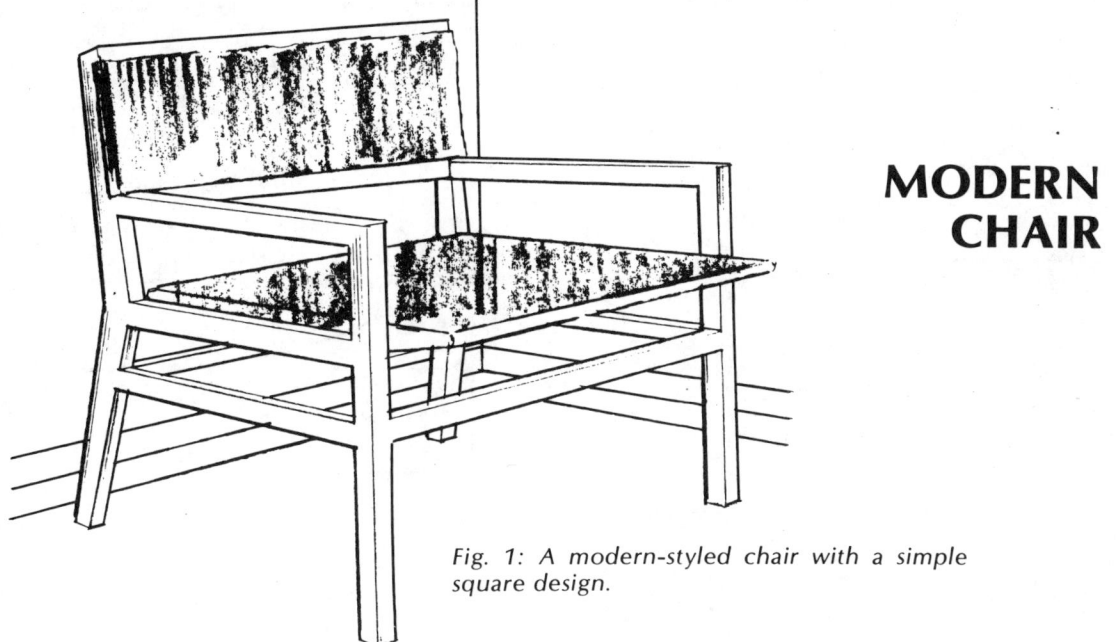

Fig. 1: A modern-styled chair with a simple square design.

MODERN CHAIR

Chairs are one of the more versatile pieces of furniture a homeshop owner can make. The many types serve a wide variety of both practical and decorative purposes. There is always room for one more chair in the house. Whether it is in the living room, dining room, or family room, a chair with this simple, square design (Fig. 1) will fit nicely with any kind of furniture.

The chair framework is made of 1-1/2" thick stock. Begin the project by laying out the rear legs, using the dimensions shown in Fig. 2. Before making the back angle cuts of the legs, cut the mortises on the drill press for the side stretcher pieces (C), (D), and (E) as shown in Photo 1. Tenons on the stretchers are made by first sawing the shoulder cuts to the proper depth. Both of the tenon cheek cuts can be made at the same time by using two saw blades of the same diameter or the two outside dado blades, with a 3/8" spacer collar between them, and a tenoning jig (Photo 2). One end of the stretcher pieces (E) and (C) is angle cut, 16° and 17° respectively, to conform with the taper on the rear leg (Fig. 2). The stretchers (F), (G), (H), (J), (N), (O), shown in Fig. 3, also use mortise and tenon joints. Every corner of each piece of the chair frame, except for the back legs, is rounded off on a table saw. The miter effects are made with a hand wood chisel.

Photo 1: Mortising the legs on the drill press for the side stretcher tenons. Note: For easier handling, the back tapers are cut after the mortising is done.

Photo 2: Cutting the stretcher tenons on the table saw, using the two outside dado blades, a spacer collar, and a tenoning jig.

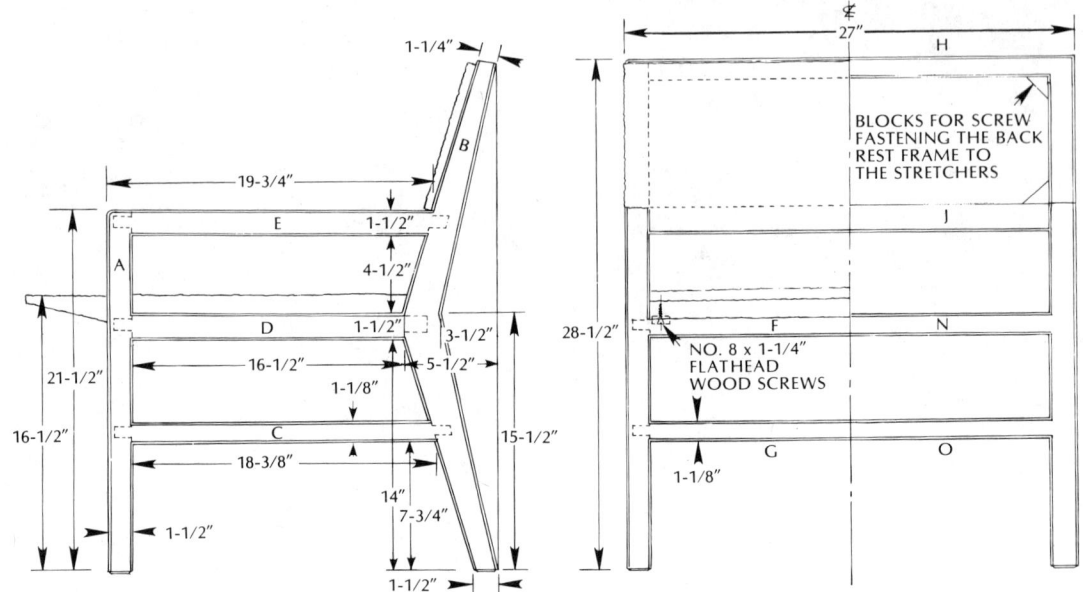

Fig. 2: Side view details of the chair. *Fig. 3: Front view details of the chair.*

MATERIALS

Quantity	Description
2 (A)	1-1/2" x 1-1/2" x 21-1/2" Front legs
2 (B)	1-1/2" x 5-1/2" x 28-1/2" Back legs
2 (C)	1-1/2" x 1-1/8" x 20-3/8" Side stretchers (lower)*
2 (D)	1-1/2" x 1-1/2" x 18-1/2" Side seat stretchers*
2 (E)	1-1/2" x 1-1/2" x 20-3/4" Arm rests*
1 (F)	1-1/2" x 1-1/2" x 26" Seat stretchers (front)*
2 (G, O)	1-1/2" x 1-1/8" x 26" Front & rear stretchers (lower)*
3 (H, J, N)	1-1/2" x 1-1/2" x 26" Back stretchers*
2 (K)	3/4" x 2" x 15" Sides (seat frame)
3 (L)	3/4" x 2" x 24" Front and back (seat & back frame)
1 (M)	3/4" x 4" x 24" Seat frame (front)
4	5/16" dia. x 4" Dowels
12	5/16" dia. x 3" Dowels
1	1" x 22" x 24" Piece of foam rubber (seat)
1	1" x 9" x 24" Piece of foam rubber (back)
8 yards	3" Wide upholstery webbing
—	Cloth or plastic covering for seat and back

*Including tenons

The wood frames for the back rest and seat can be constructed with mortise and tenon joints, or they can be doweled as shown in Figs. 4A and 5A. Note that the front piece (M) on the seat frame is taper cut from 3/4" to 3/16" (Fig. 4B). Conventional 3" seat webbing is used on both frames, utilizing a basket weave. Cover the webbing with 1" foam rubber and fasten a plastic or cloth covering over everything.

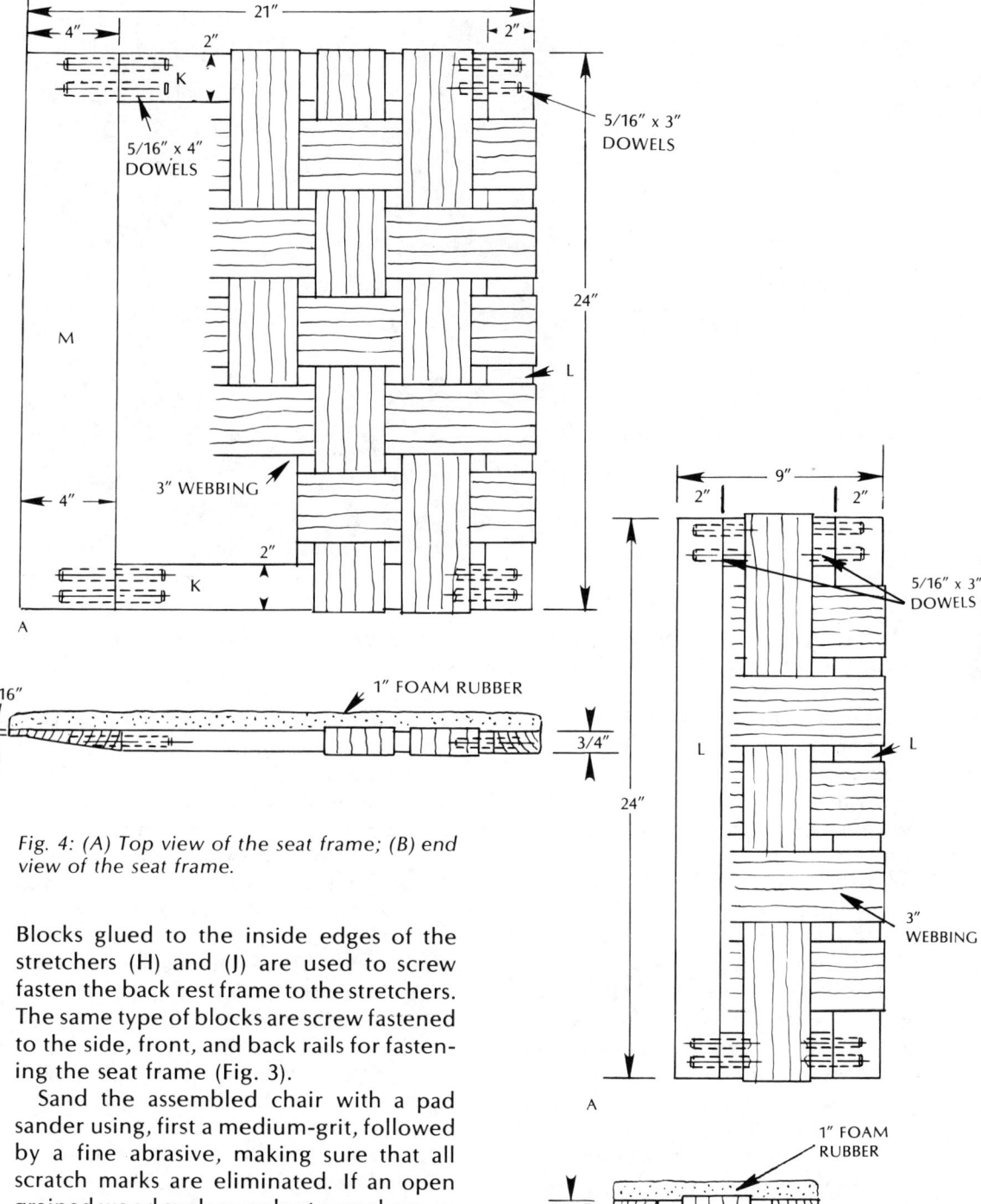

Fig. 4: (A) Top view of the seat frame; (B) end view of the seat frame.

Blocks glued to the inside edges of the stretchers (H) and (J) are used to screw fasten the back rest frame to the stretchers. The same type of blocks are screw fastened to the side, front, and back rails for fastening the seat frame (Fig. 3).

Sand the assembled chair with a pad sander using, first a medium-grit, followed by a fine abrasive, making sure that all scratch marks are eliminated. If an open grained wood such as walnut or mahogany is used, fill and stain per manufacturer's instructions. Seal the surface with two thin coats of white shellac, followed by a coat of satin synthetic varnish.

Fig. 5: (A) Top view of the back frame; (B) end view of the back frame.

CHINA CABINET

Photo 1: An easy-to-make china cabinet.

Although designed primarily to hold china, this cabinet (Photo 1) can readily serve as a bookcase or storage cabinet. For example, one of the side compartments in the bottom section of the cabinet could be converted into a liquor dispenser, as shown in Photo 2. The center section has four drawers for storing linens and silverware. Of course, a china cabinet should be able to store china; there is ample space in the upper section of this cabinet to appropriately display the best china.

The cabinet is made in two sections, with most of the parts made of 3/4" hardwood plywood. First, the sides of the base are cut to the proper width and height (Fig. 1). If dado and rabbet joints are used to fasten the top (Fig. 2B) and bottom (Fig. 2C) of the lower part of the cabinet to the sides, the height of the sides must be increased 1/4" and the length of the bottom 1/2" to allow for the dadoes. Assemble the two sides and the four center section sides to the top and bottom, gluing the joints and using 6d finishing nails for a solid construction. Note that the center section sides are paired together and fastened with glue. They are set in full width dadoes cut into the top and bottom panels (Fig. 2D). The base frame, made of 3/4" by 2" stock, is offset from the contour of the cabinet and assembled with glued butt joints. The front and sides of the frame are set back 1-1/2" for toe room (Fig. 3), except beneath the center door section, where the base frame juts out flush with the cabinet bottom and the door surface (Photo 1). Glue blocks keep the assembled base true and sturdy (Figs. 1 and 3). The back panel also helps to keep the cabinet rigid.

The four drawers in the center section are joined with rabbet and groove joints. Hand hole pull openings on the drawer fronts are cut on a band saw. If metal extension drawer slides are used, the drawers will have to be made 1" narrower than the opening, to allow 1/2" clearance between the drawer sides and the cabinet sides and center section sides (Fig. 5). The drawer fronts are 3/4" thick; the sides and back are made of 1/2" stock, and the bottoms are 1/8" hardboard.

MATERIALS

Base Section

Quantity	Description
2	3/4" x 20" x 24-1/4" Sides (ends)
4	3/4" x 20" x 24-1/4" Center section sides
1	3/4" x 21" x 72" Top
1	3/4" x 20" x 69-1/2" Bottom
2	3/4" x 17-1/2" x 23" Doors (side)
2	3/4" x 15-1/2" x 23" Doors (center)
4	3/4" x 6" x 10" Door overlays
1	1/4" x 24" x 71-1/2" Back panel
4	3/4" x 19" x 17-1/4" Shelves
2	3/4" x 2" x 66" Base frames (front and back)
1	3/4" x 2" x 31" Base frames (center front)
2	3/4" x 2" x 17-3/4" Base frames (sides)
2	3/4" x 2" x 1-1/2" Base frames (center sides)
1	3/4" x 9" x 31" Drawer front
1	3/4" x 5-1/4" x 31" Drawer front
1	3/4" x 4-1/2" x 31" Drawer front
1	3/4" x 3-3/4" x 31" Drawer front
2	1/2" x 9" x 19" Drawer sides
2	1/2" x 5-1/4" x 19" Drawer sides
2	1/2" x 4-1/2" x 19" Drawer sides
2	1/2" x 3-3/4" x 19" Drawer sides
1	1/2" x 8-3/8" x 29-1/2" Drawer back
1	1/2" x 4-5/8" x 29-1/2" Drawer back
1	1/2" x 3-7/8" x 29-1/2" Drawer back
1	1/2" x 3-1/8" x 29-1/2" Drawer back
4	1/8" x 18-3/4" x 29-1/2" Drawer bottoms
4 sets	Extension drawer slides
16	Shelf supports
4	Door pulls
4	Door catches

Top Section

Quantity	Description
2	3/4" x 17-1/4" x 41" Sides (ends)
4	3/4" x 17-1/4" x 41" Center section sides
1	3/4" x 17-1/4" x 68-1/2" Top
1	3/4" x 18" x 70" Bottom
1	3/4" x 1-1/4" x 32-1/2" Top rail (center doors)
2	3/4" x 1-1/4" x 17-1/2" Top rails (side doors)
1	1/4" x 41" x 68" Back panel
2	3/4" x 2-1/4" x 16" Top rails (side doors)
8	3/4" x 1-1/4" x 38-1/4" Door stiles (side and center doors)
2	3/4" x 2-1/2" x 16" Bottom rails (side doors)
2	3/4" x 2-1/4" x 14" Top rails (center doors)
2	3/4" x 2-1/2" x 14" Bottom rails (center doors)
1	3/4" x 1-1/2" x 70" Molding strip
2	3/4" x 1-1/2" x 18" Molding strips
4	16" x 29-3/4" Glass shelves
2	12-3/4" x 17-1/2" Glass shelves
16	Shelf supports
12	1-1/2" x 2-1/2" Butt hinges
4	Door catches

Photo 2: This versatile cabinet can be used for storing many items other than china; for example, it can serve as a liquor closet, as shown here.

Details for the optional overlay trim used on the four bottom doors are given in Figs. 6 and 7. The bevel cuts on the overlays are made most easily and safely on a radial saw after the pieces have been cut to a diamond shape. The blade is set at 25° to make the bevel cuts. After sanding to a smooth finish, glue and nail the overlays on the center of each door.

Joints in the framework of the top section of the cabinet are made identical to the ones used in the base cabinet. The four glass doors are assembled with either dowels or mortise and tenon joints. Blind chamfers on the outside face of the doors are made after they have been glued together (Fig. 2A). Details for the blind chamfers are given in Fig. 8. The beveled top trim molding (Fig. 1) is cut on a radial saw or table saw with the blade tilted approximately 29°. For a smooth cut, a hollow ground blade should be used. The corners of the moldings can be mitered; the entire molding is glue fastened to the cabinet. Molding details are shown in Fig. 9.

Exposed plywood edges can be covered with a flexible wood veneer, often called edging tape, to match the rest of the stock. The veneer should be fastened with contact cement, applying it with hand pressure, and then tapping it down with a rubber headed mallet to insure a good bond.

The cabinet can be given a natural finish with two coats of sealer, followed by at least one coat of synthetic varnish. However, the best way to finish the cabinet is to match it with the furniture in the room in which it will be located.

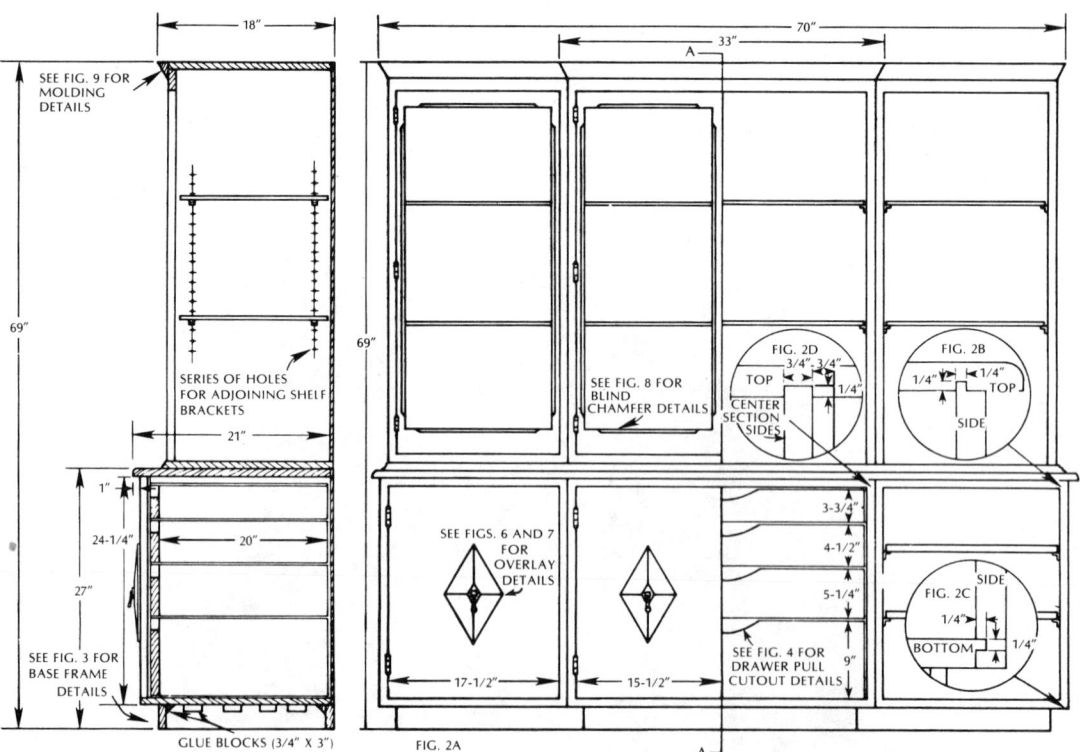

Fig. 1: Cross section of the china cabinet.

Fig. 2: (A) Front view of the china cabinet; (B) dado and rabbet joint fastening the top and side of the base cabinet; (C) dado and rabbet joint fastening the bottom and side of the base cabinet; (D) simple dado joints connecting the center section sides to the top and bottom of the base.

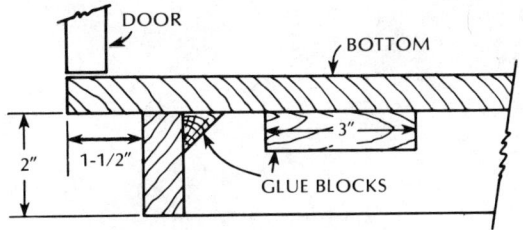

Fig. 3: Base frame details showing the indentation for toe room.

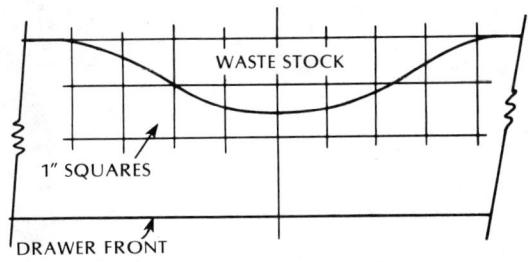

Fig. 4: Details for the drawer pull cutout.

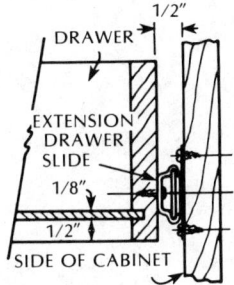

Fig. 5: Clearance needed if metal extension drawer slides are used.

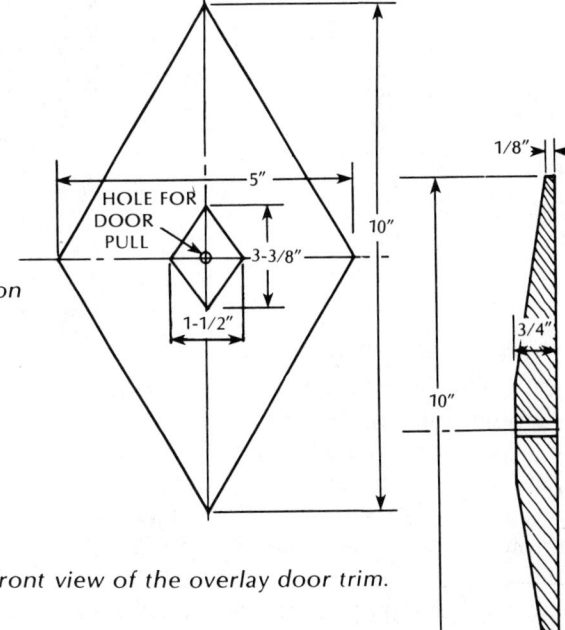

Fig. 6: Front view of the overlay door trim.

Fig. 7: Cross section of the overlay door trim.

Fig. 8: Details for the blind chamfers on the doors in the upper cabinet.

Fig. 9: Top molding details.

63

COMPACT DESK

Students and those with a business office at home will find this compact desk a perfect work center. It is just 39 inches wide, 24 inches deep, and 30 inches high, but the desk has a spacious work surface, and ample space underneath for office supplies.

Cut all the parts as shown in the panel layout (Figure 1). For hand-sawing, use a 10 to 15 point crosscut. Support the panel firmly with the face up. For power-sawing, a plywood blade gives the best results, but a combination blade may be used. The panel should lie face down for hand power-sawing; the panel should be face up for power sawing on a table or radial saw.

Once the parts are cut, proceed as follows:

1. Glue-nail each pair of A sections together to form the double-thickness desk sides. Cut the 1-1/2" half round to fit A section dimensions, allowing enough length to cut the 45° mitered half round corners, as shown in Figure 2.

2. Glue-nail 3/4" half round to section B, as shown in Figure 2. Cover the entire piece with vinyl.

3. Glue-nail 3/4" half round to sections C and D as shown in Figure 2.

4. Assemble the desk as shown in Figs. 3 and 4. Fill the joints with wood putty as needed; sand as needed; paint.

MATERIALS

Quantity	Description
1 panel	3/4" x 4' x 8' Plywood
16 lin. feet	1-1/2" Wood half round
14 lin. feet	3/4" Wood half round
1 yard	Vinyl material
-	8d finishing nails
-	Wood dough or putty
-	Fine abrasive paper
-	White glue
-	Interior semi-gloss enamel paint

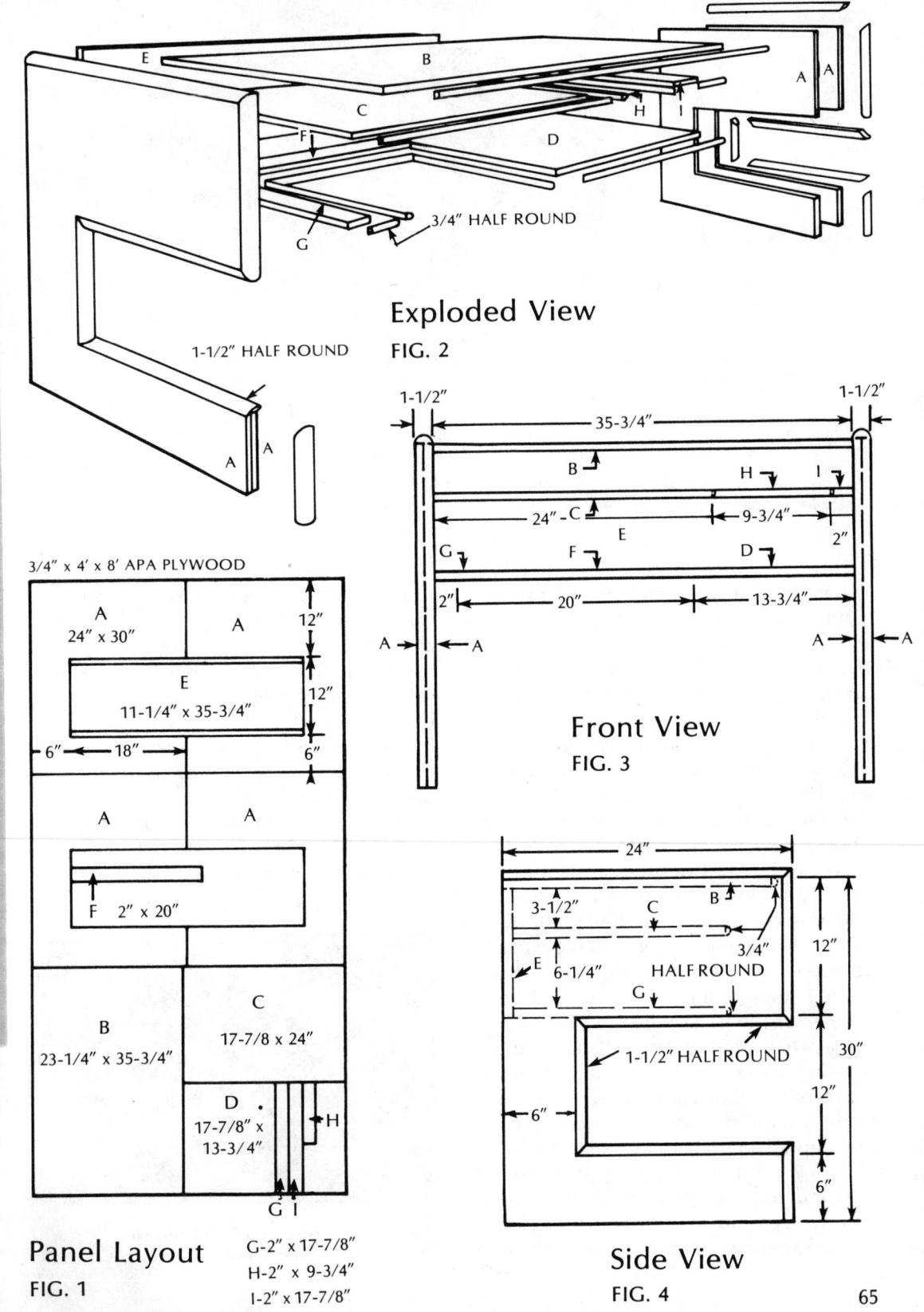

COCKTAIL TABLE

Photo 1: An eighteenth century style cocktail table with a veneered inlay top.

This period design cocktail table (Photo 1) has been strongly influenced by eighteenth century trends, especially the style exhibited in the original furniture of Thomas Sheraton. Sheraton was a Baptist preacher, Tractarian, cabinet maker, drawing master, designer, and publisher, whose work exemplifies the classical simplicity of American furniture made during the eighteenth century.

A characteristic, typical of Sheraton's work, is the round, tapered, reeded leg shown in Fig. 1. If desired, a plain turned leg may be used with equally effective results. Also, by extending the length of the legs to 28", an interesting card table can be developed. A jig for cutting the flutes in the legs on a shaper is shown in Photo 2. Details for the jig are given in Fig. 2.

To ornament the cocktail table, crossbanding the table top and inlaying the rim with holly or boxwood is recommended. However, the designs illustrated here can be adapted to individual tastes. Although either white holly or boxwood is recommended for the inlay, rosewood, tulipwood, sycamore, apple, whitewood stained green, sycamore stained brown, or harewood are all excellent possibilities for the imaginative woodworker. Because the shaped top and wood pattern decoration are typical Sheraton characteristics, the treatment of the table top may be varied to suit individual preferences without affecting the overall period design. In any case, the table top is laid into the frame on top of corner blocks which fasten to the legs and the side rails (Photo 3).

The finished project should be completed with either two coats of a satin synthetic varnish or a coat of penetrating resin finish and wax.

Photo 2: A fluting jig for making the four reeded legs on a shaper.

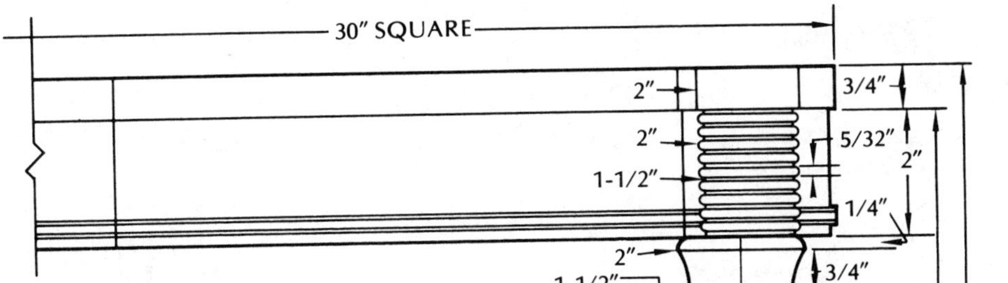

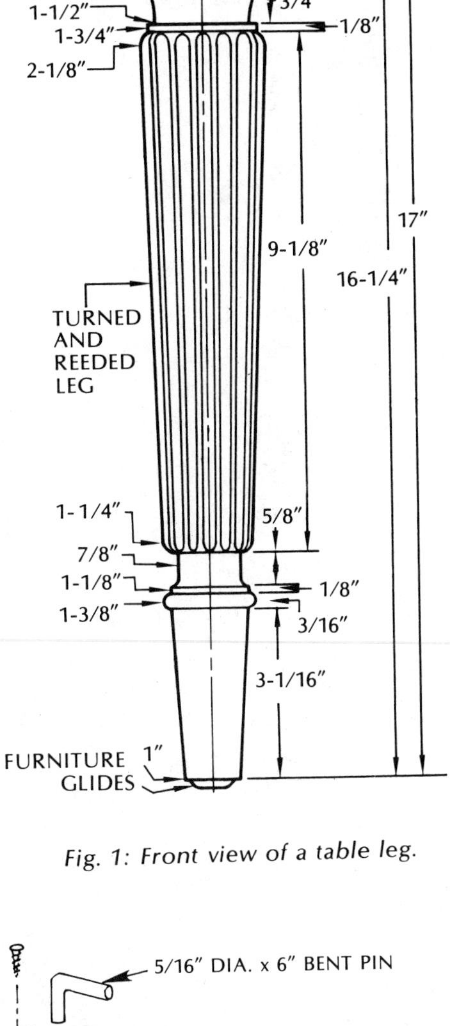

MATERIALS

Quantity	Description
1	3/4" x 30" x 30" Top
4	2" x 2" x 26" Side rails
4	1/8" x 1/2" x 2" Rail splines
4	1" x 1-1/2" x 4" Corner blocks
4	2-1/8" x 2-1/8" x 17" Legs
36	No. 10 x 1-1/2" Flathead wood screws
—	Veneering or overlay as required
—	1/4" wide Inlay strip as required
4	3/4" dia. Furniture glides

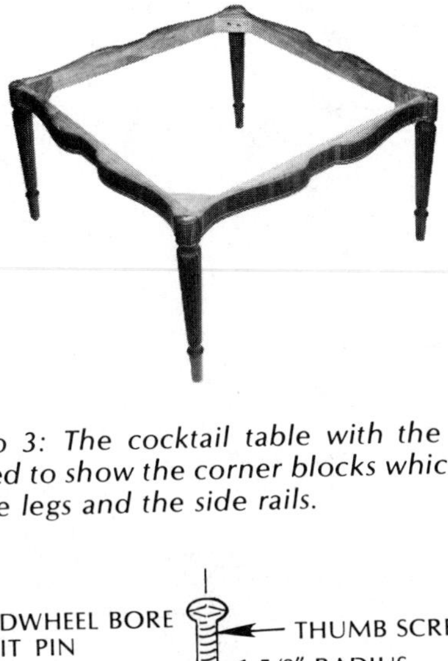

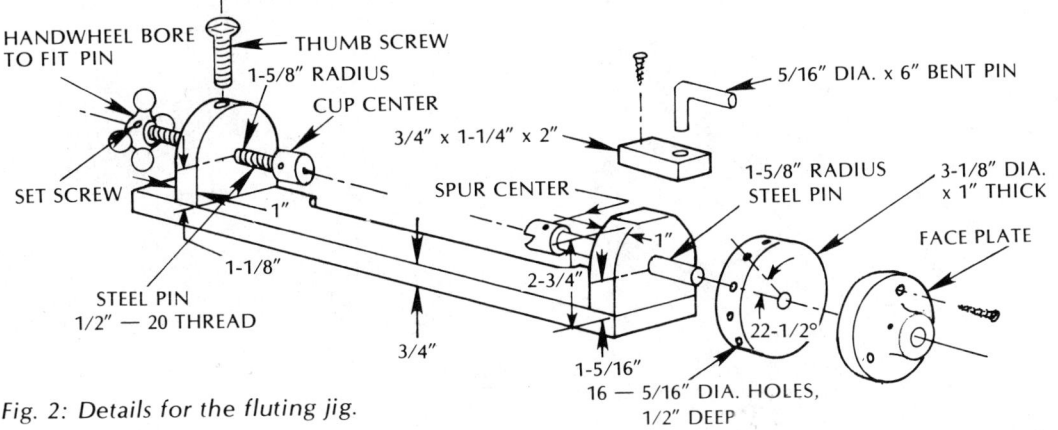

Photo 3: The cocktail table with the top removed to show the corner blocks which fasten to the legs and the side rails.

Fig. 1: Front view of a table leg.

Fig. 2: Details for the fluting jig.

67

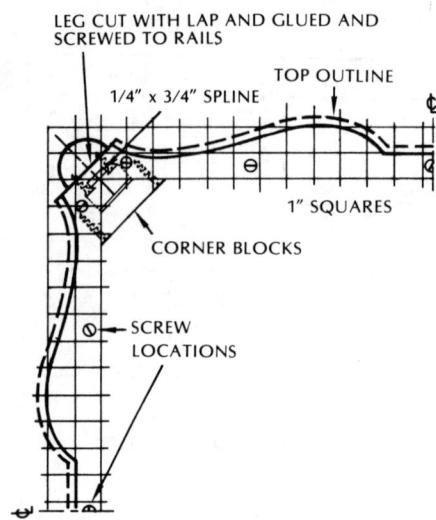

Fig. 4: Method of fastening the top to the frame.

Fig. 3: Details for the rail construction.

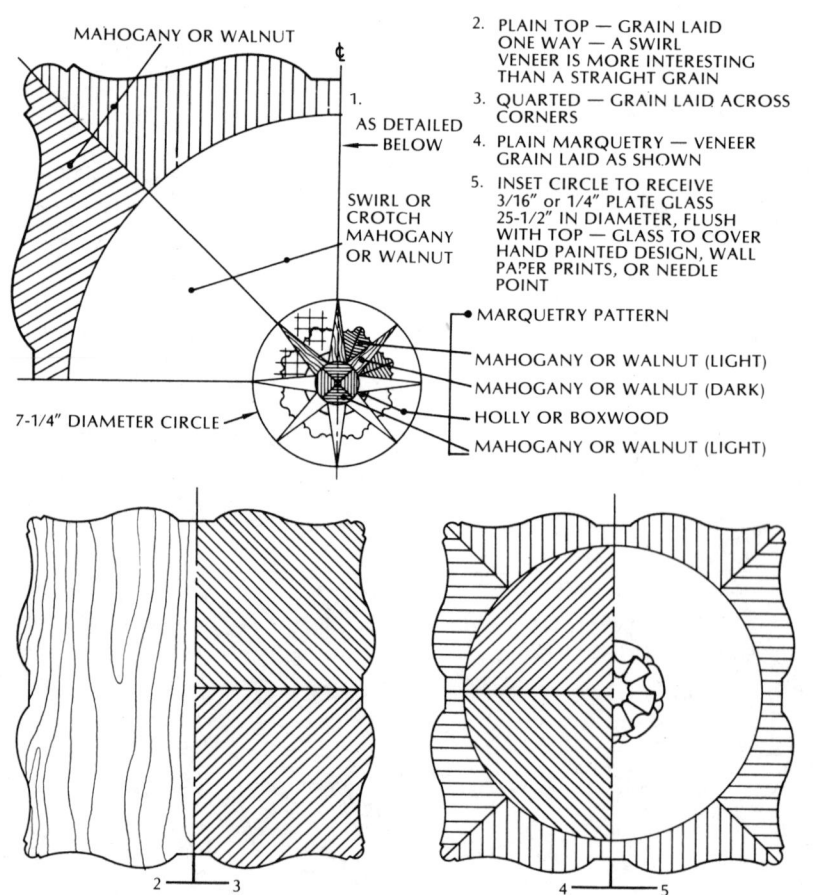

Fig. 5: Several table top veneering suggestions.

Photo 1: A student's desk with a clean, modern design.

STUDENT'S DESK

This modern desk design (Photo 1) is ideal for the student needing plenty of room for studying and writing. Making the desk also offers the homeshop owner an opportunity to try a hand at designing a ceramic or tile inlay panel for the side of the desk.

Begin the project by turning the tapered legs (Fig. 3) on a lathe, as shown in Photo 2. The two longer legs are 29-1/4" in length, while the shorter pair are 15-1/4". Commercial ferrules and swivel glides for the desk legs are available at any local hardware dealer. The longer legs can be doweled into the front, side, and back stretchers, as shown in Fig. 3, or they can be mortised for 3/8" by 1" by 1-1/2" tenons. The short legs are screw-fastened to the inside of the bottom board of the drawer compartment, using a No. 10 by 2" flathead wood screw (Fig. 4A).

The outside panel of the drawer compartment can be made with a tile insert, although artistically-inclined woodworkers might want to make an inlaid picture design panel with a scroll saw. This panel is set into a frame with a plastic insert, as shown in Fig. 6. A drawer slide frame supports the top drawer. Use mortise and tenon joints for the frame (Fig. 7). The mortises are cut on the table saw using the two 1/8" outside cutters of a standard dado head. The tenons can be made with one regular combination blade or outside dado blade cut on each side of the workpiece. A butt joint with dowels can also be used for the end frame assembly (Fig. 8).

A drawer slide frame supports the top drawer. The lower drawer slides over a solid panel. This bottom panel supports the two shorter legs and acts as a dust panel as well. Filler cleats 3/4" thick are glued in place to prevent the drawer from riding unevenly. The front and sides of the drawer can be jointed the conventional way with a 1/8" tongue and groove joint or the stronger rabbet and groove. However, cutting dovetail joints will give the project a professional touch and will provide great strength (Photo 3). This joint can be easily cut using a high speed router with a dovetail bit and a dovetail template. The cuts should be sanded before assembly. The back of the drawer can be jointed to the sides with simple dado and rabbet joints. The entire drawer assembly with both dovetail and dado and rabbet joints is shown in Fig. 9. The back panel is set into a 1/4" by 1/2" dado in the bottom of the desk top, and rabbets of the same size in the side panel of the drawer compartment and the rear end frame piece.

The desk top is made of 3/4" solid stock. The front and side edges can be shaped on the table saw with thumb-molding cutterhead knives (Fig. 4B).

Sand the entire project thoroughly with fine to very fine abrasive paper. For a natural finish apply two coats of synthetic varnish. Clear penetrating resin may be substituted for varnish if desired.

MATERIALS

Quantity	Description
2	2" x 2" x 29-1/2" Legs
2	2" x 2" x 15-1/4" Legs
1	3/4" x 2" x 15" Side rail
2	3/4" x 2" x 29" Front and back rail
1	3/4" x 14" x 20-1/4" Center panel
4	3/4" x 2-1/2" x 14" Stiles, top and bottom rails (for end panel)
1	9" x 14" Plastic insert
1	3/4" x 12-1/2" x 18" Bottom panel
1	1/4" x 13-3/4" x 18-1/2" Back panel
4 lin. feet	1/4" x 1/4" Glass molding (for end panel)
2	3/4" x 2" x 14-1/4" Drawer frame side rails
1	3/4" x 2" x 12-1/2" Drawer frame front rail
1	3/4" x 2" x 9" Drawer frame back rail
2	3/4" x 2" x 18-1/4" Drawer support cleats
1	3/4" x 6-1/8" x 12" Drawer front (top)
1	3/4" x 7-7/8" x 12" Drawer front (bottom)
2	1/2" x 5" x 18-1/2" Drawer sides (top)
2	1/2" x 6-3/4" x 18-1/2" Drawer sides (bottom)
1	1/2" x 4-3/8" x 11-1/2" Drawer back (top)
1	1/2" x 6-1/8" x 11-1/2" Drawer back (bottom)
2	1/8" x 11-1/2" x 18-1/4" Drawer bottoms
1	3/4" x 21" x 48" Desk top
4	Leg ferrules
4	Leg swivel glides
2	No. 10 x 2-1/2" Flathead wood screws

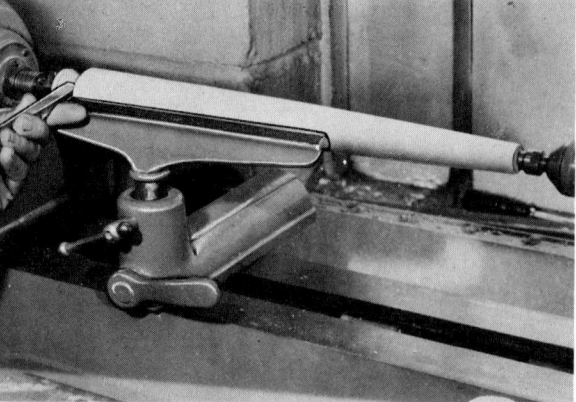

Photo 2: Turning the legs on a lathe. The bottom ends are turned down to take standard ferrules.

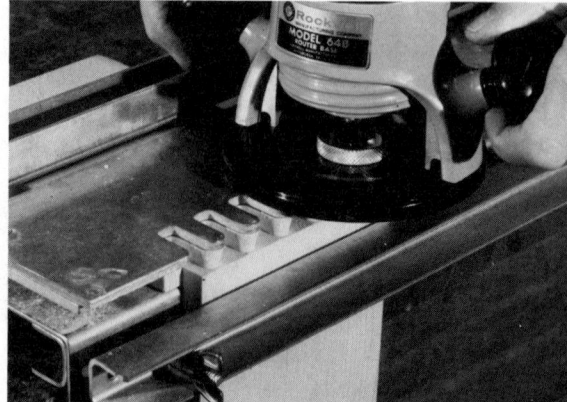

Photo 3: Dovetail joints give the front of a drawer a professional look, as well as providing great strength.

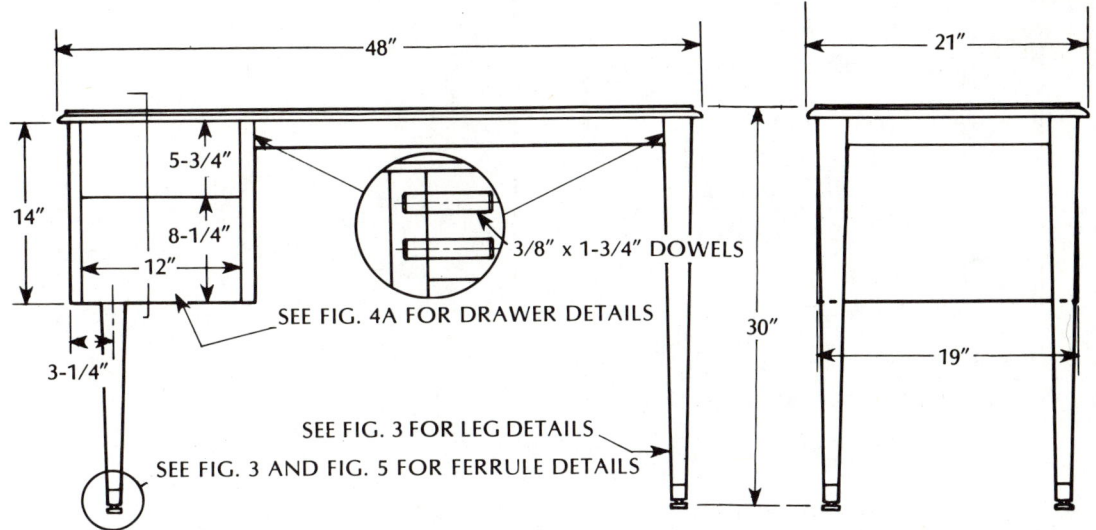

Fig. 1: Front view of the desk.

Fig. 2: End view of the desk.

FIG. 3

FIG. 5

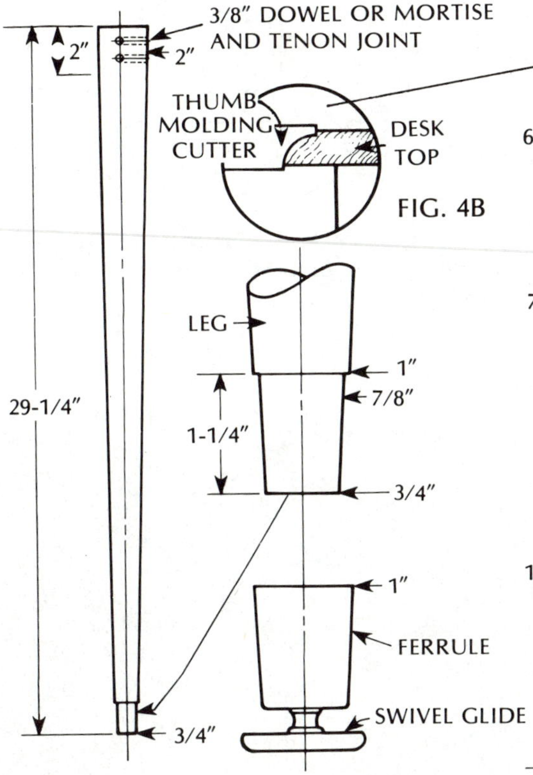

Fig. 3: Details for the longer desk legs and for the bottom of the legs.
Fig. 5: Details for the ferrule on the legs.

FIG. 4A

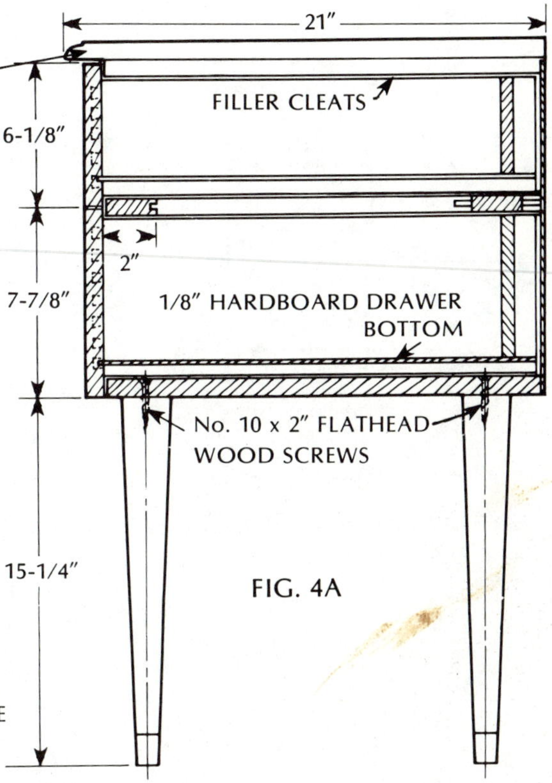

Fig. 4: (A) Cutaway view of the drawers; (B) using thumb molding cutterhead knives to shape the top of the desk.

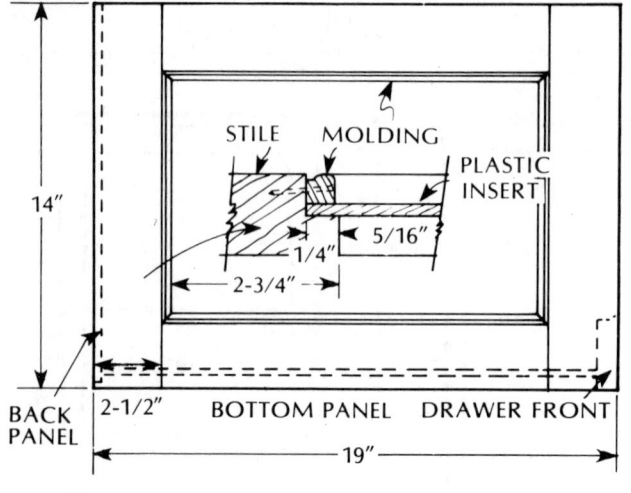

Fig. 6: Details for the end panel frame.

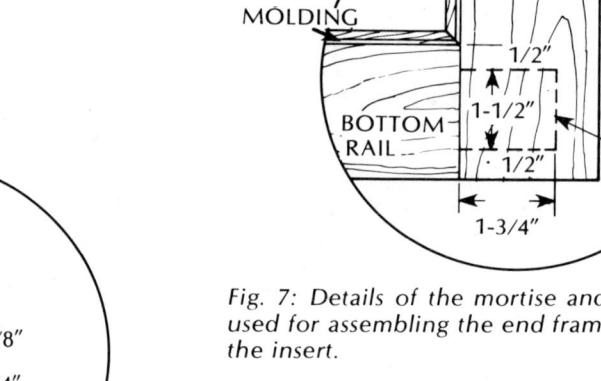

Fig. 7: Details of the mortise and tenon joint used for assembling the end frame supporting the insert.

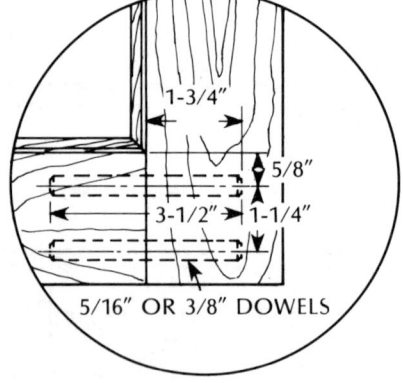

Fig. 8: Alternate doweled butt joint for the end frame assembly.

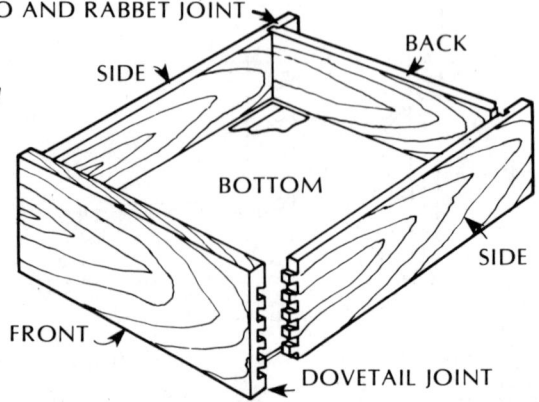

Fig. 9: Drawer assembly showing dovetail and dado and rabbet joints.

SHAKER PEDESTAL TABLE

Photo 1: A nineteenth century Shaker pedestal table.

The Shakers are a millenarian sect originating in England in 1747, who practice celibacy and lead an ascetic communal life. They came to the United States in 1774, and became known for their craftsmanship, especially woodworking. There are only a few members left today and they no longer build the furniture for which they were famous. However, their furniture design is becoming increasingly popular with woodworkers.

This handsome cherry table (Photo 1) is a classic expression of the Shaker philosophy of design. Completely devoid of ornamentation, its beauty is entirely the result of seeking a truly utilitarian form. The graceful shape of the turned center post is the result of trimming away excess material (and weight) where it is not needed for

MATERIALS

Quantity	Description
1	3" x 3" x 18" Cherry stock
-	3/4" Cherry boards, enough to make an 18" diameter table top
1	3/4" x 3-1/2" x 15" Cherry stock
3	3/4" x 4" x 14" Cherry stock
4	No. 10 x 1-1/4" Flathead wood screws
-	Glue
-	Finishing materials
-	Scrap wood for mortising jig

strength; the elegant, tapered curve of the legs provides the most material at the point of the greatest stress—the joint with the center post—and follows the grain of the wood for maximum strength.

From the modern woodworker's point of view, the most difficult part of this project is the dovetailed leg joints. While they can be cut with a router or hand tools by those who have the patience and skill required, simpler mortise and tenon joints, sealed with glue, will provide adequate strength. However, for those willing to tackle it, the dovetail provides solid construction. Details for the dovetail joint are shown in Fig. 5. The easier mortise and tenon joint is described in greater detail.

To build the table, first, joint the edges of enough 3/4" boards to make an 18" circle, and glue them together. When the glue is dry, level both faces of the workpiece with a portable disk sander or belt sander.

Set the table of a band saw or scroll saw, or the base of a portable jigsaw, at 30° and cut an 18" circle. The edge can be rounded to the contour of the template, shown in Fig. 2, with a pad sander and medium-grit paper (Photo 2). This will reduce the finished diameter to about 17-3/4". Finish sand the edges and the top surface with very fine-grit paper. If preferred, the top may be turned on the outboard end of the lathe.

Make the cleat shown in Fig. 3. Then, make a full-sized turning template for the center post, using the squares method (Fig. 2). Turn and sand the center post with its bottom end at the right end of the lathe.

Build the mortising jig shown in Fig. 1. Rout three mortises in the center post, as shown in Photo 3, cutting them 1/2" deep with a 1/4" bit first, and then 9/16" deep with a 3/8" bit (Fig. 4). Use a 3/4" template guide on the router and position the work with the lathe's indexing head. Note: Guide the router firmly against the back side of the slot in the jig.

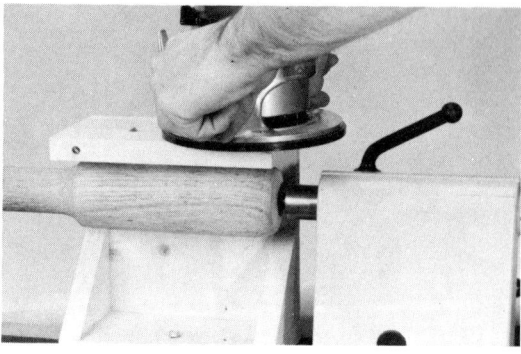

Photo 3: Routing mortises, using a high speed router, a lathe, and the mortising jig shown in Fig. 1.

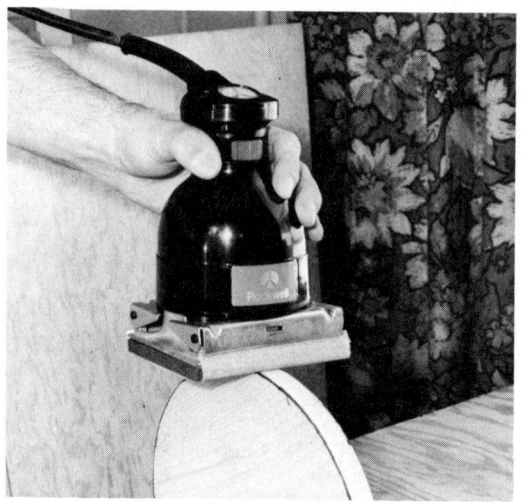

Photo 2: Contouring the table top edge with a pad sander.

Photo 4: Cutting the first rabbet in the leg. The second rabbet is cut the same way, but with the radial arm (or miter gauge) swung to the opposite direction the same number of degrees.

Draw the leg pattern shown in Fig. 6 onto one of the leg boards. Set the miter gauge of the table saw or the arm of the radial saw at 38° and cut the ends of the legs. With a dado head, cut a 3/16" by 1/2" rabbet in one side of each leg. Use the leg with the pattern drawn on it to set up a stop block that will properly position the cuts for all of the legs (Photo 4).

Reset the miter gauge or radial arm to 38° on the other side, and again use the first leg to set up a stop block that will position the rabbet cuts on the other side for all of the legs. Gradually adjust the depth of the cut to make a tenon that fits into the mortises in the center post. The tenon will be slightly shorter than the mortise to allow for gluing.

Cut out the leg with the pattern drawn on it. Use this leg as a pattern for the other two. The three legs may also be stacked and cut at one time with a band saw. Flush-sand the legs with a fine-grit paper. Assemble the table, attaching the cleat to the top, across the grain, with screws and glue for maximum strength.

Colors and kinds of finishes permissible for use by Shaker artisans were determined by their Elders who were often craftsmen themselves. All of the earliest furniture was painted, usually in various shades of red and brownish orange. Early in the nineteenth century they began to use thinned paint as a stain, and then oil-base and water-base stains, followed by varnish, to allow the natural wood grain to show through. The earliest stains were generally similar in color to the paints used previously: shades of red, orange-brown, and reddish yellow were common. Later furniture was often stained in mellow, fairly light brown tones.

In short, most fairly light stains, especially those with distinct reddish or orange tones, can legitimately be used on Shaker reproductions. Spray lacquer will provide a good imitation of a Shaker varnish finish with a lot less time and effort.

Darker woods, especially walnut and

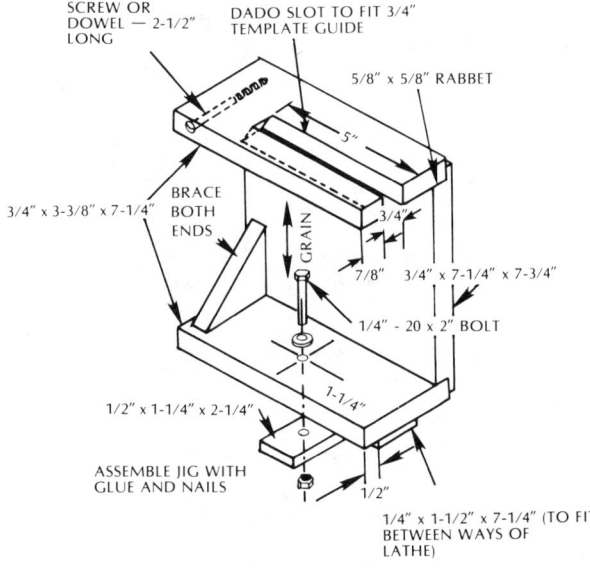

Fig. 1: Jig for routing mortises in the center post. Note: For lathes with an 11" swing, reduce the height 1/2".

cherry, were often finished with linseed oil. This pedestal table can be oil-finished to good effect. After finish-sanding the wood with very fine-grit paper, rub it with 4/0 (superfine) steel wool. Apply boiled linseed oil straight from the can with a rag and rub it in, but not too strenuously. After the oil has had time to soak in (usually not more than an hour), wipe off all of the excess with a dry rag. Dispose of the rags in a fireproof container or burn them immediately; this is a good policy with all oils and finishing materials, but linseed oil is especially notorious for spontaneous combustion.

After four or five days, another coat of linseed oil may be applied if desired, and 10 days later a good paste wax may be used if a lustrous finish is desired.

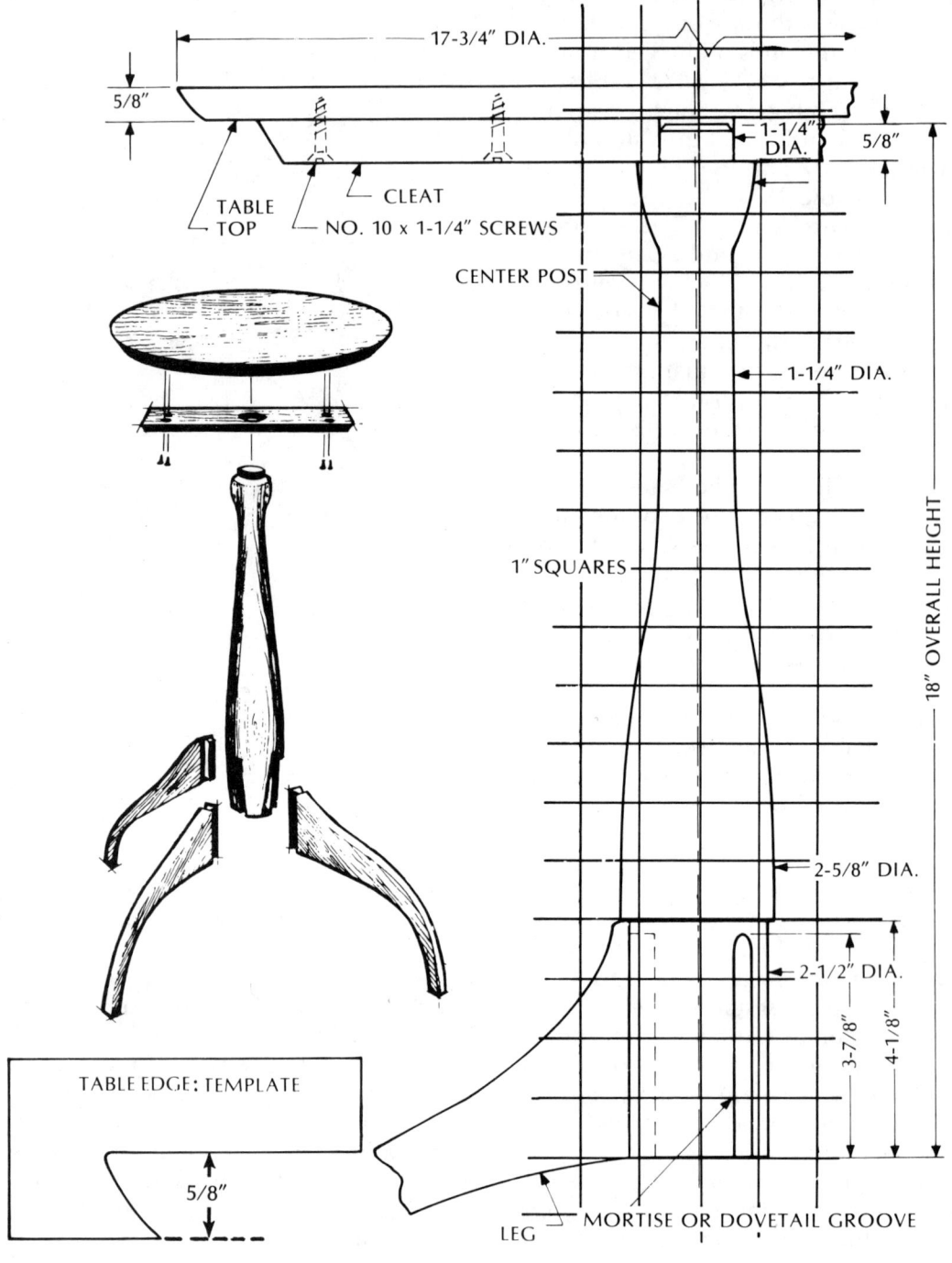

Fig. 2: Overall construction details for the pedestal table.

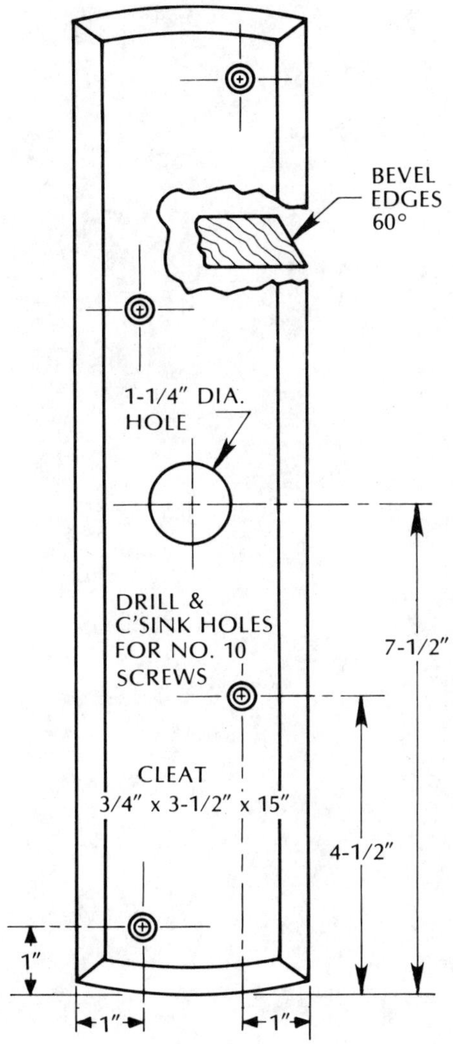

Fig. 3: Details for the cleat.

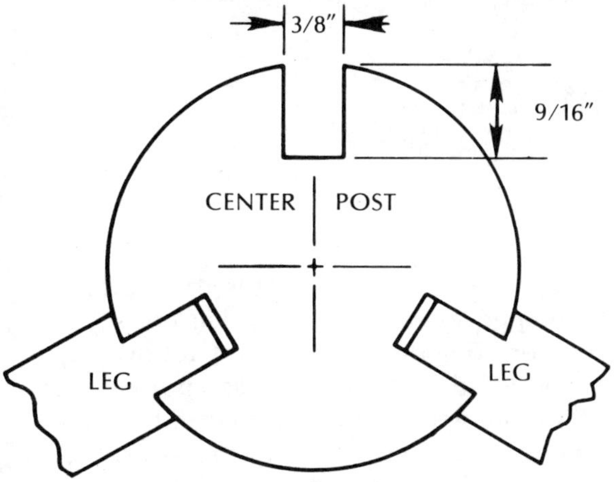

Fig. 4: Details if mortise and tenon joints are used for the center post and table legs.

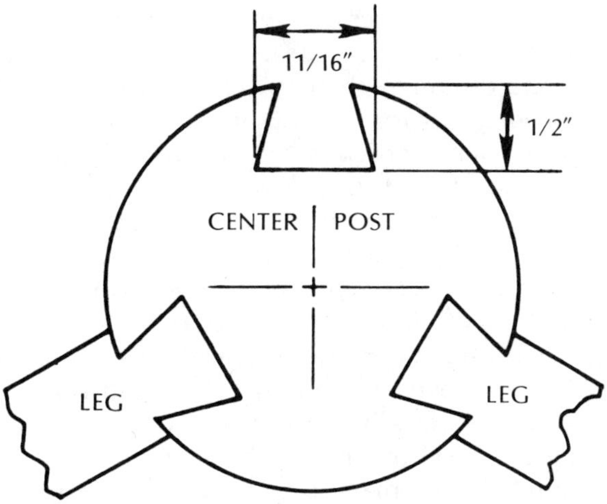

Fig. 5: Details if dovetail joints are used for the center post and table legs.

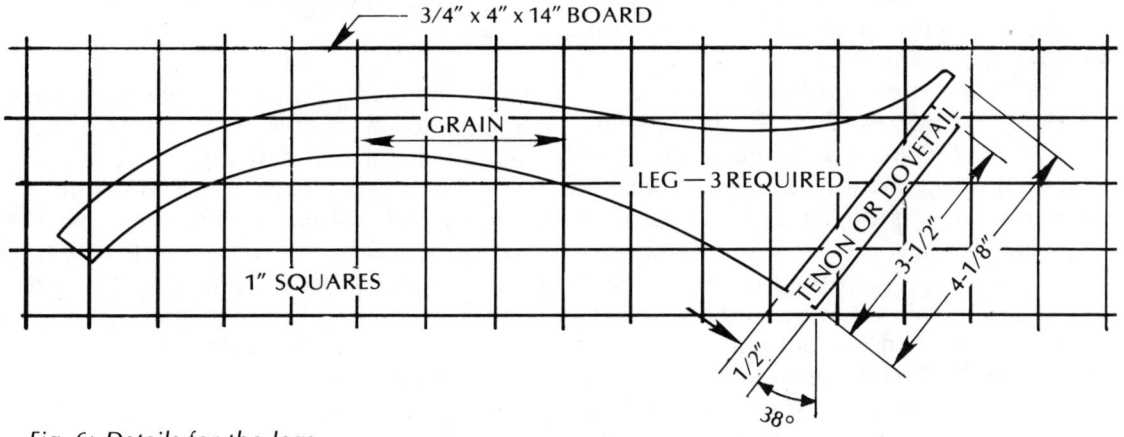

Fig. 6: Details for the legs.

77

BOOK CABINET

This book cabinet should be quite a challenge, even for the experienced woodworker. The design does not follow any time period. It can be used as a book case, china cabinet, or as a display case for figurines or trinkets. The various carvings (which are optional) will provide a noteworthy conversation piece for the living room or master bedroom. The cabinet is made in two sections and is taken apart by loosening four screws, one at each corner post, through metal brackets.

You can begin the project by cutting the corner posts for the top and bottom sections. Make grooves 1/4" wide and 3/8" deep for the side panels with 1/2" wide and 1/8" deep rabbet cuts on the back posts for the 1/8" thick hardboard back panels. Stop chamfers on the posts are made on the jointer by tilting the jointer fence inward at 45°. Several passes are required by feeding the stock over the jointer cutterhead very slowly, especially on the start and finish ends of each chamfer. The stop chamfer could also be made on the band saw with the aid of a holding block (Fig. 9B). Using the same holding block, the portion cut with a band saw can then be sanded smooth on a drill press fitted with a 1-3/4" diameter sanding drum.

Top and bottom moldings are made of various thicknesses of stock using the cutters indicated in Figs. 5 and 6. The trim molding used on the side panels of the lower section is of the commercial type available at local picture frame suppliers.

The front doors of the top section have glass and metal grills mounted into frames with the top and bottom rails scrolled as shown in Fig. 7. The edges of the frames are molded by using a high speed router fitted with a sash bead cutter. The bottom doors are also made of 3/4" stock with solid stock panels. Should you wish to try your hand at carving, use the design suggested in Fig. 9A. Continuous hinges are used on both the top and bottom doors. Metal shelf standards and brackets are used in both sections. Or, a series of holes can be bored in the side rail panels and conventional shelf brackets can be used instead of the metal standards.

The drawer front is made with rabbet and groove joints as detailed in Fig. 8. The

MATERIALS

Quantity	Description
	Top Cabinet
4	1-1/2" x 1-1/2" x 43" Corner posts
4	3/4" x 1-1/2" x 43" Stiles (side panel frames)
2	3/4" x 3-1/4" x 8-1/2" Top rails (side panel frames)
2	3/4" x 2-1/4" x 8-1/2" Bottom rails (side panel frames)
2	1/4" x 8-1/4" x 38" Side panels
1	1/4" x 33-3/4" x 43-7/8" Back panel
1	3/4" x 3-1/4" x 30-1/4" Top rail
4	3/4" x 1-1/2" x 39-3/4" Front door stiles
2	3/4" x 8-1/2" x 15-3/8" Front door top rails (1-1/2" for tenon)
2	3/4" x 3-1/2" x 15-3/8" Front door bottom rails (1-1/2" for tenon)
1	3/4" x 1-3/4" x 67-1/4" Top molding (A) (front and sides)
1	7/8" x 1-5/16" x 64-7/8" Top molding (B) (front and sides)
1	1" x 1-3/16" x 62" Top molding (C) (front and sides)
1	3/8" x 7/16" x 59" Top molding (D) (front and sides)
1	3/4" x 13-3/4" x 32-3/4" Top board
3	3/4" x 12-1/2" x 29-1/2" Shelves
2	11-7/8" x 34-1/4" Single strength glass sheets (for doors)
2	11-7/8" x 34-1/4" Metal grills (for doors)
2	1/4" x 3/4" x (as required) Back door moldings (E)
2	1-1/4" x 39-3/4" Continuous hinges
	Base Cabinet
4	1-1/2" x 1-1/2" x 26-1/4" Corner posts
4	3/4" x 1-1/2" x 26-1/4" Stiles (for side panels)
4	3/4 x 2-1/4 x 10-1/4" Top and bottom rails (for side panels)
2	1/4" x 10" x 22-1/4" Panels (for side panels)
1	3/4" x 1-1/2" x 30-3/4" Top rail (above drawer)
2	3/4" x 16" x 31-1/4" Top and bottom boards
1	3/4" x 1-1/2" x 30-1/2" Drawer slide frame (front)
2	3/4" x 1-1/2" x 14-1/4" Drawer slide frames (sides)
1	3/4" x 1-1/2" x 28" Drawer slide frame (back)
2	3/4" x 2-1/4" x 30-1/4" Base frames (front and back)
2	3/4" x 2-1/4" x 14-1/4" Base frames (sides)
1	3/4" x 1" x 63-3/4" Base molding (F)
1	3/4" x 1-3/8" x 65-1/4" Base molding (G)
1	5/16" x 3/8" x 63" Molding (K)
1	3/4" x 1-3/4" x 68-1/4" Base molding (H)
18	3/4" x 3/4" x 3" Glue blocks
4	3/4" x 1-1/2" x 19" Door stiles
2	3/4" x 6" x 16-5/8" Door top rails (1-1/2" for tenon)
2	3/4" x 2-1/4" x 16-5/8" Door bottom rails (1-1/2" for tenon)
2	1/4" x 12-7/8" x 15-1/4" Door panels
2	1-1/4" x 19" Continuous hinges
1	3/4" x 5" x 30-1/4" Drawer front
2	1/2" x 5" x 15-1/4" Drawer sides
1	1/2" x 4-3/8" x 29-3/4" Drawer back
1	1/8" x 15-1/4" x 29-5/8" Drawer bottom (hardboard)
1	3/4" x 14-1/2" x 30-1/8" Shelf

drawer front is 3/4" thick, the sides and back are 1/2" thick, and the drawer bottom is 1/8" thick hardboard. The drawer slide frame is made of 3/4" stock. The frame is held in place by the 1/4" deep blind grooves in the corner posts.

If the project is made of hardwood with an open grain like walnut or mahogany, use a wood filler to suit. Apply the appropriate stain and follow with two coats of satin polyurethane finish or a similar synthetic varnish.

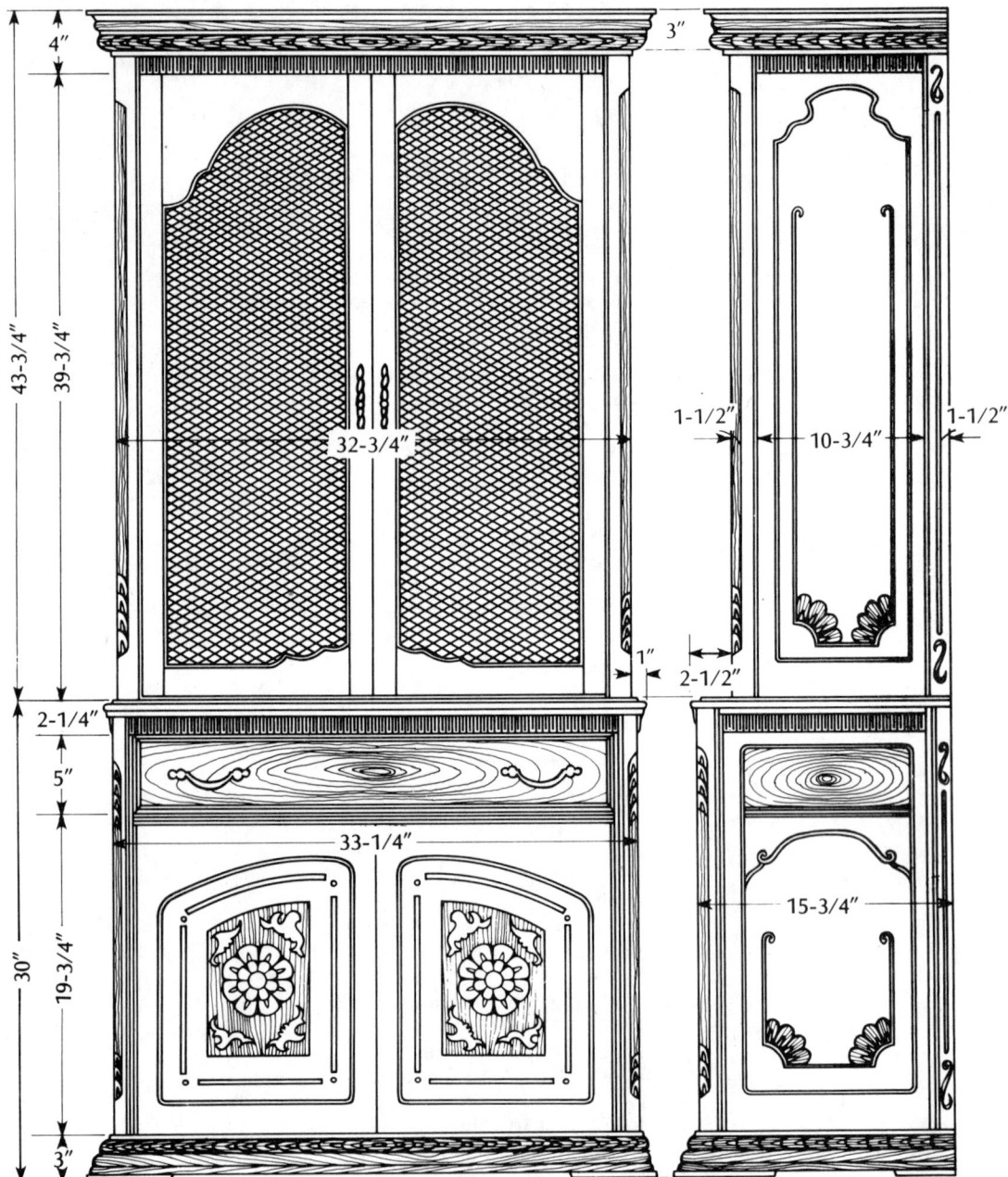

Fig. 1: Front elevation of the book cabinet. Fig. 2: Side elevation of the book cabinet.

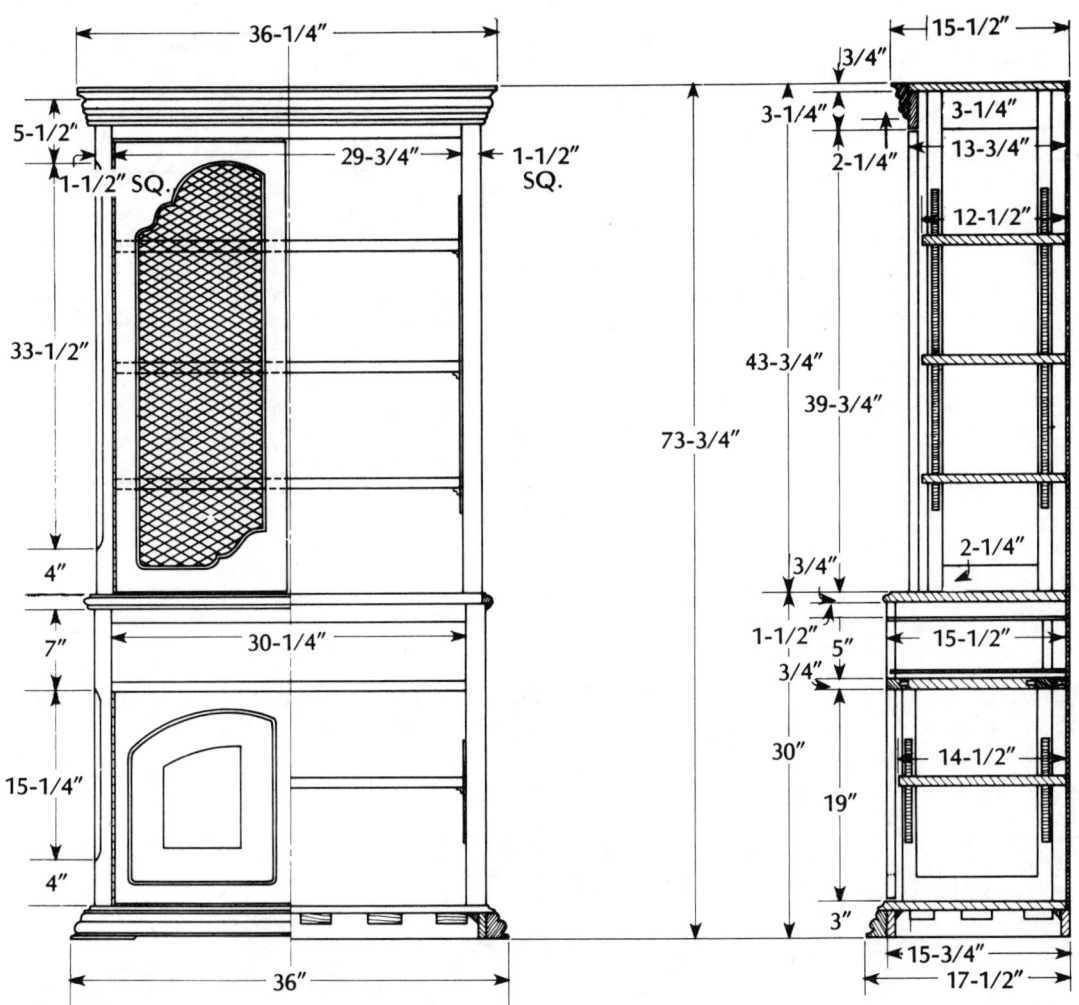

Fig. 3: Front view of the book cabinet.   *Fig. 4: Sectional view of the book cabinet.*

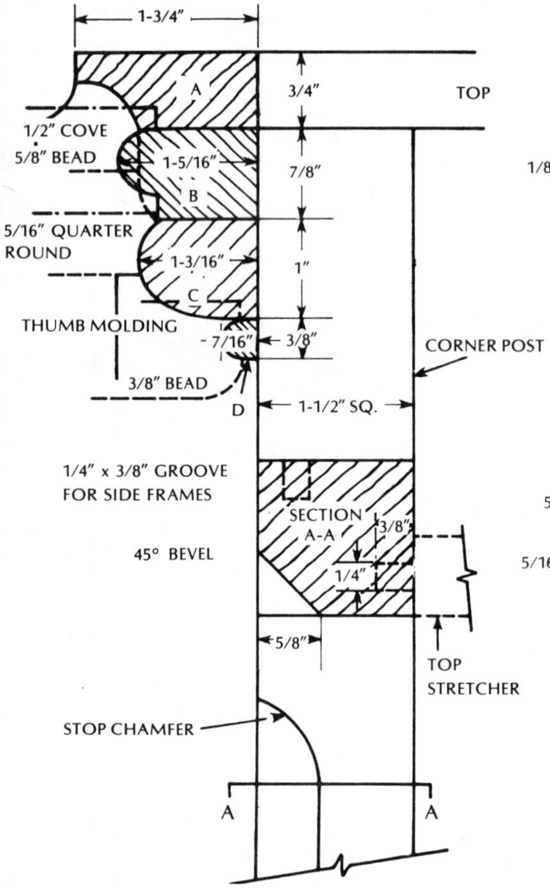

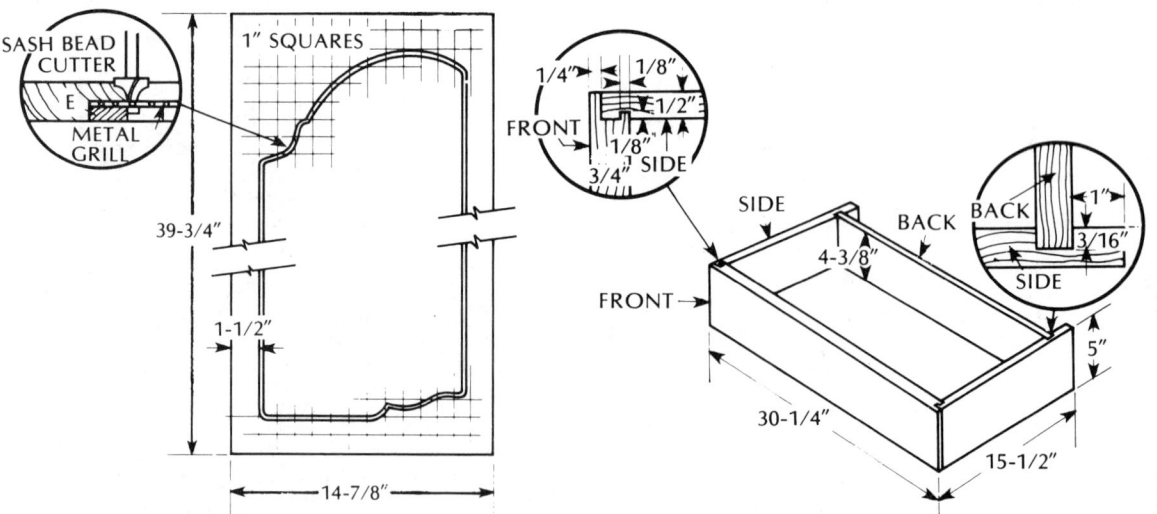

Fig. 5: Top molding details with the molding cutterhead knives shown.

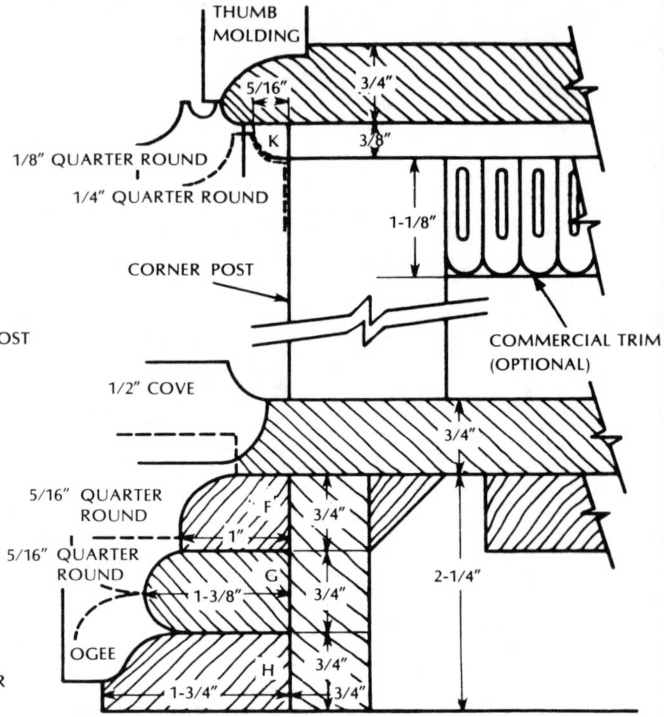

Fig. 6: Base molding details with the molding cutterhead knives shown.

Fig. 7: Top door scroll design.

Fig. 8: Drawer details.

A

B

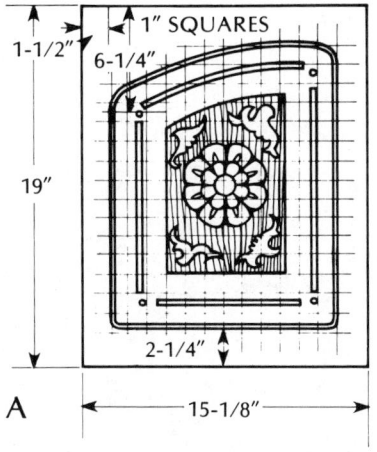

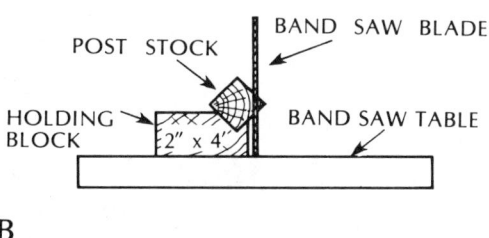

Fig. 9: (A) Bottom drawer carving details; (B) cutting the post chamfer on a band saw.

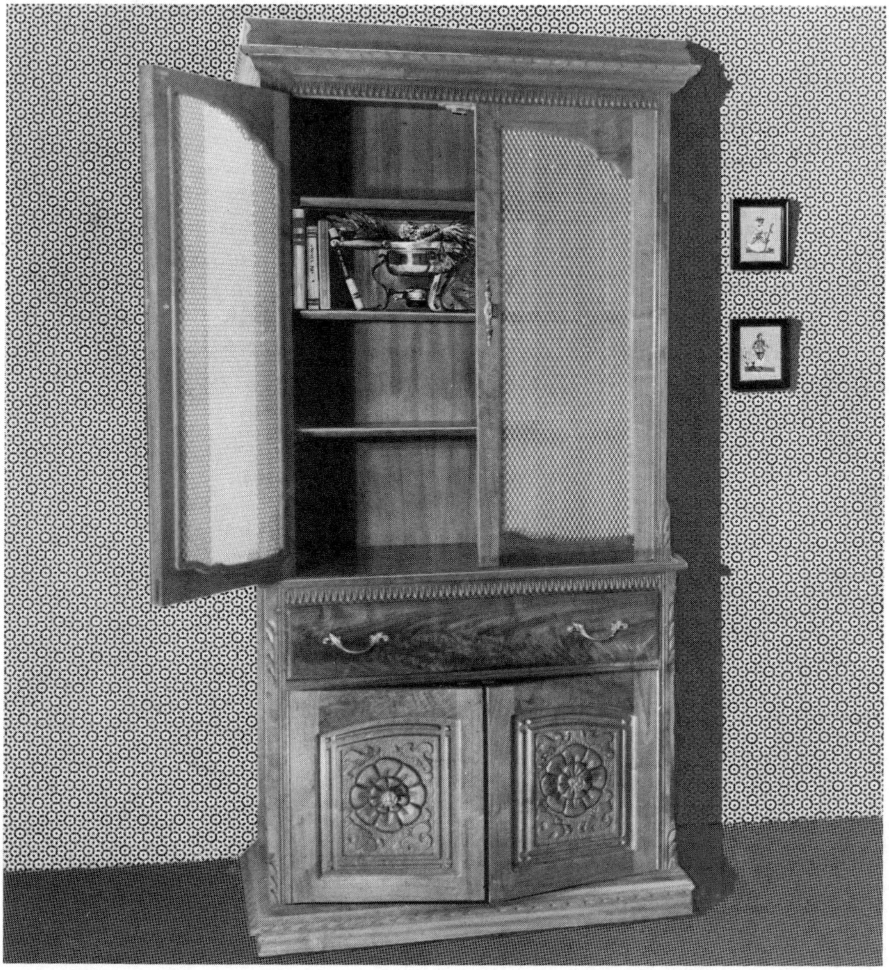

SCHOOL DESK AND CHAIR

Photo 1: A sturdy chair and desk set designed for schoolchildren.

Children will get plenty of use out of this sturdy, easy-to-make desk and chair set (Photo 1). The overall dimensions are appropriate for youngsters in the 5- to 10-year-old group; however, the dimensions can be changed to suit younger or older children as desired. Also, the cutout designs on the desk sides and the chair back can be changed to meet individual preferences. For instance, initials might be used for the cutouts.

The desk and chair can be made entirely of 3/4" birch or maple or 3/4" plywood. If plywood is used, a medium density overlaid type or a similar kind that is easy to work with and will take a nice finish is recommended.

First, trace the outline of the sides of the desk on a piece of brown wrapping paper, using the squares method, as shown in Fig. 1. Before cutting the outline on the band saw, make a 3/4" dado in each side piece for the school supply shelf (Photo 2). Next, cut the top taper, setting the miter gauge at 4° (Photo 3). A 1/4" rabbet to accommodate the desk top is made on a table saw with one pass of the two 1/8" outside blades of the dado head or with two passes of a regular saw blade. The two outside dado blades are then used to make 1/4" blind dadoes in the side pieces for the dado and rabbet joint. All curve cutting is done on a band saw (Photo 4). Decorative holes in the sides of the desk and the back of the chair can be bored on a drill press with a hole saw or multi-spur bits (Photo 5), or cut out on a scroll saw with the appropriate blade.

On the underside of the desk top, three 1/4" by 1/4" blind grooves are made; two are for the desk sides, and one for the 1/4" back panel. A 1/2" by 1/2" round-edge stop strip is glued to the desk top, 1/2" from the edge (Fig. 1). The pencil groove is made on the table saw with a molding cutterhead and 1/2" flute cutter knives (Fig. 2). The desk pieces are glued and screw-fastened together with No. 8 by 1-3/4" flathead wood screws (Fig. 3). No screws are needed for the top and the back panel.

The chair parts are cut to the dimensions shown in Figs. 5, 6, and 7. The back of the chair has a bevel cut of 7° at the bottom. The front leg brace is also bevel cut 7° on the bottom edge only. The entire chair is butt jointed and held together with glue and No. 8 by 1-3/4" flathead wood screws.

Smooth all sharp corners with a portable belt or disk sander. Use a pad sander to thoroughly finish sand both the desk and the chair. For a natural finish, apply two coats of polyurethane finish, sanding lightly between applications. A penetrating resin clear finish may also be used. For an enamel finish, apply undercoating and one or two coats of non-toxic enamel.

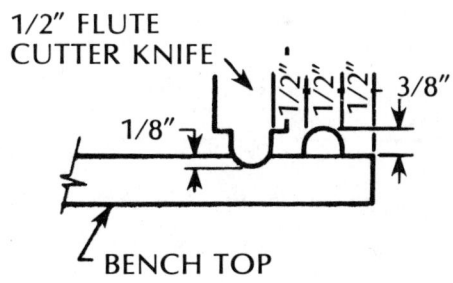

Fig. 2: Bench top details.

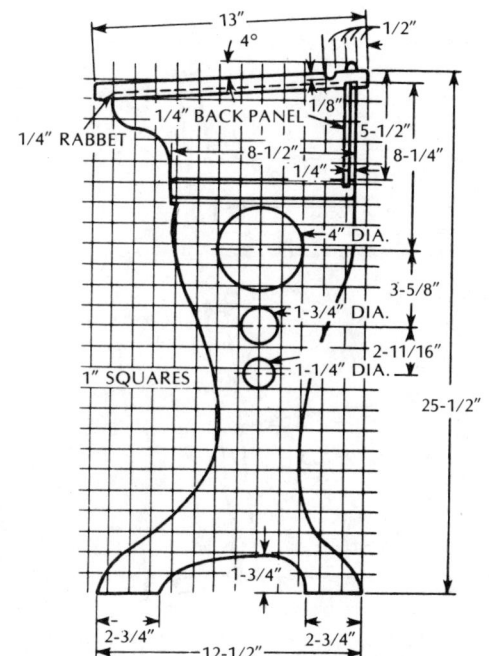

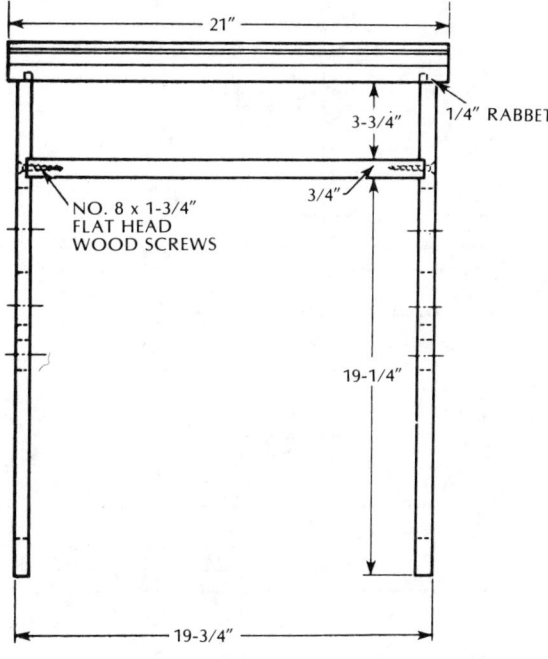

Fig. 1: Side view details of the desk.

Fig. 3: Front view details of the desk.

85

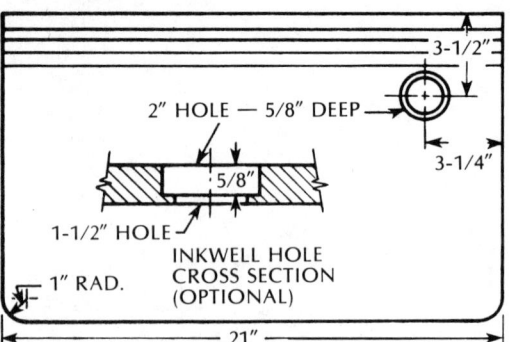

Fig. 4: Top view details of the desk.

MATERIALS

Quantity	Description
2	3/4" x 12-1/2" x 23" Sides
1	3/4" x 13" x 21" Top
1	3/4" x 8-1/2" x 18-3/4" Shelf
1	1/2" x 1/2" x 21" Top stop strip
1	1/4" x 5-1/4" x 18-3/4" Back panel
4	No. 8 x 1-3/4" Flathead wood screws
1	3/4" x 13" x 26-3/4" Chair back
1	3/4" x 13" x 13" Chair seat
1	3/4" x 13" x 11-1/2" Chair center support
1	3/4" x 3" x 13" Chair front leg brace
9	No. 8 x 1-3/4" Flathead wood screws

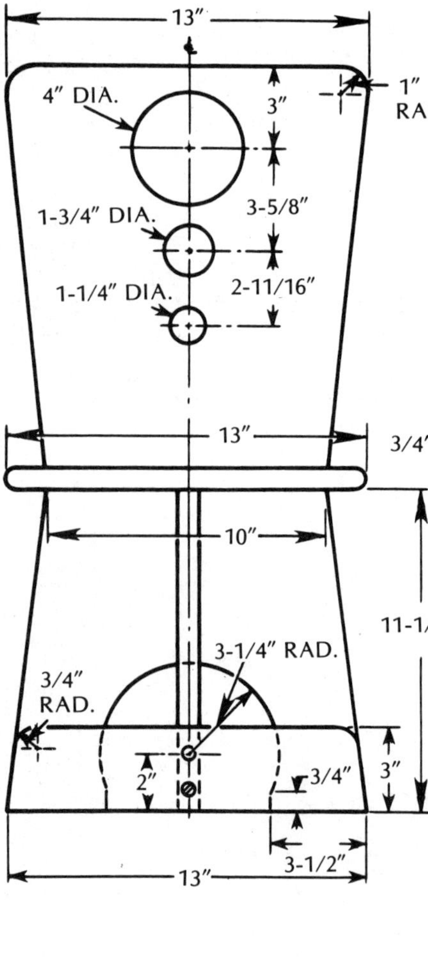

Fig. 5: Front view details of the chair.

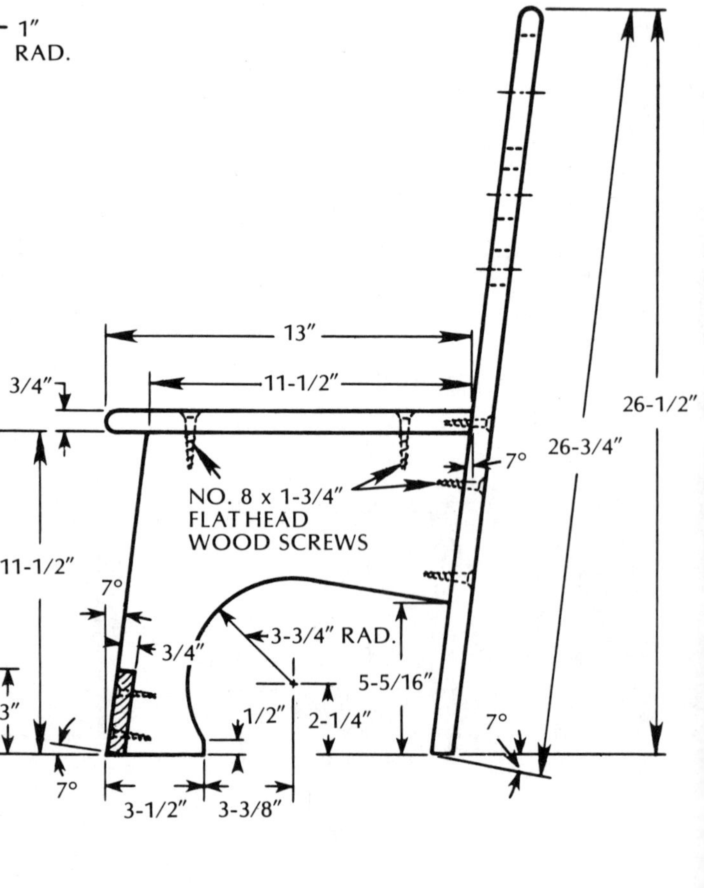

Fig. 6: Side view details of the chair.

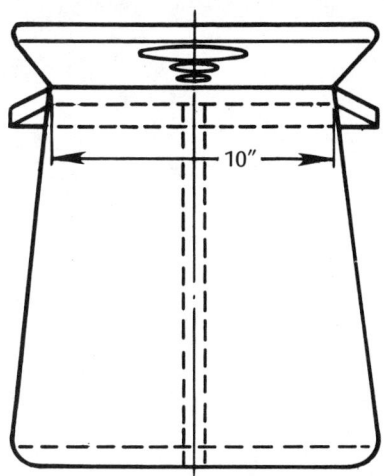

Fig. 7: Top view details of the chair.

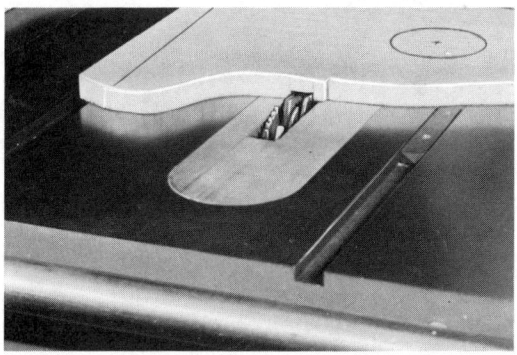

Photo 2: Cutting 3/4" dadoes in the desk sides for the school supply shelf. The dadoes are made on the table saw before cutting the sides to shape on the band saw. Note: The blade guard is removed for clarity.

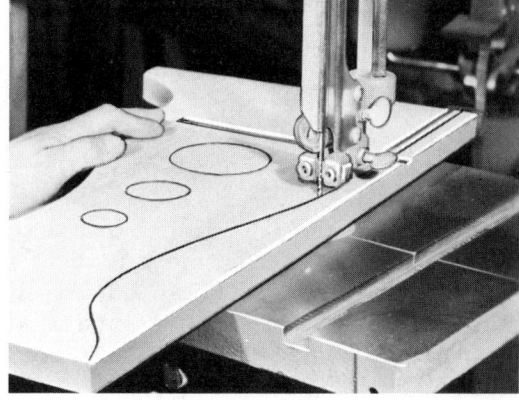

Photo 4: Cutting the curved portions of the side pieces of the desk on a band saw.

Photo 3: Making a taper cut on the top of the desk side with the miter gauge set at 4° on the table saw. Note: The blade guard is removed for clarity.

Photo 5: Boring holes in the sides of the desk on a drill press with multi-spur bits. Hole saws can also be used.

NESTED TABLES

Photo 1: (A) A three-legged table, ideal for serving at a casual get-together; (B) the set of three tables can be nested for easy storage.

These nested or stacked tables (Photo 1A) will serve many purposes. They are designed to solve the problems normally involved with informal serving. Their sturdy, well-balanced, three-legged construction makes them ideal as a setting for drinks and canapés. They are light in weight and can be nested when not in use (Photo 1B).

The three legs are taper turned on a lathe or they can be turned, using a duplicator attachment, as shown in Photo 2. The template for turning the legs is cut on a band saw from 1/8" tempered hardboard (Photo 3). Draw the template, using half of the leg design shown in Fig. 1. The edge of the template should be sanded smooth after cutting. An undercut is made on the small tapered end for a metal ferrule. Commercial leg mounting plates can be used to attach the legs to the table top, or homemade plates can be used. Homemade plates should be cut from 1/8" cold rolled steel and screw fastened to the table top. It is best to counterbore holes for the leg mounting plates, so that the leg is flush with the table top stock when assembled.

The table top (Fig. 2) can be made from solid stock or 3/4" hardwood plywood with two good sides. The edges of the plywood can be covered with edging tape to match the appearance of the plywood surface. The table top is most easily cut to shape on a band saw (Photo 4). Use a 1/4" skip tooth blade for fast cutting. The edges of the table top can be sanded smooth on a disk sander, using a coarse abrasive disk

MATERIALS

Quantity	Description
3	1-1/2" x 1-1/2" x 15-1/4" Table legs
1	3/4" x 15-3/8" x 16" Table top
3	5/16" x 1-1/2" Leg hanger bolts
3	Hanger bolt plates (for straight mounting)
3	7/8" to 1/2" Tapered leg ferrules

(Photo 5). Remember to sand on the down rotation side of the disk. All pieces of the table are then sanded thoroughly with first, a medium-grit and then a fine-grit abrasive.

If open grained wood is used, stain it and apply a matching wood filler. Apply two coats of a synthetic varnish, such as a satin polyurethane finish.

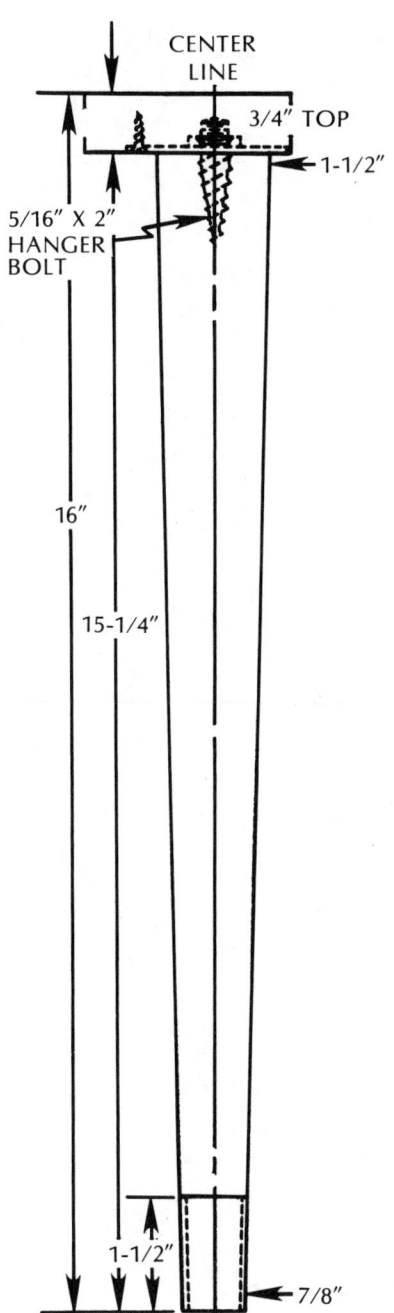

Fig. 1: Leg details.

Photo 2: With the template screw fastened to a duplicator attachment, identical tapered legs are turned on a lathe.

Photo 3: Cutting the leg template from tempered hardboard on a band saw, using a skip tooth blade.

Photo 4: Cutting a solid stock table top on a band saw, using a 1/4" skip tooth blade.

Photo 5: Sanding the edges of the table top on a disk sander.

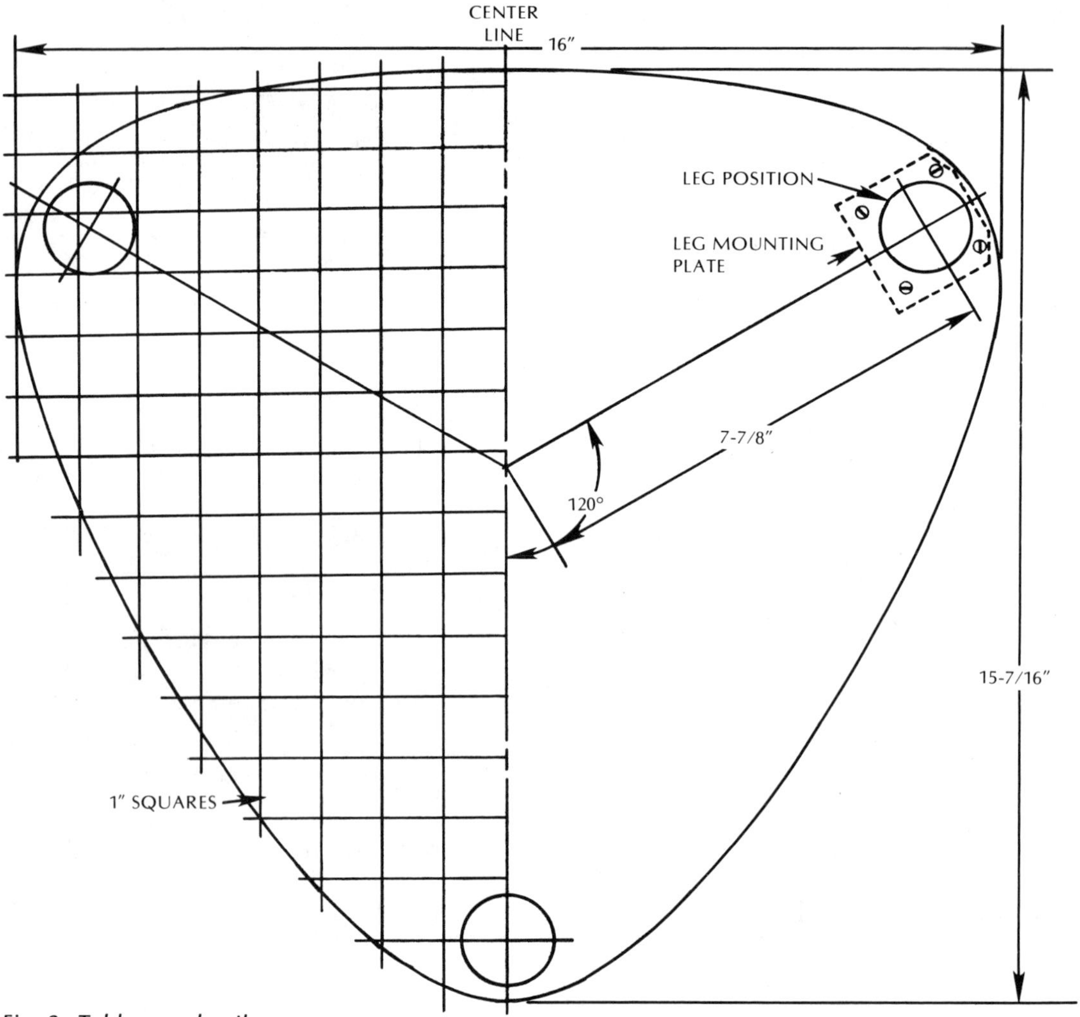

Fig. 2: Table top details.

SOFA

This handsome contemporary sofa project is designed for the average woodworking skills. It is based on standard lumber sizes and grades available at the local lumberyard. Dimensions are planned to minimize extensive cutting and most lengths can be transported in the family car to save delivery charges. Basic construction is featured, with no tricky dovetail or mortise and tenon joints called for. Simple butt joints, secured with screws, are all that is necessary.

Steps in the construction of the modern roll-around wood sofa are shown on the next two pages. When the project is completed, it must be finished to protect it from the soil and fingerprints of daily household activity. Clear finishes will show the natural grain to the best advantage and are available in dull, satin or high gloss types.

MATERIAL

Quantity	Description
2	2" x 10" x 16' Lumber (sides)
1	2" x 3" x 10" Lumber (top trim)
1	1" x 4" x 16' Lumber (base trim)
6	2" x 4" x 10' Lumber (framing)
1	1" x 12" x 5' Lumber (front)
1	3/4" x 4' x 8' Plywood panel (A-C Interior)
4	600 lb. Ball casters
16	1/4" x 4" Lag bolts/washers
48	2-1/2" No. 9 Flathead wood screws
—	Wood putty
—	Medium and fine abrasive paper
—	16d Finish nails
—	8d Finish nails
—	8d Box nails
—	Clear natural oil finish
—	White glue

MATERIALS FOR SEAT COVERS

Quantity	Description
2	24" x 28" x 4" Foam (seat)
2	16" x 28" x 3" Foam (back)
1	30" x 30" Dacron fiber fill (padding)

Standard sewing techniques are used to create the zippered seat covers.

Wrap the foam in dacron padding material and insert it in the completed seat covers.

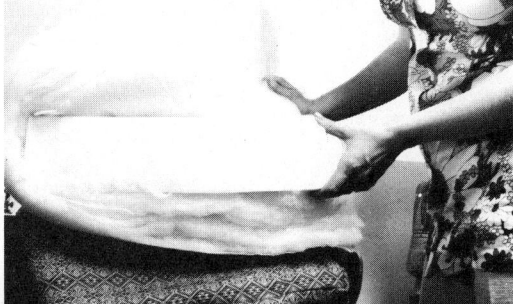

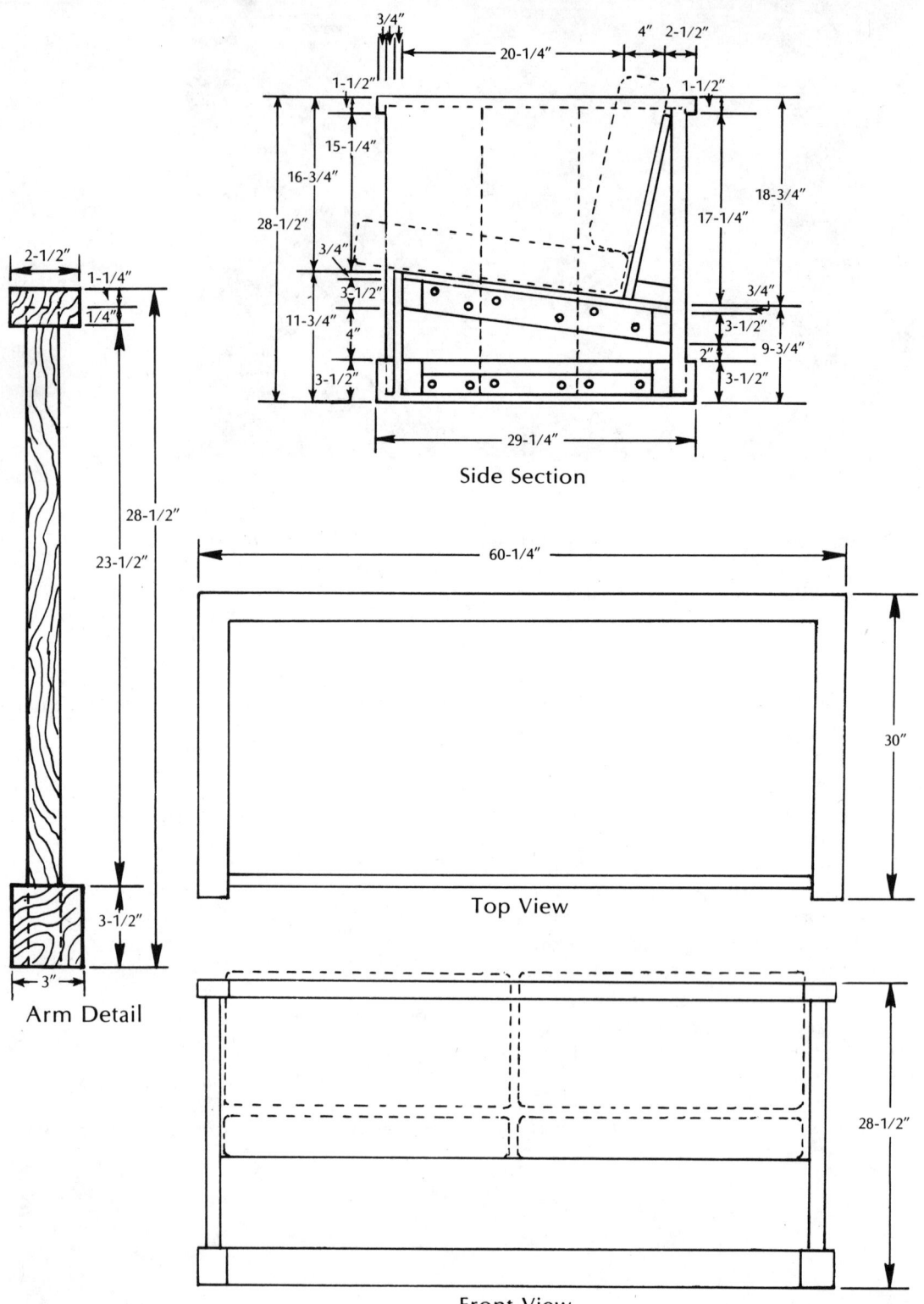

(A) Begin by assembling the 2" by 4" framework with the countersunk lag bolts and washers. (B) Fasten the assembled frame to the 2" by 10" back pieces with 2-1/2" flathead wood screws. (C) Position the seat frame 2" from the bottom of the frame in the back, and 3" apart in the front.

 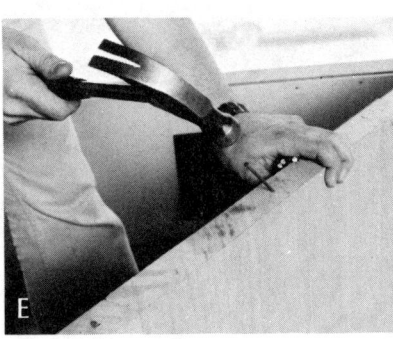 

(D) Use a 3" spacer block while screwing the seat frame to the couch sides and back. (E) Drive the 16d finish nails at an angle to secure the 2" by 10" pieces in place. (F) Cut the 3/4" plywood to size and apply the seat bottom to the frame with 8d box nails.

  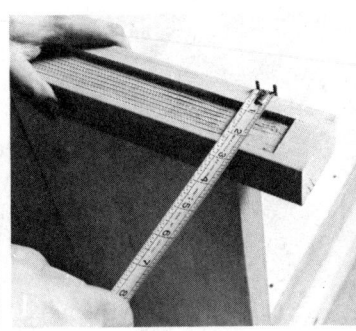

(G) Cut a 2" by 4" spacer, angling the front edge slightly, then nail it to the back of the seat. (H) After trimming the edge of the plywood seat back to a 30° angle, nail it in place with 8d nails. (I) Passes with a saw will create a 1-1/2" wide channel in the top of the trim. Chisel the ends square. (J) Apply the 2" by 3" top trim to the sides and back with 8d nails and countersink the heads. (K) Install the front panel, miter and apply the 1" by 4" base trim with 8d finish nails. (L) Fill all nail holes with wood putty and sand the completed sofa.

 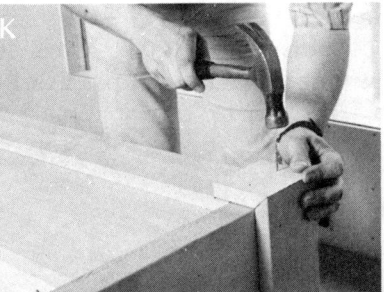 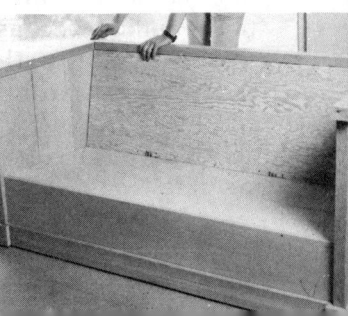

FOLDING DINING TABLE

Photo 1: This folding dining table can seat ten people.

For unexpected company, this folding table (Photo 1) will serve up to ten people and can be folded away to a compact size of 16" by 32". The versatile design of the table will readily lend itself to most dining areas.

The table top sections are cut on a table saw from 3/4" plywood for the various sizes needed (Fig. 1).

Lay out the legs, using the squares method, on a piece of brown wrapping paper (Fig. 2). Nail two pieces of 3/4" by 6-1/2" by 28-1/4" plywood together and tack the pattern onto the top piece and proceed to cut the outline. The inside cut is made on a scroll saw (Photo 2). The outside cut can be made faster on a band saw (Photo 3). Drill a hole 1/2" deep and with a 1" diameter on the inside of all four legs (Fig. 2). These holes are for dowel stretchers (Fig. 3).

Figure 4A shows the assembled leg. Cut two 4-7/8" by 25-1/2" workpieces (B) from 3/4" plywood. From solid stock, cut four 3/4" by 3/4" by 4-7/8" cleats (C). The cleats (C) and workpiece (B) are predrilled as shown in Figs. 4A and 4B.

Assemble the leg (A) shown in Figs. 4A and 4B to the workpiece (B) with glue and 6d finishing nails; then, strengthen the leg with a cleat (C). Attach the top (D) to the workpiece (B) with six No. 8 by 1-1/4" wood screws.

Make four gatelegs following the layout and dimensions shown in Fig. 5A. Notches — both dadoes and rabbets — for the gatelegs can be cut on a table saw with two passes of a dado head (Photo 4).

One leg of each gateleg assembly is 1/4" shorter (Fig. 5B), allowing the top rail to clear the continuous hinge barrel (Fig. 2).

MATERIALS

Quantity	Description
4 (A)	3/4" x 6-1/2" x 28-1/4" Legs
2 (B)	3/4" x 4-7/8" x 25-1/2" Leg bottom boards
4 (C)	3/4" x 3/4" x 4-7/8" Leg cleats
2 (D)	3/4" x 6-1/2" x 32" Leg top boards
2 (E)	1" dia. x 26-1/2" Leg stretcher dowels
8 (F)	3/4" x 1-1/2" x 28-1/4" Gateleg front and back uprights
8 (G)	3/4" x 1-1/2" x 23-1/8" Gateleg top and bottom cleats
4 (H)	3/4" x 20-1/4" x 32" Table tops
1 (J)	3/4" x 1-3/4" x 32" Table top
4 (K)	3/4" x 3/4" x 1-1/2" Gateleg stop blocks
13	Rolls of flexible wood trim
4	1-1/4" x 22" Continuous hinges
16	5/8" Furniture glides
4	Brass hooks
8	Brass round head wood screws
8	1-1/2" x 2" Brass butt hinges
12	No. 8 x 1-1/4" Flathead wood screws

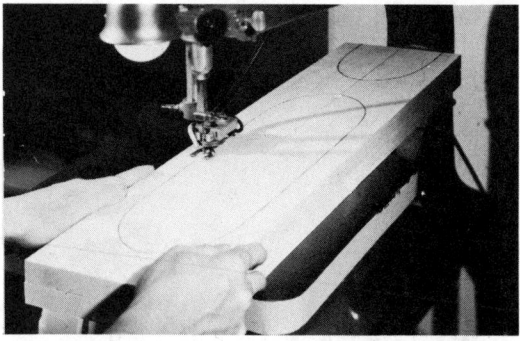

Photo 2: The inside cutout in the table legs is made most easily on a scroll saw.

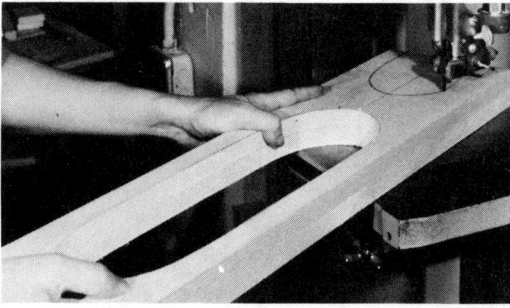

Photo 3: The outside cutout at the bottom of the legs can be cut faster on a band saw.

Photo 4: Notches — both dadoes and rabbets — are cut on a table saw with two passes of a dado head.

Assemble with glue and 6d finishing nails. Attach the gatelegs to the leg assemblies with 1-1/2" brass butt hinges (Fig. 6). Two hinges for each gateleg are required.

To assemble the table, turn the table top panels (H) shown in Fig. 1 and the leg assemblies (Fig. 3) bottom side up. Place one panel (H) on each side of the leg assembly and join them together with continuous hinges. The continuous hinge is screw fastened at the gateleg assembly end of the leg assembly to within 1-3/4" of the leg (A), opposite the hinged side of the gatelegs. Gateleg stop blocks are mounted 3-1/2" from the end of each table panel (H), as shown in Fig. 7A.

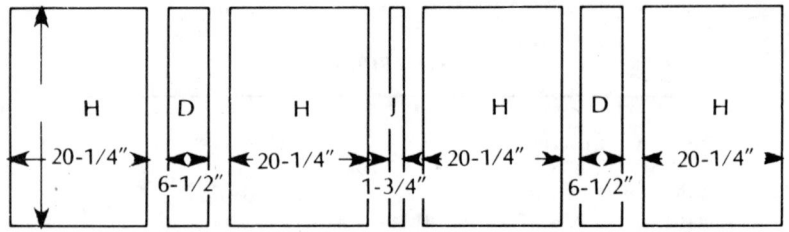

Fig. 1: Layout of the table top boards (cut from 3/4" plywood).

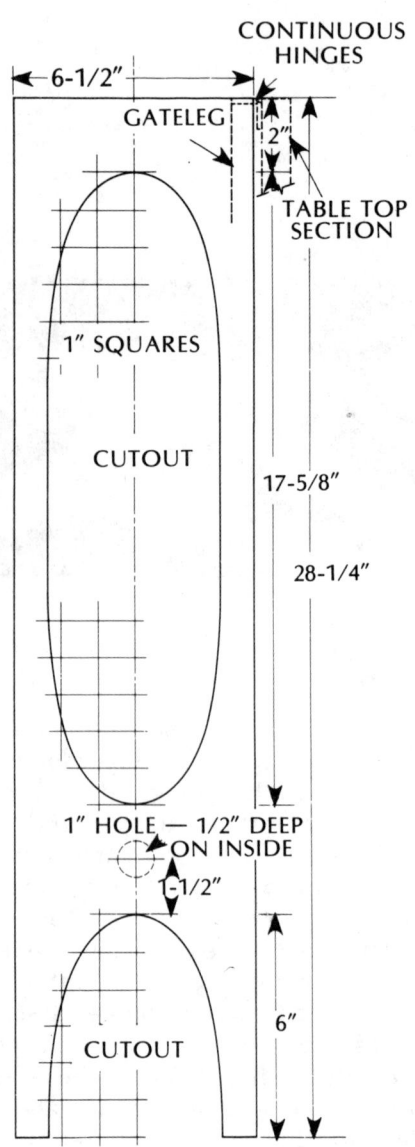

Fold both leg assemblies with the attached panels (H) and join together the two center panels (H) with a continuous hinge. Note that the continuous hinge is the full width of the panels (H), as shown in Fig. 7B. Also, install furniture glides on all 16 table leg bottoms.

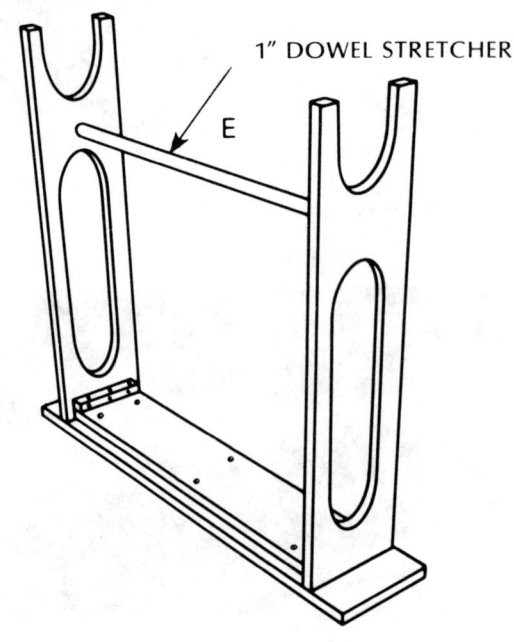

Fig. 2: Details for the table leg.

Fig. 3: Bottom view of the table leg assembly, showing the 1" dowel stretcher.

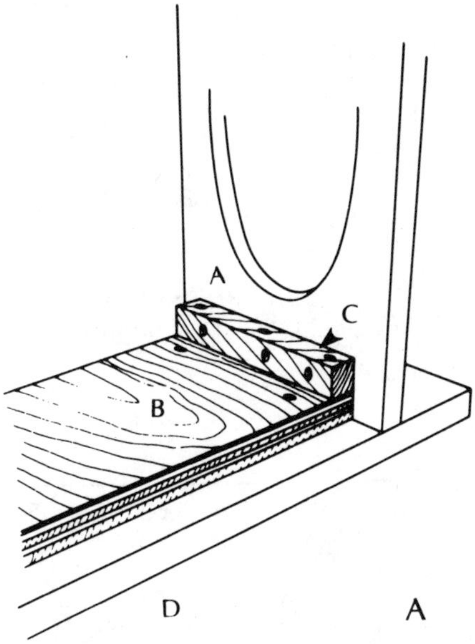

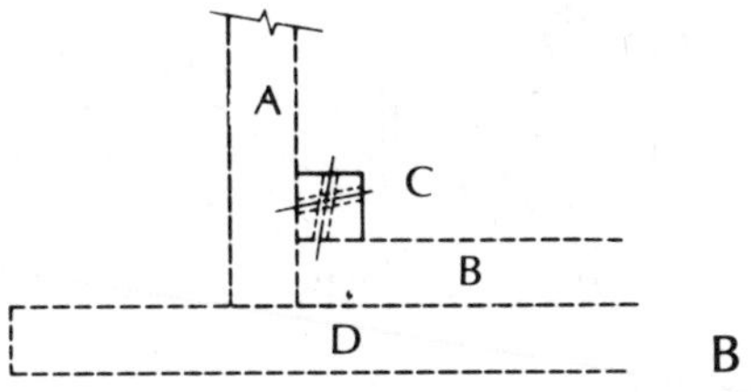

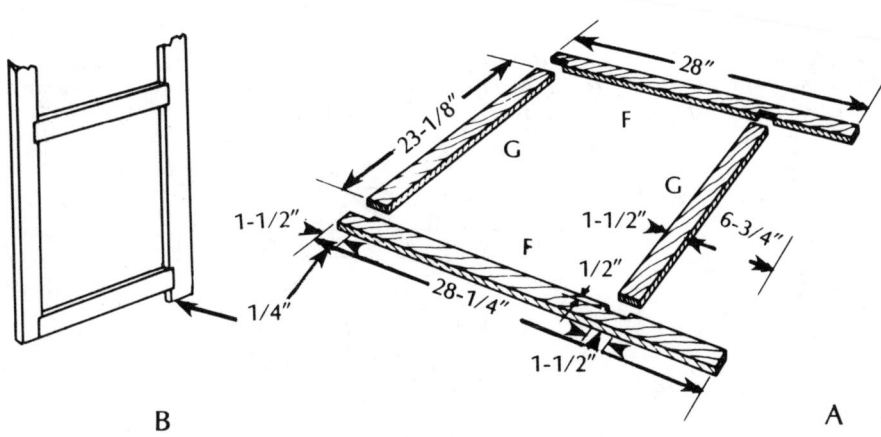

Fig. 4: (A) How the leg is assembled; (B) positioning and mounting of the cleat.

Fig. 5: (A) Gateleg assembly details; (B) gateleg assembly showing a 1/4" difference between the two legs.

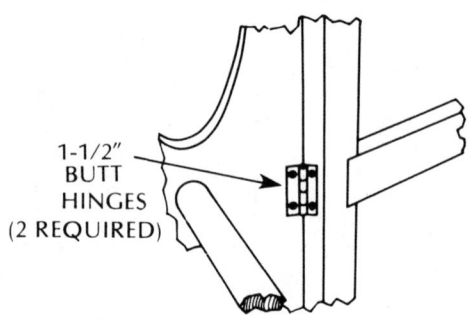

Turn the table right side up and attach the flat brass hooks to the panel (J), as shown in Fig. 8. The panel (J) is only used to fill space when the table is closed. Use flexible wood trim to cover the exposed edges of the plywood. This type of veneer should be applied with contact cement, and tapped with a rubber-headed mallet to achieve a good bond. Use a penetrating oil resin finish per manufacturer's instructions to complete the project.

Fig. 6: Gatelegs are attached to the table leg assemblies with 1-1/2" butt hinges.

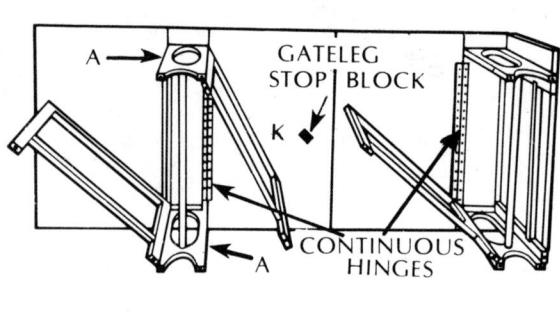
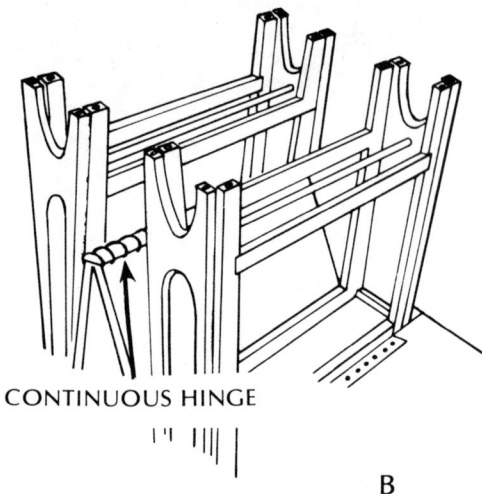

Fig. 7: (A) Bottom of the complete table assembly, showing the continuous hinges holding the table top sections and the gateleg stop block, to the table top sections to the table leg assemblies; (B) a bottom view of the table with both leg assemblies folded.

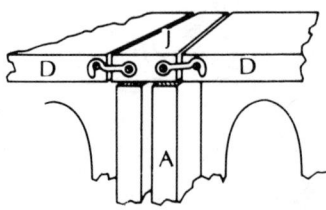

Fig. 8: Hooks for holding the table leg assemblies together when the table is closed.

EARLY AMERICAN NIGHT STAND

Photo 1: An Early American night stand.

This night stand (Photo 1) will be a challenging and rewarding project for anyone who has a collection of Early American furniture and wants to add to it. The stand should be made from a hardwood, like maple or white birch, and finished with a maple stain, a common finish for furniture of this style.

The four legs are turned on a lathe (Photo 2) from 2-3/16" stock, according to the details shown in Fig. 2. The side and back rails, the drawer front and drawer slide frames, and the top of the table are all made of 3/4" thick stock. The drawer sides and back are made of 1/2" thick stock; the drawer bottom is made from 1/8" hardboard (Fig. 3).

The side and back rails are mortised and tenoned into the legs (Fig. 3). Note that the side and back rails are set 1/8" in from the outside edges of the legs (Fig. 4). The drawer slide frames and the drawer front are flush with the legs on the front of the stand. A dado 1/4" deep must be cut into the legs for the drawer slide frames to fit into. Glue 1" wide filler strips on the lower drawer slide frames between the front and back legs and along the side rails, to prevent the drawer from binding when being opened or closed (Fig. 4).

The drawer front is made with a rabbet and groove joint; the drawer back has a 1/4" by 1/4" dado and rabbet joint (Fig. 5). The hardwood drawer bottom is held in place by 1/8" by 3/16" deep grooves in the drawer front and side pieces. The drawer bottom is inserted into these grooves before the back of the drawer is joined to the sides. Details for the wooden drawer knob are given in Fig. 6.

Sand all pieces with first a medium-grit and then a fine-grit abrasive. Apply the maple stain, followed by two coats of satin or rubbed effect polyurethane finish. Then wax to complete.

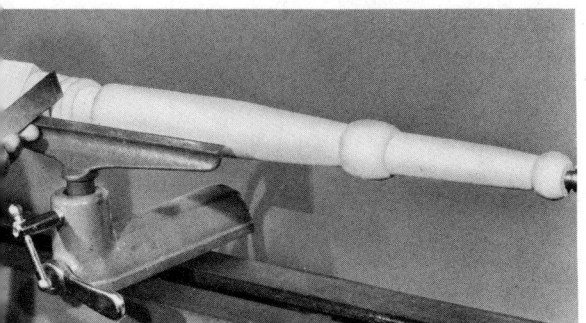

Photo 2: Turning one of the night stand legs on a lathe. The finishing cuts are being made with a skew.

MATERIALS

Quantity	Description
4	2-3/16" x 2-3/16" x 28" Legs
2	3/4" x 5" x 17-3/8" Side rails
1	3/4" x 5" x 17" Back rail
2	3/4" x 2" x 15-1/2" Front drawer slide frame pieces
4	3/4" x 2" x 17-1/4" Side drawer slide frame pieces
2	3/4" x 2" x 14-3/8" Back drawer slide frame pieces
2	3/4" x 1" x 15-3/8" Drawer filler strips
1	3/4" x 3-1/8" x 15" Drawer front
2	1/2" x 3-1/8" x 18-5/8" Drawer sides
1	1/2" x 2-5/8" x 14-1/2" Drawer back
1	1/8" x 14-3/8" x 18-5/16" Drawer bottom (hardboard)
1	1" x 1" x 1-1/4" Drawer knob
4	3/4"dia. Furniture glides

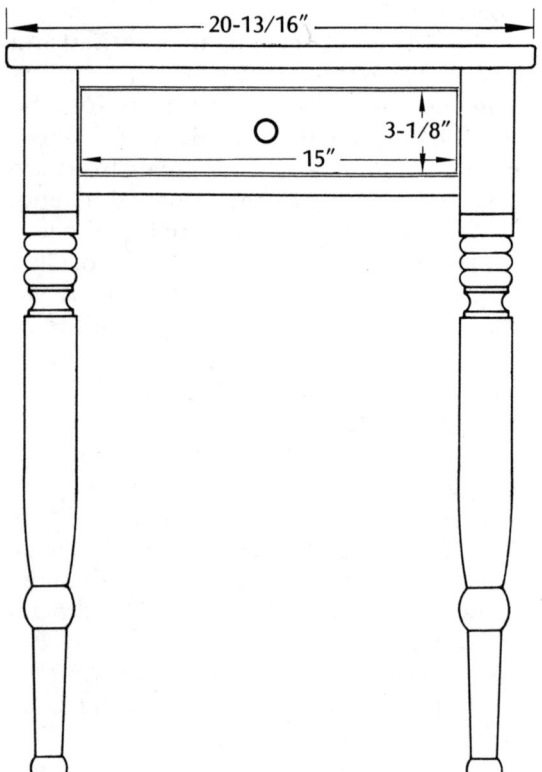

Fig. 1: Front view of the night stand.

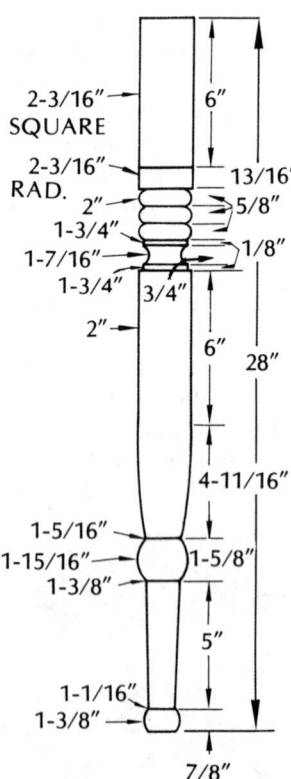

Fig. 2: Details for the legs.

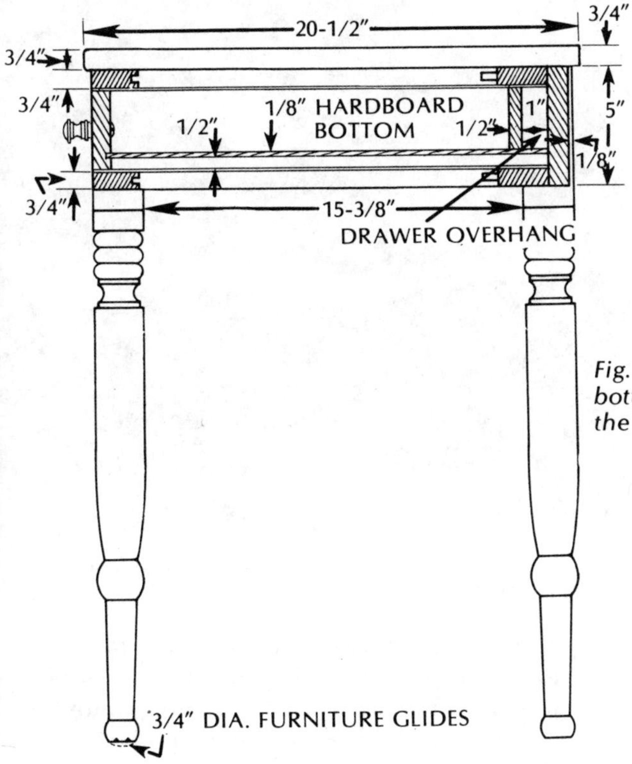

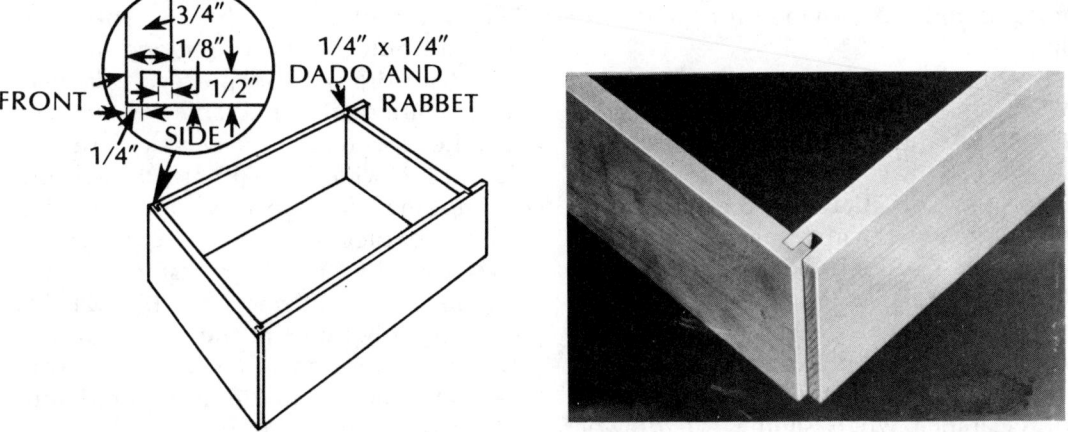

Fig. 3: Side view of the night stand.

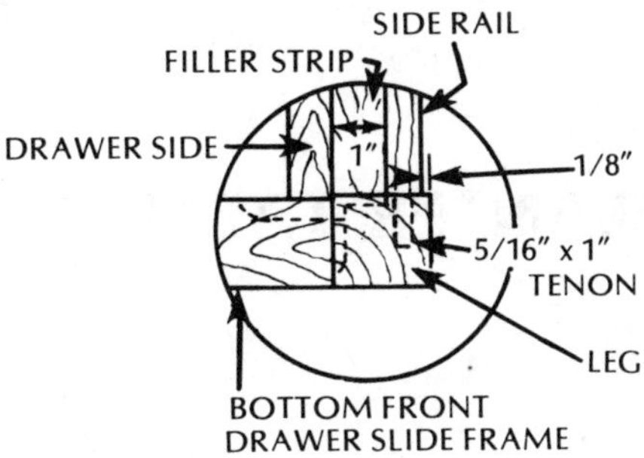

Fig. 4: Lower front corner details, where the bottom front drawer slide frame, the leg, and the side rail join.

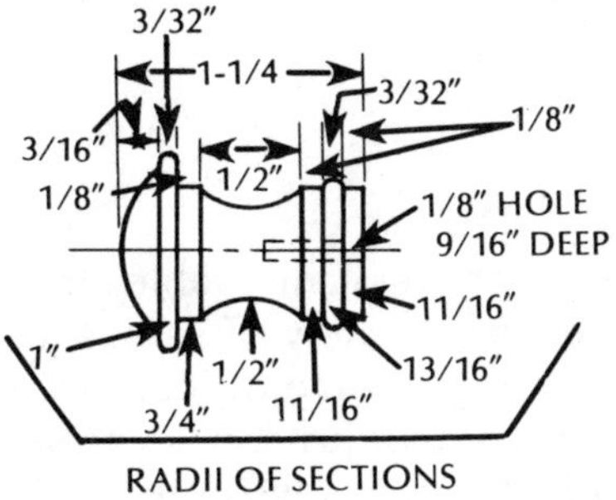

Fig. 6: Details for the wooden drawer knob.

Fig. 5: Drawer construction details.

PLANTER TABLE

Photo 1: An easy-to-build planter table, which can serve a variety of uses.

This attractive planter table (Photo 1) can be built for a variety of uses. It can serve as a desk for a home office, a vanity table in a bedroom, or just a place to set household plants in a living room.

The entire project requires only one sheet of 3/4" thick fir plywood, plus two pieces of 1/4" thick plywood for the drawer bottoms and 1/2" plywood for the drawer sides.

Lay out the parts required on a panel of plywood, as shown in the cutting diagram (Fig. 1). Use the materials list for the proper dimensions. Be sure to allow for the width of the saw kerfs between the parts when measuring. The panel can be easily cut apart with a portable electric circular saw. To ensure straight and square edges, finish cuts to the exact size can be made on a table saw. Cut the drawer fronts and sides about 1/16" short of the 4" width, to allow for clearance when sliding the drawer. After cutting, smooth all edges with first a fine-grit, and then a very fine-grit abrasive.

Assemble the sides, partitions, and back to the bottom, as shown in Fig. 2. Use glue and nails to fasten the butt jointed pieces. For a neater finishing job, paint the inside surfaces of the open shelves before fastening the top in place. The inside surfaces of the drawer compartments are not painted.

The drawer fronts can be dadoed for the sides to fit into, or butt jointed and fastened with screws counterbored from the front and covered with wood plugs (Fig. 3). The drawer backs and sides are fastened with dado and rabbet joints (Fig. 3). The partitions are butt jointed or dadoed into the back. If the drawer front pieces are dadoed, the cuts are made on a table saw, using a dado head with enough inside chippers to make a 1/2" wide dado (Photo 2). Glue and 6d finishing nails are used in assembling the drawer pieces. Hardwood guide strips, 1/4" by 3/4" by 20-1/4", are fastened on the outside of the drawer sides (Fig. 2). Set them in rabbet cuts in the drawer fronts. The drawer bottoms can be made from 1/4" plywood or hardboard, fitted into 1/4" wide grooves in the drawer sides and front. These grooves are cut on the table saw, using the two 1/8" outside blades of the dado head (Photo 3).

If the table will be a setting for household plants and must be located under a window, the apron under the sill of the desired window must be removed. Screw

MATERIALS

Quantity	Description
2 (A)	3/4" x 4" x 21-3/4" Sides
1 (B)	3/4" x 4" x 73" Back (add 1/2" to the length if a dado and rabbet joint is used.)
3 (C)	3/4" x 4" x 21" Partitions (add 1/4" to the length if these pieces are dadoed into back.)
2 (D)	3/4" x 21-3/4" x 74-1/2" Top and bottom
2 (E)	3/4" x 4" x 17" Drawer fronts
4 (F)	1/2" x 4" x 20-1/2" Drawer sides
2 (G)	3/4" x 3-3/8" x 16" Drawer backs
2 (H)	1/4" x 16" x 20-1/2" Drawer bottoms
4 (J)	1/4" x 3/4" x 20-1/4" Drawer guide strips
1	3/4" x — x 72" Wall fastening cleat (for table fastened to wall)
2 or 4	3/4" x (Length determined by window height) Aluminum pipe (with pipe flanges)
2	1" dia. Wood drawer pulls

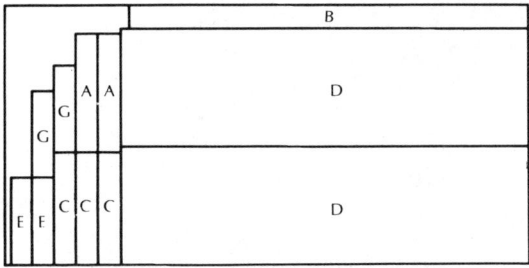

Fig. 1: All of the table parts, except for the drawer fronts, drawer sides, and the legs can be cut from a single 3/4" by 48" by 96" panel of fir plywood.

fasten a cleat to the table top along the back edge and fasten it with screws into the wall studs. Details for hanging the table under a window are given in Fig. 4.

The table legs are made from 3/4" aluminum pipe fastened to pipe flanges on the table bottom. The legs are attached 3" from the front and back of the table and 9" in from each end.

All nail holes and exposed plywood edges are filled with wood filler and then sanded smooth. A coat of enamel undercoat, followed by two coats of semi-gloss enamel completes the project.

Photo 2: Cutting dadoes in the drawer front pieces on a table saw, using a 1/2" wide dado head. Note: The blade guard is removed for clarity.

Photo 3: Cutting the grooves for the 1/4" thick drawer bottoms in the drawer front and sides, using the two 1/8" outside dado blades. Note: The blade guard is removed for clarity.

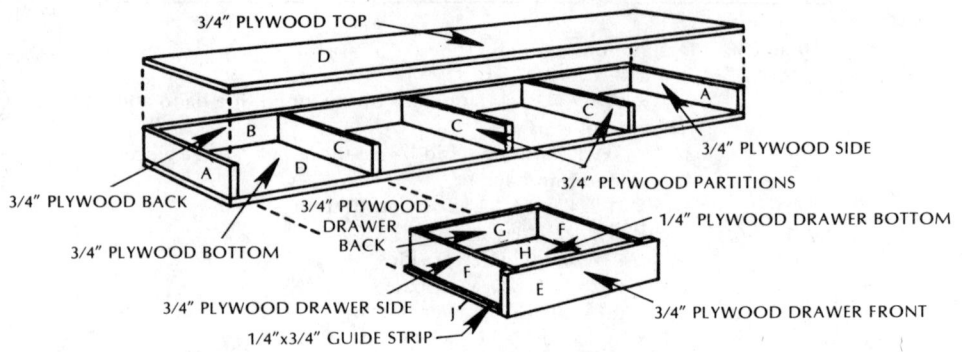

Fig. 2: Assembly of the planter table parts.

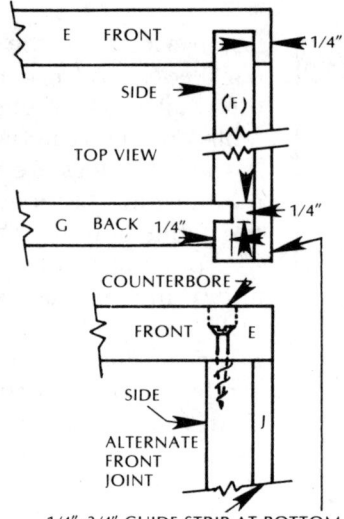

Fig. 3: Drawer joint details.

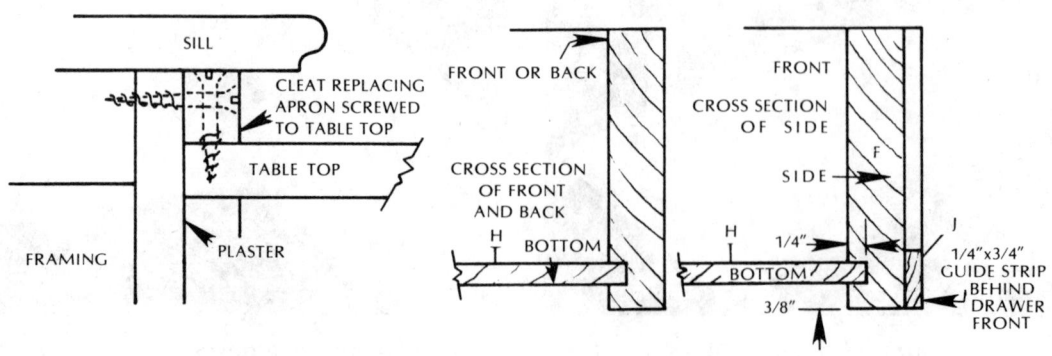

Fig. 4: Details for hanging the planter table under a window.

All of these projects, which utilize plastic laminates, appear either in this book or in the Rockwell publication, **Projects for the Weekend.**

PLASTIC LAMINATED FURNITURE

Many beautiful furniture pieces can be made with plastic laminate covered plywood. The lamination is easy to make and the laminate is available in a variety of decorator colors, attractive motifs, and wood-grain patterns. Sheets come in widths of 24", 30", 36", 48" and 60"; lengths are 72", 84", 96", 120" and 144". Any combination of width and length may be ordered; actual sizes are usually slightly oversize so you can obtain a desired rectangle by trimming after bonding.

When bonding the plastic laminate to a plywood (A-D grade is preferred for most of the projects shown in this book) corestock, the temperature in the room in which you are working should be no lower than 65° F. At the same time, relative humidity should be no less than 35 percent and no more than 80 percent.

It is very important that you read and follow the instructions on the labels of all the materials before using them, particularly adhesives and solvents. If you have a choice when picking a contact cement, select a nonflammable type. Contact cement should be applied in a well-ventilated room only and there should be no open flames or sparking equipment in the same room. The adhesive is applied so as to cover well, but not in thick globs. Generally it is best applied with a short nap

Photo 1: The edge is usually laminated first. Apply contact adhesive to the laminate and plywood edge.

Photo 2: Bond the strip of laminate to the edge using the fingertips to keep the surface apart as you go.

paint roller. To determine the amount of adhesive for do-it-yourself projects, remember both laminate and underlayment must be covered. Figure one gallon for each 50 square feet.

High-pressure plastic laminate can be cut with a number of different tools. Because of the toughness of the product, carbide cutting edges are preferred; ordinary cutting edges dull too quickly. It is important that you cut from the correct side when cutting plastic laminates or the decorative surface will be chipped. Keep in mind that the cutting tool must always enter—never exit—on the decorative side. Here are the most common methods of cutting plastic laminate:

Jig Saw. Cut with the decorative side down using a hacksaw blade (in the jig saw). The workpiece must be adequately supported. If the work is permitted to hang in the air while cutting, you stand a good chance of damaging the laminate by splitting.

Table or Radial Saw. Use a carbide-tipped blade, and cut with the decorative side up. This is the best way to cut smaller, easy-to-handle pieces—larger ones can be somewhat difficult.

The six easy steps for applying laminate are as follows:

1. Make certain the core stock (surface to which laminate is to be bonded) is absolutely clean and smooth. Clean with solvent if necessary; sand using a belt or pad sander. At this stage study the piece to determine the order in which you will apply laminate to the surfaces. Keep in mind that the order in which to apply various panels is determined by the edge most visible to the eye, and therefore, subject to the most abuse. An edge strip always goes on before the top piece which then neatly covers the joint. A drawer front, on the other hand, would violate this rule and go on after the strips—including the top one—because the appearance will be better.

2. Once you have decided upon sequence, start by applying the contact cement to the core-stock surface and its mating piece of laminate. Check the instructions on the label for drying under the right climatic conditions. The parts should be ready for bonding in about 30 minutes. To check, touch the surface in several places with clean kraft paper; when the adhesive no longer adheres to the paper, the surfaces are ready for bonding.

3. Keep the mating pieces apart until they are ready for contact. Fingers alone can guide small pieces, but when bonding larger pieces, a "third-hand" helper to prevent accidental contact will be needed. There are several ways to keep the pieces apart until you are ready to bond them. One is to use a large sheet of clean kraft paper as a slip sheet; another is to use clean 3/4" diameter dowels or square sticks to keep the laminate and core stock separated. Align the laminate over paper or sticks; check all four sides to make sure the core stock will be covered; then, starting at one end, remove the paper or sticks and bond the laminate to the core stock.

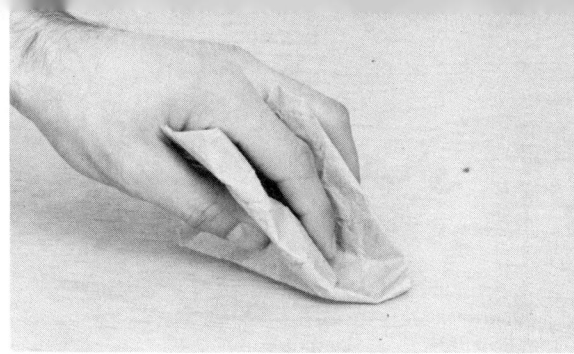

Photo 3: Apply the pressure immediately after the bonding, using a hammer and a clean block of hardwood.

Photo 6: Surfaces are ready for bonding when the adhesive does not adhere to a piece of clean kraft paper.

4. Most contact cements need only momentary pressure after bonding. But do not mistake momentary for light. Immediately upon bonding the laminate to the core stock, apply as much pressure as you can over the entire surface. A "J-Roller" is an inexpensive tool and is preferred to assure adequate pressure. However, a rolling pin may be used. You can also slide a block of clean wood about the surface and give it hefty blows with your hammer. Do not worry about giving the laminate too much pressure; you cannot. Just make certain you are careful when applying pressure near overhanging edges.

5. The final step is trimming. The easiest method, of course, is with a router and carbide cutter. Lacking this power tool, you will have to trim the overhang using a block plane and smooth file. Either way, the overhang is first trimmed flush (i.e. 90°) and then beveled slightly—to about 20° to 22°. Finish the beveling work with a smooth file.

6. Cleanup. To remove contact cement remnants from the surface, use the contact cement solvent recommended on the label instructions, and use scraps of plastic laminate—*never use metal*—to scrape off the heavy globs. Be sure to follow safety precautions for the solvent's use and provide adequate ventilation.

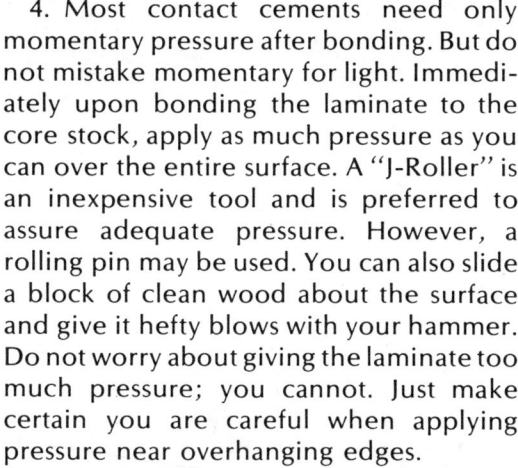

Photo 4: Trim the excess plastic with a straight carbide cutter in a router, or use a block plane and file.

Photo 7: Align the laminate over the surface. As the 3/4" sticks (or dowels) are pulled out, it is bonded.

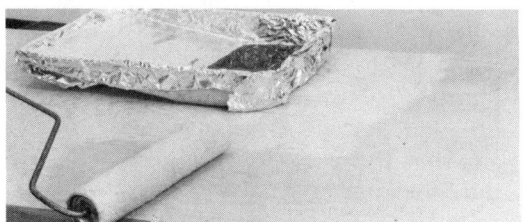

Photo 5: For larger surfaces, use a short-nap roller and work from the tray. The foil speeds the cleanup later.

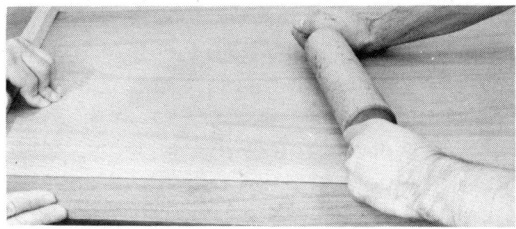

Photo 8: Immediately apply pressure over the entire surface. Here, a rolling pin is used to bond the laminate.

MODERN COCKTAIL TABLE

MATERIALS

Quantity	Description
2	3/4" x 16-1/2" x 22-1/2" Plywood (top and bottom)
2	3/4" x 12" x 17-1/4" Plywood (ends)
2	3/4" x 12" x 23-1/4" Plywood (sides)
4	3/4" x 3/4" x 8-3/4" Pine lumber (corner cleats)
1	17" x 23" Plastic laminate (top)*
2	13" x 24" Plastic laminate (sides)*
2	13" x 18" Plastic laminate (ends)*
4	Platetype casters, 2" balls
-	Plastic wood putty
-	Fine sandpaper
-	1-1/4" Ringed nails
-	White glue
-	Contact adhesive
-	Adhesive solvent

*Note: All necessary laminate pieces can be cut from one 36" by 72" laminate sheet. Take the time to lay out the table part sizes before cutting to assure proper yield.

A super easy but practical project, this handsome contemporary cocktail table can be completed easily in a single Saturday shop session, if you follow these steps:

1. Start by cutting the parts to size as shown in Fig. 1, or to your specification.
2. Assemble the ends and sides to the bottom using ringed nails and white glue.
3. Using ringed nails and glue, secure the corners.
4. Then, securing with white glue and ringed nails, add the top-supporting corner cleats to the box.
5. Lower the top onto the cleats; secure it with glue and nails. Use additional nails through the sides and ends into the top, as well.
6. Fill all the voids in the plywood; sand and dust.
7. Apply the plastic laminate to the ends; trim.
8. Apply the laminate to the sides; trim.
9. Finally, apply the laminate to the top and trim.
10. Taking care to protect the laminate, flop the workpiece and install the four ball-type casters.
11. Right the table, clean with adhesive solvent recomended on label instructions. Be sure to follow safety precautions for the solvent's use and provide adequate ventilation.

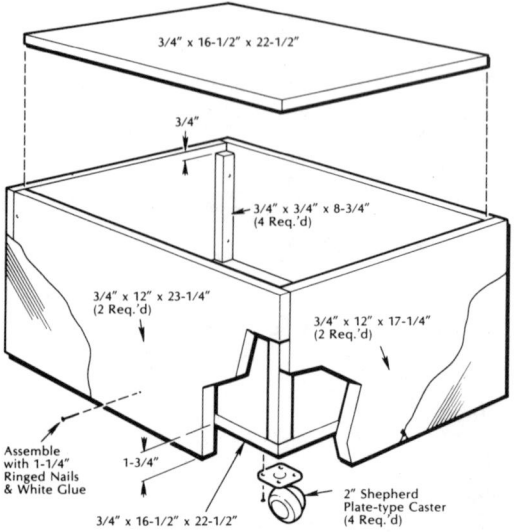

FURNITURE CUBE

This furniture cube base has many uses around the home. In fact, the cube may be fabricated for any size requirement. (An 18" cube was used for the coffee table shown here.)

The basic construction of the furniture cube and modern coffee table shown above are the same. That is, begin the project by cutting the plywood to your specifications or to the proper size for the coffee table. Assemble all the side panels with simple butt joints and fasten, using 1-1/4" No. 8 flathead screws and white glue. Wipe away excess white glue and check to assure that the structure is square. Then, install the top panel and secure it with white glue and wood screws. Wipe away any excess white glue and set it aside to dry for at least one hour. After the glue is dried, fill all voids and sand smooth.

MATERIALS

Quantity	Description
4	3/4" x 17-3/4" x 17-3/4" Plywood (sides)
1	3/4" x 16-1/2" x 16-1/2" Plywood (top)
5	18-1/2" x 18-1/2" Plastic laminate (can be cut from 1—48" x 60" sheet)
4	Furniture glides
—	White glue
—	1-1/4" No. 8 Flathead wood screws
—	Fine sandpaper
—	Contact adhesive
—	Adhesive solvent
—	Plastic wood filler

Now, begin the application of the laminate. Start on two opposite ends; apply the laminate according to the procedures outlined previously and rout flush at all edges. Continue laminating the other two end panels, again, routing all edges flush. Finally, apply the laminate to the top, and bevel rout.

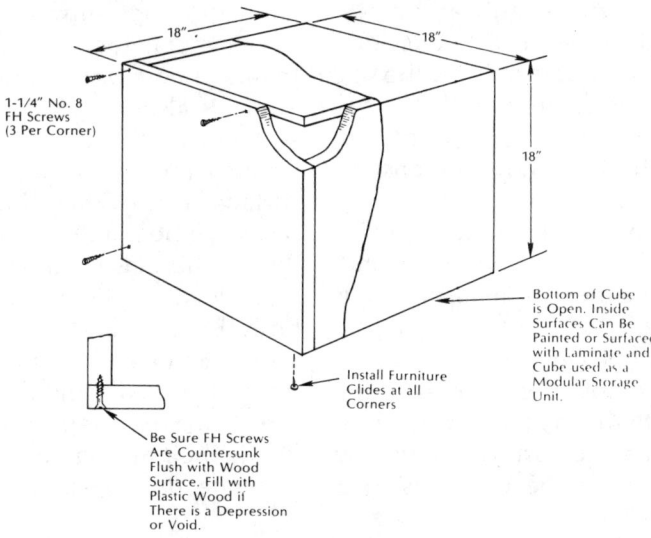

TELEVISION CABINET

MATERIALS

Quantity	Description
—	White glue
2 pair	Hettich pivot hinges
2	Tutch latches
—	Brads
—	1-1/4" No. 8 Flathead wood screws
—	3d Common nails
—	Plastic wood filler
—	Fine sandpaper
—	Contact adhesive
—	Adhesive solvent

Lumber and plastic laminate: 3/4" plywood is used to construct the TV cabinet, except for the back which is of 1/4" plywood. Since the cabinet dimensions will be determined by the size of your television set, measure it and indicate the necessary dimensions on the drawing. From this, you can then determine the amount of plywood and decorative plastic laminate required.

Here is an ideal way to convert your portable television into an attractive furniture piece. The cabinet is easy to construct when proceeding as follows:

1. Start by measuring your television set and transferring the measurements to the drawing. To make certain you build the cabinet large enough to easily accommodate the set, add at least 1/8" to its width, height, and depth for determining the size of the pocket in the cabinet for the TV set. When these dimensions are determined, you can fill in the remaining dimensions on the drawing (Fig. 1).

2. Cut all plywood parts to size. Fill voids in the edges with plastic wood filler; sand.

3. Test assemble the cabinet using brads only.

4. When satisfied with the cabinet fit, permanently assemble the cabinet, using No. 8 by 1-1/4" flathead screws and white glue. After joining the parts, immediately wipe off any glue squeeze-out using a damp cloth. Set the cabinet aside so the glue can dry (about 1 hour).

5. Meanwhile, go to work cutting the cabinet doors to fit. *Important:* When measuring for door sizes, note the spacing between the door and cabinet as shown in Fig. 1. This space is a must to allow for hardware and for the door swing.

6. To finish the cabinet, start by bonding the plastic laminate to the sides; trim any overhang. Next, apply the laminate to the 3/4" wide surfaces at the front and to the 3" wide rail at the bottom. (Note that these laminate strips simply butt each other at the corners; there is no need to cut 45° miters unless you so desire (See Fig. 1). There is also no need to cover the inside surfaces of the cabinet pocket with the plastic laminate (the TV set will hide those surfaces from view). If desired, these surfaces can be painted with a color compatible to the plastic laminate used.

7. Next, apply the plastic laminate to both the front and back surfaces of doors. The door edges can be simply painted, if desired, but if laminated edges are preferred, make certain you cut the doors 1/8" less in height and width to allow for the laminate thickness. After the doors have

been laminated, the hardware can be installed.

8. Install hinges on the doors (see Fig. 2). Note that two drill bits are required to bore the holes for the hinges. In the cabinet, you will have to bore 15/32" diameter holes 3/8" deep. The two pairs of holes in the door edges have a 1/4" diameter and are 1-1/4" deep. Locate the hole positions and bore the required holes. Install the hinges. *Important:* The fixed-pin hinge is always installed at the bottom. The pin with the spring goes in at the top. For the latter, it is necessary to bore an access slot on the inside door surface (as shown in Fig. 2) so that the spring can be depressed for door installation or removal.

9. Finally, clean up, using adhesive solvent recommended on the adhesive label instructions. Be sure to follow safety precautions for solvent use and to provide adequate ventilation.

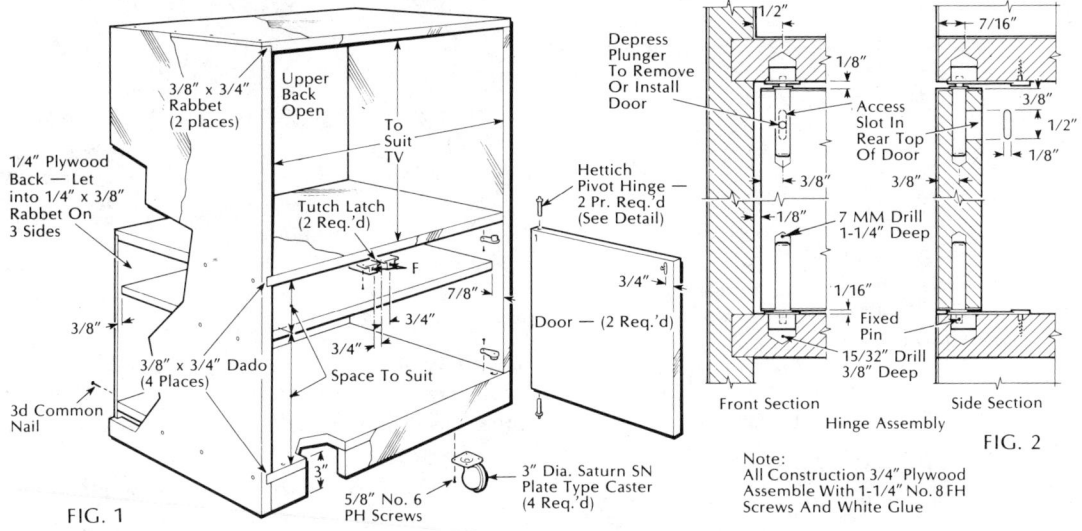

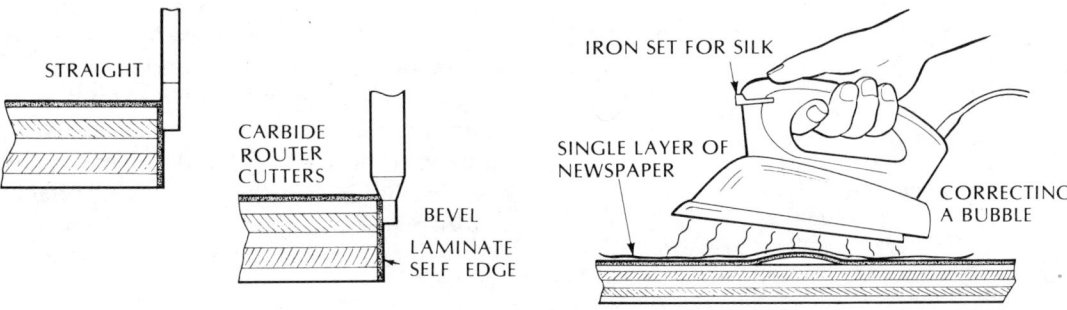

Fig. 3: When trimming, make the first cut with a straight cutter. Then complete the operation with a carbide bevel cutter. To prevent scorch marks, protect the edge with petroleum jelly.

Fig. 4: If a bubble should form, place an iron on it and press down until the heat penetrates the area. If the newspaper scorches, lower the heat setting. Then roll out the blister.

UTILITY CABINET

MATERIALS

Quantity	Description
1	3/4" x 16" x 16" Plywood (top)
2	3/4" x 16" x 19-5/8" Plywood (sides)
1	3/4" x 15-1/4" x 19-5/8" Plywood (back)
1	3/4" x 15-1/4" x 15-5/8" Plywood (shelf)
1	3/4" x 5" x 14-1/2" Plywood (false front)
1	3/4" x 10-1/2" x 14-1/2" Plywood (false front)
1	1/2" x 9-3/4" x 13" Plywood (drawer front)
2	1/2" x 9-3/4" x 14-1/2" Plywood (drawer sides)
1	1/2" x 9" x 13" Plywood (drawer back)
1	1/2" x 4-1/4" x 13" Plywood (drawer front)
2	1/2" x 4-1/4" x 14-1/2" Plywood (drawer sides)
1	1/2" x 3-1/2" x 13" Plywood (drawer back)
2	1/4" x 13" x 14-1/4" Plywood (drawer bottoms)
1	16-1/2" x 16-1/2" Plastic laminate (top)*
2	16-1/2" x 20" Plastic laminate (sides)*
1	16" x 20" Plastic laminate (back)*
1	11" x 15" Plastic laminate (drawer front)*
1	5-1/2" x 15" Plastic laminate (drawer front)*
2	3/4" x 21" Plastic laminate (edging)*
1	3/4" x 17" Plastic laminate (edging)*
1	3-1/2" x 17" Plastic laminate (apron)*
2	Drawer pulls
2 pairs	14" Drawer slides, Knape & Vogt model #1250
—	Fine sandpaper
—	Plastic wood filler
—	White glue
—	1-1/4" Ringed nails
—	1-1/4" No. 8 Flathead wood screws
—	1-1/2" Finishing nails
—	Contact adhesive
—	Adhesive solvent

*Note: All necessary laminate pieces can be cut from one 48" by 48" laminate sheet. Take the time to lay out the cabinet part sizes before cutting to assure a proper yield.

This handy utility cabinet fits comfortably into several areas of the home and if the instructions are followed, it is easy to construct:

1. Cut all parts to size as shown in Fig. 1.
2. Next, locate and cut the grooves (for the bottom shelf) in the sides, and the edge rabbets in the top and side pieces. Use either a router and 3/4" straight cutter, or a dado head setup in a table saw or radial saw, to make the grooves and rabbets.
3. Using brads, temporarily assemble the cabinet to check the fit and squareness. When satisfied, permanently assemble the cabinet using white glue and 1-1/4" No. 8 flathead screws. Fill and sand the nail holes.
4. Apply laminate to the cabinet back; trim overhang.
5. Apply laminate to the cabinet sides; trim.
6. Apply the strips of laminate to the front edges, including the apron of the bottom shelf. Use butt joints (not miters) at the corners as shown in Fig. 1; trim.
7. Apply the laminate to the top; trim.

8. Next, measure the opening for the two drawers and adjust drawer component sizes, if necessary. Construct the drawers, making certain to allow adequate clearance for the drawer slides as shown. *Note:* Make certain you read the manufacturer's instructions and diagrams for mounting the drawer slides and drawers.

9. Construct the drawers as shown in Fig. 1; temporarily tack the drawer pieces together without glue and check for fit by installing them in the cabinet. When satisfied with the fit, permanently assemble the drawers using white glue and 1-1/2" finishing nails.

10. Cut the drawer false fronts from 3/4" stock; fill all voids in the plywood edges and sand smooth. Bond the laminate to the drawer false fronts; trim any overhang. (*Note:* The edge of the drawer fronts on the cabinet shown were finished with paint. If you opt for plastic laminate edges, cut the core stock for drawer faces 1/8" less in width and length.) Fasten the false fronts to the drawer, using white glue and 1-1/4" No. 8 flathead screws, through the drawer fronts and into the back of the false fronts.

11. Locate the drawer pulls and bore appropriate size holes for pull-screws. Install the pulls. Mount the drawers in the cabinet. If necessary, clean up the laminate surfaces using the adhesive solvent recommended on the label instructions. Be sure to follow safety precautions for the solvent's use and to provide adequate ventilation.

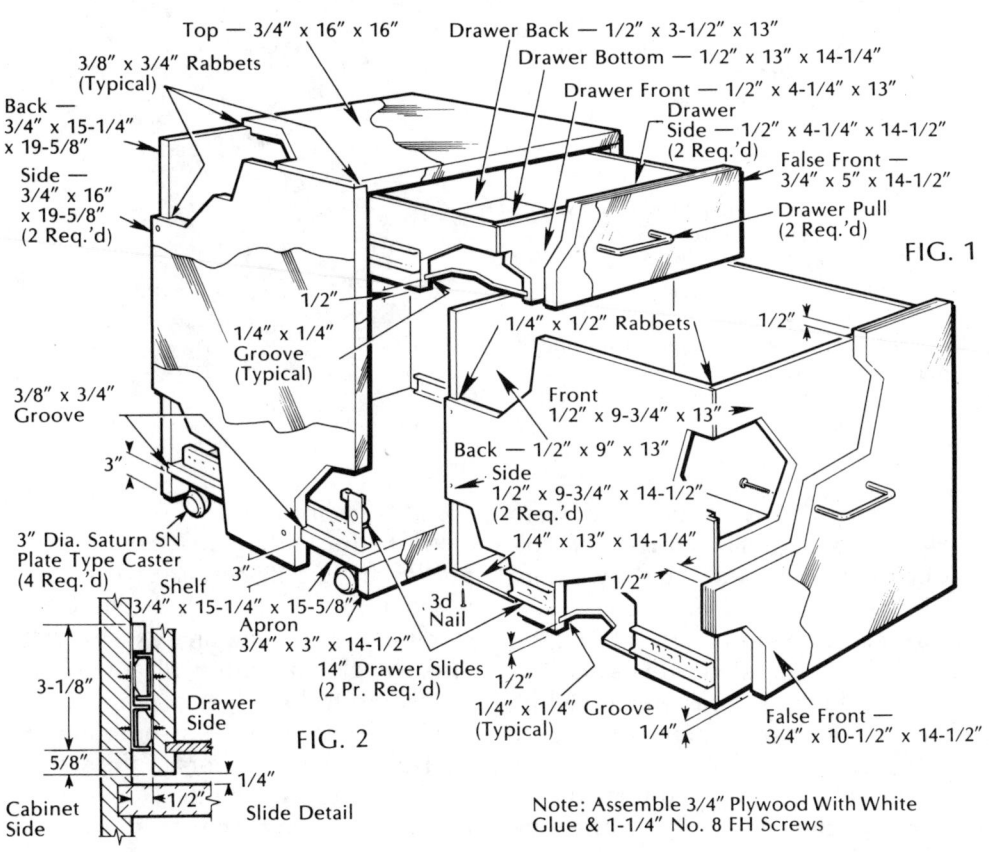

ART PEDESTAL

MATERIALS

Quantity	Description
2	3/4" x 18" x 36" Plywood (side members)
2	3/4" x 16-1/2" x 36" Plywood (opposite side members)
2	3/4" x 18" x 18" Plywood (top element)
4	3/4" x 16-1/2" x 16-1/2" Plywood (various parts)
4	18-1/2" x 36-1/2" Plastic laminate (sides)
4	2" x 17" Plastic laminate (edge strips)*
4	2" x 18-1/2" Plastic laminate (edge strips)*
2	18-1/2" x 18-1/2" Plastic laminate (top elements)*
—	Fine sandpaper
—	Plastic wood filler
4	Furniture glides
—	White glue
34	1-1/4" No 8. Flathead wood screws
4	2" No. 8 Flathead wood screws
—	Contact adhesive
—	Adhesive solvent

*Note: All plastic laminate pieces can be cut from one 48" by 96" and one 24" by 38" laminate sheet. Take the time to lay out the pedestal part sizes before cutting to assure proper yield.

A problem in many homes is how to properly display statuary and other collectors items. The art pedestal shown here may help solve this problem.

The project is begun by assembling the 18" by 36" pedestal base side elements. Butt the panels as shown and fasten with white glue and 1-1/4" No. 8 flathead screws. Wipe off any excess white glue. Fit the 16-1/2" square top and bottom members flush with the sides, again using white glue and wood screws. Wipe off any excess white glue. Set it aside and allow it to dry for at least an hour.

While the white glue is drying, fasten together the two 18" square top pieces, again with white glue and 1-1/4" No. 8 flathead screws. Clean away any excess glue, and after the glue has dried, fill any voids, sand, and smooth the edges. Continue the carpentry preparation by assembling the two 16-1/2" reveal members in the same manner as the top elements.

Before joining any of these pedestal components, laminate the two sides of the pedestal and the two sides of the 16-1/2" square reveal member and the 18" top member. Flush rout at all edges. Then, laminate the other two sides of the pedestal, reveal, and top elements. Flush rout the top and bottom edges of the pedestal, top, and reveal components. Bevel rout the vertical edges of the pedestal base. Continue the laminating operation, applying laminate to the 18" square top of the pedestal base. Bevel rout the edges.

Now, fasten the 16-1/2" square reveal member to the top of the pedestal base, taking care to position it symmetrically. Use five 2" No. 8 flathead wood screws and countersink. *Do not use glue.* Then, fasten the 18" square top component to the reveal, using four No. 8 flathead screws and white glue. Wipe away any excess glue and allow the bond to dry. Be sure to countersink the screws flush with the wood; fill and sand any depressions. Finally, laminate the 18" square top and bevel rout.

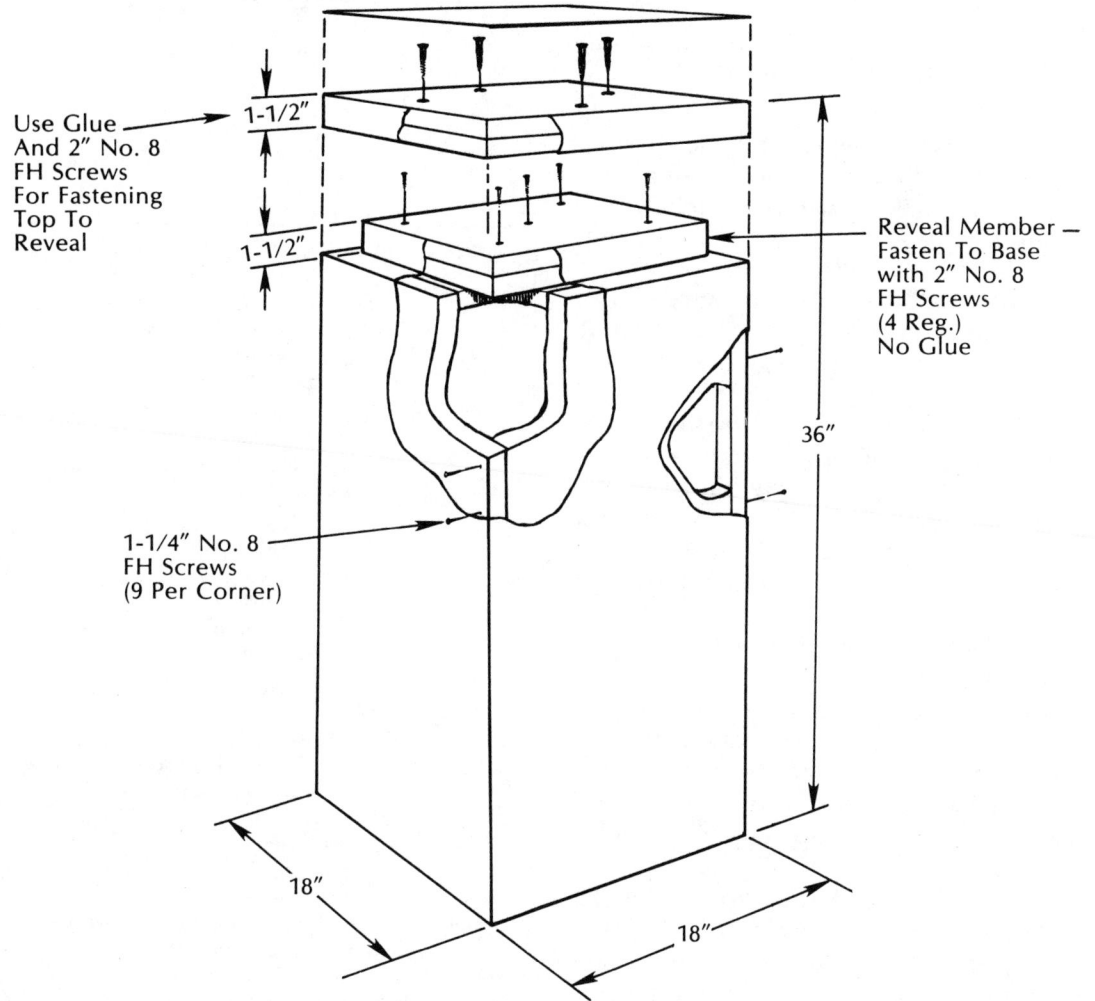

DINING ROOM PEDESTAL TABLE

This 48" by 48" dining room table is ideal for a small eating area. You can select any wood grain pattern that will match the rest of the room's furniture.

To build the pedestal table, start by cutting all base, top side and corner assembly parts to the precise length and width. Fill all the voids in the edges with plastic wood filler, sand smooth, and dust thoroughly. Next, bond the laminate to the *decorative surface only* of all inside corner assembly strips; trim the laminate overhang flush on each strip. Then, create the four corner assemblies by joining pairs of strips with white glue and 1-1/4" No. 8 flathead screws as shown.

Now, assemble the pedestal. Use a pair of 1" by 1" corner braces at *each* corner-joint as shown (i.e., four per corner). Fasten the braces with 5/8" No. 5 panhead sheet-metal screws. Install the pedestal bottom so that it is flush; fasten it with ringed nails, then carefully flop the workpiece right-side-up.

Using glue and 1-1/4" No. 8 flathead screws, install the top cleats 3/4" down from the top edge of the sides. Then, install the top with glue and 1-1/4" No. 8 screws. Set the piece aside overnight so the white glue dries thoroughly.

MATERIALS

Quantity	Description
1	30" x 72" Plastic laminate (sides)*
1	30" x 30" Plastic laminate (top)*
1	30" x 30" Plastic laminate (inside corners)*
4	3/4" x 16-1/2" x 27" Plywood (sides)
4	3/4" x 3" x 27" Plywood (corner assemblies)
2	3/4" x 22-1/2" x 22-1/2" Plywood (top and bottom)
4	3/4" x 1-1/2" x 16-1/2" Pine lumber (top-supporting cleats)
16	1" x 1" Corner braces
1	1/2" x 48" x 48" Polished plate glass
4	Plastic non-slip bumpers to keep glass top from slipping
8	Furniture glides
—	White glue
—	1-1/4" Ringed nails
—	No. 8 x 1-1/4" Flathead wood screws
—	No. 5 x 5/8" Panhead screws
—	Fine sandpaper
—	Plastic wood filler
—	Contact adhesive
—	Adhesive solvent

*Note: Before buying your laminate, take the time to lay out the table parts—in scale—on graph paper. The dimension of sheets to buy have to vary from the plans somewhat if you purchase a patterned laminate; i.e., if you pick a woodgrain, all the pieces should run vertically for proper aesthetics.

To finish, apply the laminate starting with the sides. Trim the laminate overhang from all edges and bond the top piece of laminate to the table top. Trim; clean up where necessary, using the contact cement solvent recommended on the label instructions. Then, turn the pedestal upside down and install two furniture glides in the bottom edge of each side panel. Turn the pedestal right-side-up and, using four plastic bumper discs (these are available from the glazier) to keep the glass fixed, position the polished plate glass on its pedestal.

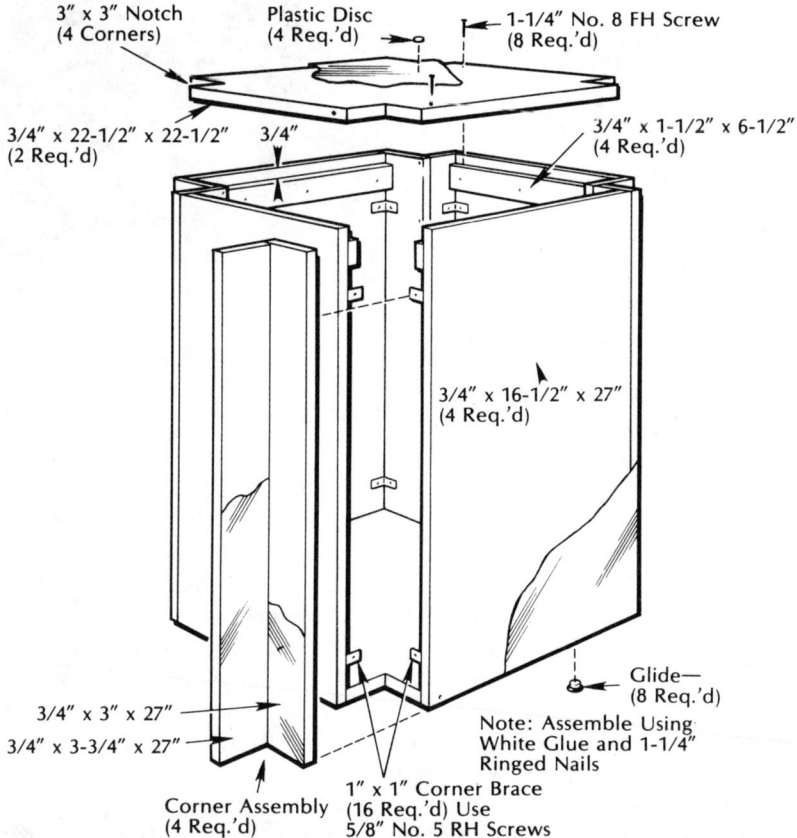

Photo 1: A laminate trimmer is handy for beveling the edges.

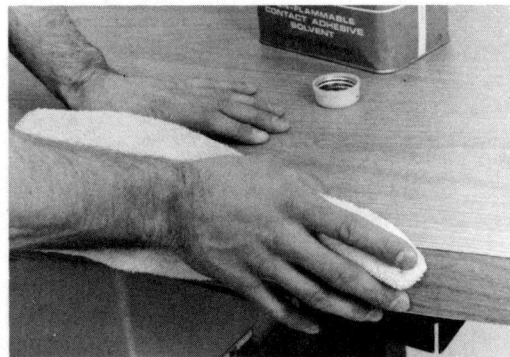

Photo 2: Use a contact adhesive solvent to the laminate surface.

BEDSIDE TABLE

This contemporary bedside table is most attractive and, thanks to its drawer unit, it is most utilitarian. Construction steps are as follows:

1. Start by cutting all parts to size as per Fig. 1.
2. Next, locate the grooves in the sides and plough them, using either a router and straight cutter, or a dado head setup in a table or radial saw. Then locate and plough the edge rabbets in both the sides and top.
3. Fasten the 1" by 2" edge thickeners to the shelf and top pieces using white glue and 1-1/4" ringed nails.
4. Cut the 3/4" by 1-1/2" notches in the side pieces and temporarily assemble the cabinet, using brads only. When satisfied that the parts fit correctly, disassemble the cabinet.
5. With the pieces disassembled, apply the laminate to the inside surfaces of the back, sides, and shelf pieces only. Take care *not* to bond the laminate to the 3" wide edge surfaces that will be let into the rabbets and grooves. *Note:* Before laminating the shelf top, apply the laminate edging to the front edge.
6. Assemble the cabinet using white glue and 1-1/4" flathead screws.
7. Apply laminate to the sides; trim.
8. Apply laminate to the front edges; trim.
9. Apply laminate to the top; trim.
10. Next, construct the drawer. Measure the cabinet and alter the dimensions shown in Fig. 1, if necessary. Note the clearances required for the drawer slides. If a different brand is selected, check the manufacturer's instructions on the package for clearance. Then construct the drawer, install all hardware and check it for fit. When satisfied, temporarily set the drawer aside.
11. Cut the piece for the drawer false front. (*Note:* If the false front edges are to be covered with laminate, allow for the laminate thickness when cutting the core stock to size.) Laminate the drawer front; locate holes for the drawer pull at the center and bore. Attach the false front to the drawer by fastening with 1-1/4" screws through the drawer front and into the back of the false front. For extra strength, also use white glue.
12. If necessary, clean up the surfaces using adhesive solvent recommended on the label instructions. Be sure to follow safety precautions for solvent use and to provide adequate ventilation.

MATERIALS

Quantity	Description
1	3/4" x 18" x 38" Plywood (top)
4	3/4" x 18" x 22-1/4" Plywood (sides)
1	3/4" x 17-3/4" x 35-3/4" Plywood (bottom)
1	1/4" x 22-5/8" x 35-3/4" Plywood (back)
1	1/4" x 16-1/4" x 32-1/2" Plywood (drawer bottom)
6-1/2 lin. feet	1" x 2" Lumber (edge thickeners)
1	3/4" x 4" x 35" Plywood (false drawer front)
1	1/2" x 3-1/2" x 33-1/2" Plywood (drawer front)
2	1/2" x 3-1/2" x 16-1/2" Plywood (drawer sides)
1	1/2" x 2-3/4" x 33-1/2" Plywood (drawer back)
1	20" x 40" Plastic laminate (top)*
1	20" x 36" Plastic laminate (inside back)*
2	18" x 20" Plastic laminate (inside sides)*
1	18" x 36" Plastic laminate (shelf)*
2	20" x 24" Plastic laminate (outside sides)*
10 lin. feet	1-1/2" Wide strips of plastic laminate*
1	4-1/2" x 36" Plastic laminate
1 pair	16" Drawer slides, Knape & Vogt model #1250
1	Drawer pull
—	Plastic wood filler
—	Fine sandpaper
—	White glue
—	No. 8 x 1-1/4" Flathead wood screws
—	Contact adhesive
—	Adhesive solvent

*Note: All necessary laminated pieces can be cut from one 48" by 96" laminate sheet. Take the time to lay out the table part sizes before cutting to assure proper yield.

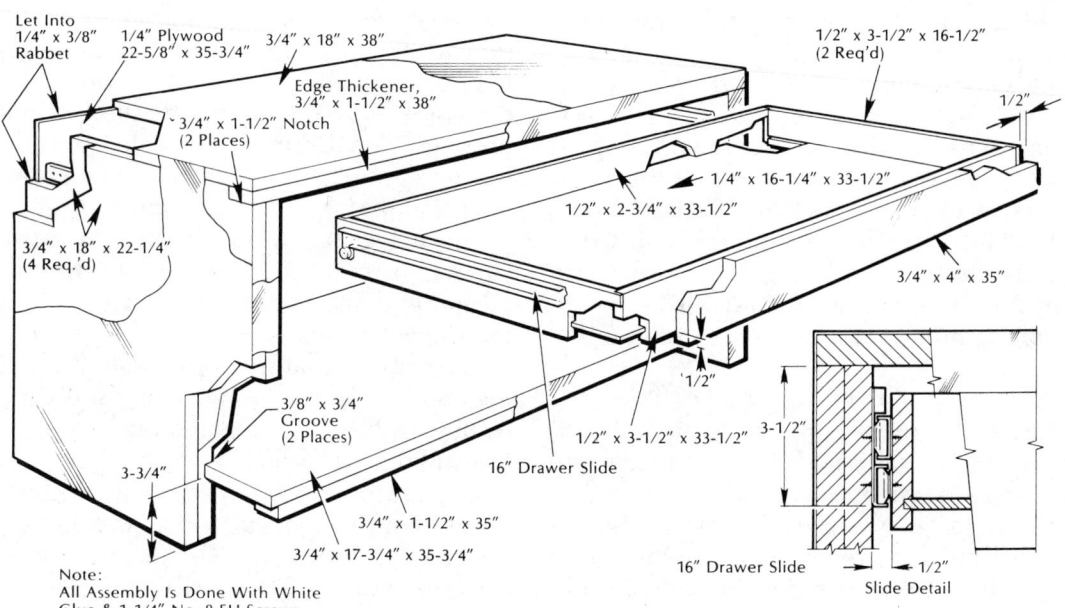

119

CONSOLE TABLE

This console table is at "home" in many rooms of the house. Thanks to the use of laminated plastic, it can be used in a hall, living room, kitchen, family room, and it can be made to match in texture or color other furniture pieces already in these rooms.

To begin the construction of the table, cut the two 18" by 36" leg panel pieces. Then, attach the sandwich construction framing strips to the perimeter of the two leg panels, holding 3/4" from the top edge. Fasten with white glue and No. 4 by 1-1/4" ringed nails. Now, fasten the two 12" by 18" shelf support base members to the sandwich with white glue and nails. Allow a 1-9/16" space for the sliding shelf. Complete the leg or end sandwich construction by attaching the 18" by 21-11/16" top support member. Wipe away any excess white glue.

Proceed with the assembly of the top sandwich structure in a manner similar to the leg or end panel. Fill any voids with plastic wood filler, sand smooth, and dust clean. Fasten the two 18" by 57" sliding shelf members together with white glue and 1-1/4" ringed nails. Fill voids, sand, and dust.

To complete the carpentry work, fasten the top sandwich to the side or leg members, using white glue and No. 8 by 1-1/4" flathead wood screws. Be sure of squareness and wipe away any excess before the glue is left to dry overnight.

Now, begin the application of the laminate on the inside and outside surfaces of the leg members. Bond material across the sliding shelf groove. After the laminate has been thoroughly rolled and bonded, rout the edges flush, including the sliding shelf groove. Then, laminate the table front and the back edges of the table. The two one-piece laminate top and leg edge shapes (as shown in Fig. 1) may be cut from one of the laminate sheets. After bonding to the surface, rout the top edge flush and bevel rout the edge/leg section joints.

The final laminating steps include applying the front edge of the sliding shelf and routing it flush, then laminating the top of the sliding shelf and the top of the table. Finally, all of the edges must be routed. Carefully turn the table on its top and install the furniture glides. Use recommended solvents or general purpose cleaners for the final cleanup.

MATERIALS

Quantity	Description
2	3/4" x 18" x 36" Plywood (leg panels)
1	3/4" x 18" x 58-1/2" Plywood (top)
1	3/4" x 18" x 57-1/2" Plywood (lower top sandwich)
2	3/4" x 12" x 18" Plywood (base support)
2	3/4" x 18" x 21" Plywood (top support)
2	3/4" x 18" x 57" Plywood (sliding shelf)
6	3/4" x 2" x 18" Pine lumber (sandwich framing)
4	3/4" x 2" x 31-1/4" Pine lumber (sandwich framing)
2	3/4" x 2" x 53-1/2" Pine lumber (sandwich framing)
1	3/4" x 2" x 14" Pine lumber (sandwich framing)
2	18-1/2" x 36-1/2" Plastic laminate (side)*
2	18-1/2" x 33-1/4" Plastic laminate (side)*
1	18-1/2" x 60-1/2" Plastic laminate (top)*
1	18-1/2" x 57-1/2" Plastic laminate (shelf top)*
1	2" x 57-1/2" Plastic laminate (shelf front edge)*
2	36-1/2" x 60-1/2" Plastic laminate (table edge)*
—	White glue
—	1-1/4" No. 8 Flathead wood screws
—	1-1/4" No. 4 Ringed nails
4	Furniture glides
—	Plastic wood filler
—	Fine sandpaper
—	Contact adhesive
—	Adhesive solvent

Note: All necessary laminate pieces can be cut from three 48" by 72" laminate sheets. Take time to lay out the table part sizes before cutting to assure proper yield.

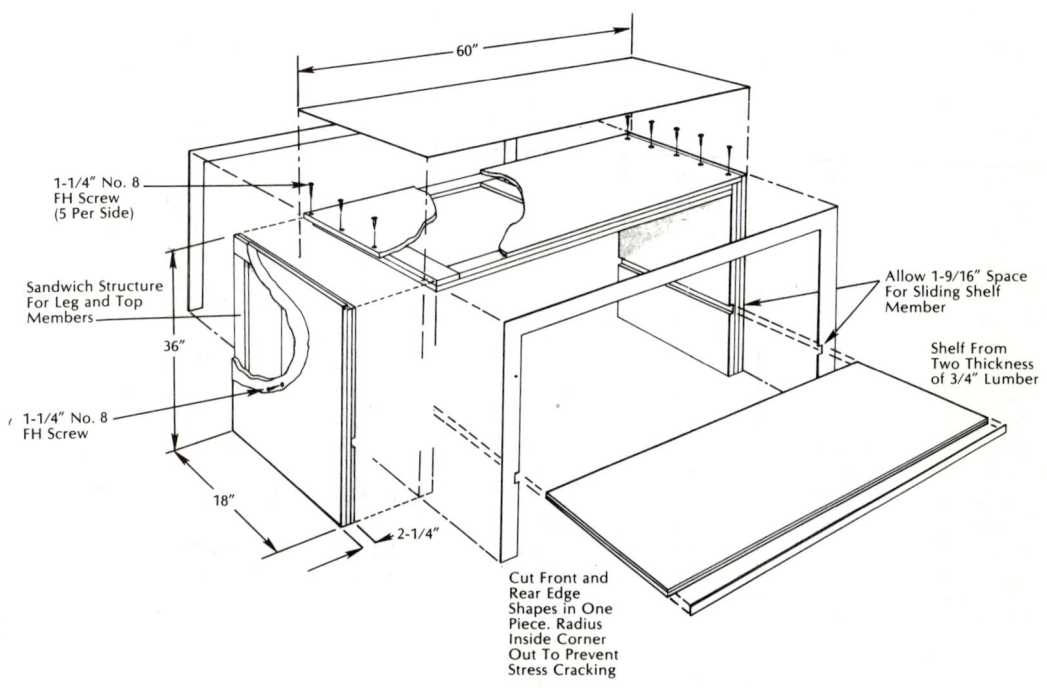